Hoof Prints
to
HIS Prints

Where the Woods
Meet the Word

Jeff May

ALSO BY JEFF MAY

Heaven: O For A Home With God

Hoof Prints
to
HIS Prints

Where the Woods
Meet the Word

Jeff May

WOODS2WORD PUBLISHING

Hoof Prints to HIS Prints

Where the Woods Meet the Word

I wasn't born in the woods,
but I got there
as fast as I could.

Dedication

Hoof Prints to HIS Prints
is dedicated to
my wonderful wife, Susan,
children, and grandchildren.
You have filled my home with
peace, joy, laughter,
and the encouragement I have
needed to keep walking the trail,
pursuing Him, and reaping
a bountiful harvest in the end.
I love you all.

Special Thanks to my Bridge Builders

On the roads I travel to teach the word of God and then recreationally to hunt the whitetail deer, I cross many bridges. Although I don't know who built them, I am thankful. Without them I could never do what I love to do. This book is dedicated to all those in my life who have built bridges for me.

First, there is my Lord, who died on the one that leads to heaven.

Next, I must thank my wonderful parents, James and Glenda May, who built the ones that gave me opportunities in life. Daddy, thank you for having such a big heart for those who hurt. And thanks for giving me a love for the words of good songs. Mama, thanks for bringing snow to the bathtub because I was too sick to build a snowman outside. I've never forgotten it and all the other acts of a mother's love. I thank my sister, Sharon, for all of her encouragement by asking, "How's the book coming along?"

I thank my in-laws, Billy and Ruth Henderson, who have always treated me like their own son and brought up the woman I love. I miss Mr. Billy (our "Paw Paw"), who passed away in the winter of 2012.

To me, the greatest woman in the world is my wife, Susan, who gave me a path to her heart. She is the "wind beneath my wings." It takes a special "breed of cat" to be a preacher's wife. And it takes a "country girl" with understanding to be a deer hunter's wife. Thank God, I got both.

To my children, Bethany and Henderson, and son-in-law, Caleb, you are a great joy in my life, and I am very proud of you. And to my first grandchild, Garrett, and all the others to come, my prayer is that you will cross the bridges I have left and build your own for others to cross.

To Chester Wright, thank you for sitting with "Bro," keeping his dreams alive and helping the winter not to be so cold and hard on him. Thanks for modeling what brotherhood really means. You've made me a better hunter and a better man.

To my landowners in Alabama, Tennessee, and elsewhere, how can I thank you enough? Your properties, which God entrusted to you, are simply beautiful! If I were a deer, I'd want to live there too. May God bless you all. You have touched my life in wonderful ways.

At last, I thank my mentors and friends who built bridges for me to cross for comfort and help in time of need. May God bless you all!

The Bridge Builder
By William Allen Dromgoole

An old man going a lone highway,
Came, at the evening cold and gray,
To a chasm vast and deep and wide,
Through which was flowing a sullen tide.
The old man crossed in the twilight dim,
The sullen stream had no fear for him;
But he turned when safe on the other side
And built a bridge to span the tide.

"Old man," said a fellow pilgrim near,
"You are wasting your strength with building here;
Your journey will end with the ending day,
You never again will pass this way;
You've crossed the chasm, deep and wide,
Why build this bridge at evening tide?"

The builder lifted his old gray head;
"Good friend, in the path I have come," he said,
"There followed after me to-day
A youth whose feet must pass this way.
This chasm that has been as naught to me
To that fair-haired youth may a pitfall be;
He, too, must cross in the twilight dim;
Good friend, I am building this bridge for him!"

Promotions & Proofs

Photo of "Rukus," the massive buck at the beginning of
each devotion, is provided courtesy of
Terry and Belinda Kennedy at
SOUTHERN YANKEES WHITETAIL FARM.
Toney, Alabama
www.southernyankees.net

Special thanks to Darren Winland at
Faith Illustrated for his work on video promotions.
Faith Illustrated is also the home of
presentation templates and design media.
www.faithillustrated.media

Thanks to Trent Faris
for the creation of the website. It's a site for additional short
devotionals, information on how to draw closer to God,
and helpful hints for avid deer hunters.
www.woods2word.com

Proofreading by:
Shirley Holt
Sharon May
B.J. Waddell

Layout Assistance:
Caleb White

Cover Design & Photography:
Susan May

Table of Contents

FALL 151

WINTER 229

Foreword
(From Jeff's Mentor in the Woods)

In 1997, my trail crossed with a young man, whom spiritually, I came to love because he was a good teacher of the Bible. Jeff was in Middle Tennessee teaching a series of classes called "Rich Bible Passages." It lived up to its name – it surely was rich!

He and I talked for the first time and I felt like we were kindred spirits. I left thinking, "He's a Jim Bob Dandy!" That's what I call someone who is just alright in my book. I later gave him some of my deer jerky, and a great friendship began. Jerky is the best way to "win friends and influence people"! In time we became two brothers whose souls were knit together in the woods and in the Word, much like David and Jonathan (1 Samuel 18:1).

In a sense, we needed each other. I had been a wayward son for a while needing the Lord and more time in the scriptures. Jeff's head was always in the Book, and to be honest, he needed to let himself "smell the roses," get away a little more, and restore his soul. Jesus did. He loved the mountains, the wilderness, and the garden. He talked about birds, and fields, and flowers. He spent a lot of time outdoors. We need to enjoy these things too. That's why He gave them to us (1 Timothy 6:17).

I confess to making Jeff a whitetail addict. What he did for me in the Word, I did for him in the woods. He would share with me what he had done for years behind a desk. I would share what I had done for years in a tree stand. In both places, God was showing us life-changing things. "Iron sharpens iron," the Bible says, and that's what we were doing for each other.

The woods became a sanctuary where all that we loved came together. Happiness filled our hearts from the time we left the truck until we descended from our stands. I watched Jeff grow from a novice deer hunter to becoming pretty savvy. He was hungry to learn. He listened intently and applied what he learned. And our daily talks about the Bible fed my hunger as well. It was awesome!

I hope you enjoy *Hoof Prints to HIS Prints*. I surely have. It's a devotional book that hopefully will lead you to think more about the greatest Book ever written: the Bible. I wouldn't be surprised if you even take this book to the stand, where life shuts down for a little while and you have time to think and meditate. Jeff's stories will make you relive some of your own.

This book is truly "live action!" There's friendship, brotherhood, adventure, deep reflection, laughter, and yes – even sadness. When Jeff and I talked about this book, I told him my copy just might be ink-stained where my tears fell to the page. It's about life, really living, the way we were meant to live. It will make you think and at times challenge your thinking.

So come along with us into a world of whitetail wonder, and our hope is to meet you on the other side of the river. To God be the glory.

Eddie Simmons

Foreword
(From Jeff's Mentor in God's Word)

A foreword is an introduction to a book, according to the dictionary. It is usually by a person other than the author of the book. I am the "other" than the author of this book. It is a privilege and an honor to write a foreword of this book because I know the author so well. Jeff May is my nephew, and I had the privilege of him listening to me preach for a number of years before he went off to college. Jeff has caused many people to know me as "Unka Thomas." I do not mind him referencing me as such as he feeds the flock of God.

I do not know Jeff as a deer hunter. I know him as a Christian hunting others to bring to Christ, and his years of preaching have been successful in his endeavor.

Jeff asked me many years ago about preaching, and my answer basically was "not now." He never asked me about deer hunting. I would have had no advice on that. When I told Jeff "not now" about preaching, I thought he was rushing into a serious matter that he might find disappointing as he worked with all types of people who were not as anxious and eager as he. Young preachers may get discouraged and, as a result, their zeal harmed for life. I advised Jeff to wait until the time was ripe for him to begin full-time preaching. He took my advice, and when I called him later about preaching, my advice was to get your "bow and arrow" ready because there is a church that needs a man like you. He loaded, got in his "stand," and has been there ever since. Thus began Jeff May's preaching the good news.

Jeff is a man who can do whatever he sets his mind to do. I am happy he set his mind to preach the simple gospel of Christ. I do not care that he is an avid deer hunter—as long as he keeps things in perspective, and I believe he has and will. If I had a son, I would like for him to be "Jeff." He would make any dedicated father happy to say, "This is my son." Not because he killed an "eight-point," but because he helped a person kill the works of Satan.

I might add that if Jeff's knowledge of deer hunting grows as his knowledge of God's word has grown, there are deer who are in trouble. He will face the obstacles to get the "big one." It takes a dedicated deer hunter to rise at three or four in the morning to sit in a deer stand patiently waiting for movement of a deer on the distant horizon. As Jeff waits, he probably is reading the book about matters that pertain to eternal life. That is the Jeff I know.

Jeff has taken a simple matter of deer hunting and given it a spiritual truth that many will enjoy reading through the years. Jeff, as you walk through the woods or sit in a tree stand seeking that trophy deer, remember what the psalmist said: *"As the deer pants for the water brooks, so pants my soul for You, O God"* (Psalm 42:1).

A sad moment in my life was when I thought Jeff had been killed in a car accident. A car fitting the description of Jeff's car had been hit by a train on the road that Jeff often traveled to work. When I arrived on the scene, I saw the car and was told a young man was inside. Not wanting to hear Jeff's name, I strolled down the railroad track out of hearing range. As I walked, I came to myself, saying I had to face the sad news. When I returned to the scene, I was told the name, and it was not Jeff. I rejoiced, and then I thought, "But it is someone's son." When I returned home, I tried to tell the story to my family, and I broke down in tears as I spoke.

What would have happened had that been Jeff? Things would have drastically changed for me and others who loved him. This book would not have been written. Jeff's wife and children would not be, and many persons would not have been taught by Jeff. Thank you, God, it was not Jeff, and thank you we have the Jeff who has done so much for so many and continues to try to help those who will listen, read this book, and understand its spiritual applications. Just another way of spreading God's truth.

You are special, Jeff.

Thomas "Unka Thomas" May

Introduction

Hoof Prints to HIS Prints was a labor of love for me. It's intended to connect the woods...to the Word. That's not hard to do. Listen to Psalm 42:1. ***"As the deer pants for the water brooks"*** (there's the hoof print), ***"so pants my soul for you, O God"*** (there's His print).

The greatest love of my life is God and His word. I am also an avid deer hunter. I find it easy to bridge those two worlds. God wants that. He desires for us to see things in the created world that cause us to meditate on His written word. The world is God's *general revelation*: it proves that He exists. We are without excuse if we fail to see His power in the things He made (Romans 1:20). But He has also given us *specific revelation*: the Bible. It tells us who this God is, why He made us, and what His plan is for our lives. It's about purpose. What we need then is more time to be alone and meditate on the things that really matter.

Americans struggle with silence. It seems we must have the radio blaring in the car or a TV on in the house, even if no one is watching. We can't handle solitude very well. Yet, solitude is the one thing a deer hunter craves and anticipates. There are a few times when the woods get so quiet you feel like you are the only living creature around. It's life-changing! People are most like themselves in nature. You can get down to the real you—no veneer, no facade, no masquerade— and it is there that God can do wonders on us. I like thinking of it as an anesthetic that puts everything to sleep so that surgery can take place.

Jesus knew the power of time alone with God, and we also need to know it — by experience. He would often slip away (Luke 5:16). The disciples would awaken, look around, and discover that Jesus was gone. He loved the early morning moments before the world came alive and began buzzing with activity (Mark 1:35-39). He knew that soon everyone would wipe the sleep out of their eyes, and He would be in high demand. So, He placed high priority on those private, devoted moments, in order to escape and be alone with His Father. He didn't just squeeze in prayer and meditation between all His preaching and miracles. Someone once said, "Jesus went from place of prayer to place of prayer with teaching and miracles in between." I like that.

Those who hunt know the adrenaline rush caused by the crunching leaves as a whitetail slowly approaches. There is also such a surge when the word of God is read. I hope you will enjoy both as you read this book. My greatest satisfaction would be to know that you have found yourself a quiet place to read this book and contemplate the spiritual lessons in it. When you have even more time, get your Bible and turn to the passages cited and read them more fully. It will deepen your understanding.

You see, a hoof print might lead you to the trophy of a lifetime, but only following His prints will lead you to eternal life (John 14:6). A song planted in my heart from childhood says it well.

> *"Then at last when on high He sees us,*
> *Our journey done.*
> *We shall rest where the steps of Jesus,*
> *End at God's throne.*
> *Footprints of Jesus,*
> *That make the pathway glow.*
> *We will follow the steps of Jesus,*
> *Where'er they go."*
> (Footsteps of Jesus, Mrs. M.B. Slade, Dr. A.B. Everett)

> *"For to this you were called, because Christ also suffered for us,*
> *leaving us an example, that you should follow His steps"*
> 1 Peter 2:21

This book will not help you to become a better hunter, but it just might be a little something to help you think more about Him. If it does, the dreams I had while writing it will come true.

Deer season always has that final tick of the clock. The sun sets on that last day, and we can hardly wait until next season when the sun rises on opening day. More importantly, one day the sun will set on our lives here below, and when it does, our relationship with Him will be all that matters. Onward and upward.

- Jeff May

Whitetail Wonder

He led me down a leaf-blanketed road that led away from one world and into another. I had no idea where the path would take me. Boy, is that a HUGE understatement!

We walked side by side, sometimes matching each other stride for stride until at last the road came to a T in the heart of the "Ponderosa," our newly acquired whitetail property. No, it's not as big as its namesake on TV, but it has grown as big in my heart.

I had no idea what to expect, but my dreams were that my landowner's "old homeplace" would hold at least one "Sid." That's what my deer mentor, Eddie Simmons, calls a really nice buck.

At the T, Eddie said, "Go left here until this path ends at the creek. Cross the creek, go a little ways up the hill, and hunker down at the bottom of a tree." He knew what he was doing. I did not. I was basically still a beginner at deer hunting. What little hunting I had done had been from shooting houses overlooking fields. You know how it is. There's great vision but little sound. I want the sounds when I can get them. They are God's symphony, perfectly orchestrated by the Conductor.

I had never really hunted in the heart of the woods. I would find out today there is a huge difference! We had no stands yet, so I would take my place on the forest floor, and the Lord would introduce me to a beautiful kingdom of its own: a place of whitetail wonder and MORE!

There is a bit of mystery to the woods before daybreak. On new property, you anticipate what your eyes will soon behold. For someone who hasn't been in the woods when it's dark, a little eeriness can be felt. Hair may rise on your arms when a nearby owl beckons *"who, who, whoooo"* or in the distance a pack of coyotes sounds frenzied. And about the time you get locked in on those sounds, something scurries about five feet away from you, causing you to jerk and think, "What was that! Oh, it's just a squirrel." The squirrels are nature's acrobats—the circus of the outdoors.

At the crack of dawn, birds begin to sing. The day shift is checking in while the rulers of the night check out. You know it will not be long until God will, in His own way, whisper, "Good morning," as His sun arises *"like a bridegroom coming out of his chamber"* (Psalm 19:4-5).

Why does God use such picturesque language like that to talk about sunrise? Because God is a lover, a poet, an artist, ever wooing us toward Him. But He is also a God of the wild...adventurous. I think this is why so many hunters feel a yearning to answer the call of the wild.

Trust me; I talk to lots of hunters asking them one question, "What is it that draws you to deer hunting?" Usually the first answer I get is, ***"I just feel so close to God when I am in the woods."*** If you are a deer hunter, something tells me at this moment you are nodding in agreement. At least I hope you are not nodding off to sleep! And if you are not a hunter, you don't have to shoot to have the same experience. Try it. I think you will like it.

NATURE, NOISES, & NERVES

After sunrise, a couple of squirrels started chattering away. I thought it was because the "great whitetail hunter" had invaded their turf. But then they became nervous and barked out some high-pitched warning sounds. *"Kuk, kuk, kuuuuk!"* Were they warning *me* or other critters *about me?*

Then I heard it! *"Chh, chh, chh, chh, chh, chh."* Something was coming from behind me. Instantly, I felt like I had been given an IV injection of adrenaline, and I could feel my heartbeat in my Adam's apple. I readied myself to see one of the most majestic creatures on earth...the American Whitetail. The crunching was right upon me. Something entered my peripheral view and there was a sudden stop.

My eyes bulged when I saw, not a whitetail, but two coyotes a mere ten yards to my right. And remember, I am on the ground with them and outnumbered. I'm told they are more afraid of us than we should be of them. I was hoping so. The squirrels, however, didn't seem to know that. So, I sat motionless. After a few moments, they moved on. Whhh!

TRYING TO EXPLAIN, THE UNEXPLAINABLE

I did not see a deer that day, but it didn't matter. I saw more. I saw God today. I had left the world humans clutter up with noise and trash. I found another world, pure and clean: a world that at times has a deafening silence but where God speaks loudly as if to say, "I am here" (Psalm 19:1-4).

Sometimes I am simply overcome with the beauty of it all. I feel so alive in the woods! I realize some hunters might not be aware that something spiritual is going on, but they do admit loving something unexplainable, and they are not quite sure what it is. I once read where one hunter said, ***"You can't explain it, but nothing would keep you from it."*** Another says, ***"If I have to explain it, you wouldn't understand it."*** And then some never really tune in. They will spend a lifetime hunting the whitetail, yet **never realizing it is not the deer they are after.**

Planted in the heart of all of us is an itch that begs to be scratched. A desire for the spiritual, the eternal, well...for God.

> *"He has made everything beautiful in its time.*
> *Also, **He has put eternity in their hearts...**"*
> Ecclesiastes 3:11

This itch will never be scratched by anything else the world offers. Money, material things, prestige, power, or sex may offer a counterfeit pleasure but, at last, only intensify the itch. Even when you get what you want, it will not be what you want (Ecclesiastes 5:10). Nothing fills the God-shaped hole only He was meant to fill. How do I know? Because a man who had the means to have everything said that nothing satisfied. His name was Solomon.

> *"Whatever my eyes desired,*
> *I did not keep from them.*
> *I did not withhold my heart*
> *from any pleasure...*

*And indeed it was all vanity
and grasping for the wind.
There was no profit under the sun."*
Ecclesiastes 2:10-11

So Solomon, what satisfies? What will scratch the itch?
What will give me lasting happiness, contentment, and purpose in
life?

*"Let us hear the conclusion of the whole matter:
Fear God and keep His commandments.
For this is the whole duty of man."*
Ecclesiastes 12:13

Come along with me. You don't even have to bring a gun. I
will be aiming at something else myself. I am aiming for you to see
there is no way we can disconnect God from ANYTHING in the
world we live in. He is in all of it. If you want to see Him, you will.
If for some reason you don't want to, you will not.

You can take any bug or animal you want, and you will see
incredible design from the Designer. Whether a tiny ant or a
massive whitetail, there are lessons to be learned and wonders to
behold (Proverbs 6:6-8). Take time to really study them. Did you
know a deer's tail can tell you so much? It can tell you if they are
happy, mad, flirty, sassy, excited, nervous, frightened, or even sick.
When they are sick they will tuck their tail down and under.

All God's creatures are unique. Learn from their abilities and
their wisdom. That's why Solomon spoke of trees, animals, birds,
creeping things, and fish (1 Kings 4:33). In their own way, they are
God's teachers.

This is why Jesus loved to teach in the natural amphitheatres
of God's creation. His Sermon on the Mount is a masterpiece (well
of course, it's from the Master). He asked His audience to stop and
behold the lilies of the field. They do nothing to produce their own
beauty. God loves them, and He tends to them. They just relax and
let God work. From the lily, His mind shifts to tell them how God
lovingly took care of Solomon and arrayed him with splendor.
What's the point? Quit worrying; seek God first in your life, and He
will love you and always give you what you *need* (Matthew 6:25-

34). See how this works? From the woods to the word and back again — learning all the while.

In an exciting article entitled "Whitetails Are Nature's Superstars," photographer Charles Alsheimer, tells of a moment when he saw a buck clear a fence at full throttle. He says, "I was shocked by the amount of ground the airborne buck covered. When things calmed, I measured the distance the jumping buck had flown through the air. It was just shy of 35 feet. I've seen a lot of running, jumping, and bounding from whitetails in my life, but nothing like that scene. It's something I'll never forget" (Whitetail News, Volume 22, No. 3, pg. 18). They can be standing still, and all they need is one step and a leap, and they have easily cleared an eight foot fence! Did that just happen, or was there design?

The more I discover about the whitetail, the more I am astounded. Did you know a whitetail's hairs are hollow like tubes? Warm air from inside their body can enter these tubes and keep them warm during the winter. Was that a fluke? I think not. It's *whitetail wonder*. They and we are *wonderfully* made (Psalm 139:14). And get this...the universe and the world we live in are just the *mere edges of His power,* and we have only heard a *faint whisper* of His greatness (Job 26:14)!

The beauty of hunting is that no two hunts are the same. Each outing is different and a story of its own, yet for the spiritually minded, each outing in the woods will cause the same thing to happen every time. The woods will make you think about things you have read in the Word: the Bible. Or if you've never read it much, you might find yourself wanting to read it more. I hope so. It's your story, written *about you* and *for you.* Your meditations will thrill the heart of God (Psalm 104:34). The great people of faith, who have gone on before us, knew about the reward of time alone with God—the path of private devotion. Uncover that old trail and walk it.

"They shut the road through the woods
Seventy years ago.
Weather and rain have undone it again,
And now you would never know
There was once a road through the woods. "
(Rudyard Kipling)

Walk with me into the woods. Let's find that old road. Join me in my adventures. Relive a few of your own. I am not a professional. I'm not in any earthly record books. I probably hunt pretty much like you do. But I do hunt something that many do not. If you find this *something*, this *Someone*, you will be eternally glad you did.

THE ARROW STRIKES As I think about my love for the woods or the whitetail, who would I credit for planting that love in my heart? Do I remember my first hunt and who was with me? Does it make sense to me that the creation can teach me much about the Creator? Do I slow down to really study and appreciate the things I see in the created world? Does it make sense to me that a world of such order and amazement just accidentally happened? Can I see that design argues for a Designer?

SPRING

As you make your way through this book, you will come across inserts for each season of the year. Just as each calendar year has seasons, so does your life. Slow down to meditate on what is likely going on in my neck of the woods and possibly yours too.

In the world: Springtime!! A time of new birth. Everything is coming alive. Buttercups bloom. Grass is greening up. A little boy walks barefoot behind his daddy on fresh-tilled dirt. Neighbors emerge from their houses. Windows are opened, and spring-cleaning begins. Kids ride their bikes. In my part of the world, the Braves are in Spring Training. The smell of popcorn and grilled hamburgers fills the air at the ballparks. Bama and Auburn fans anticipate their A-Day games. Excitement abounds! And although we don't like to mention it...tornadoes arrive in the deep south! Life "under the sun" always brings its trials.

In the woods: Tender leaves are popping out on the trees, decreasing our visibility. Bucks that made it through their winter wars emerge wiser and smarter. They grow bigger headgear. Little fawns will soon be born. Within twenty minutes after birth, they are able to stand and walk. Their coats are reddish-brown. Little white spots will keep them camouflaged against the sun-dappled forest floor and better hidden from predators. They will double their weight within the first two weeks and drink their mother's milk until about three months old. They will soon know which foods are good to eat and where to find them. They are watching Mom and learning very fast.

In the Word: Let's use springtime to represent the beginning of your journey as a Christian. You have just become a Christian. You have repented and been baptized into Christ and thus born again (John 3:5; 1 Peter 1:23). You are a new creation (2 Corinthians 5:17). You are rejoicing that the burden of your past sinful life is now gone (Romans 6:1-6). As a babe in Christ, you too need milk and lots of it!

In the local church, God is giving you spiritual fathers, mothers, brothers, and sisters to encourage you and to give you someone faithful to watch and imitate (Mark 10:29-30; 1 Corinthians 11:1).

When you make mistakes, maybe even the same ones you made before becoming a Christian, you quickly correct them, ask God's forgiveness, and resolve to never do it again (1 John 1:7-10). And once again, you are perfect in the blood of Christ! So much to learn, yet so much to enjoy. Alive in Christ. It feels so good!

"As newborn babes,
desire the pure milk of the word,
that you may grow thereby,
if indeed you have tasted
that the Lord is gracious."
1 Peter 2:2-3

"Mister, Do You Still Get Buck Fever?"

When I first began deer hunting, I was totally unprepared for the way "Buck Fever" takes over a man's body. The sight of a huge buck slowly approaching or even the sudden appearance of a mature doe are both enough to instantly trigger an adrenaline explosion.

Here is where a man finds out if he can "come through in the clutch" much like an athlete has to do in a close, tense ballgame. The ability to settle the nerves and focus can make all the difference in the world. Some people get better in such moments. They live for it. Others lose it completely. Maybe that's because the chance to get a "good un" is very rare, and the average amount of time to get the job done is less than seven seconds. I read that somewhere. I do know from experience, the window of opportunity is indeed small. And mature bucks are seldom about giving second chances.

Buck fever can cause some wild and varied reactions. I've had to talk myself down a number of times just to become controlled enough to shoot. I've seen men struggle to catch their breath and gasp between words as they try to speak after their shot. I've had cold shivers afterward that were virtually uncontrollable for a time. I've even heard of it causing a man to completely lose his senses and walk off the tree stand. And to be sure, that first step's a doozy! It is a hunter's greatest detriment but also a hunter's greatest joy. We pursue that rush of excitement.

I remember once watching an outdoor TV show and seeing a little boy approach a professional hunter. The man had been doing this stuff for years. The little boy looked up at his hunting hero and said, *"Mister, do you still get buck fever?"* I'll never forget his answer. With great compassion and understanding he looked into this little hunter's eager eyes and said, *"Yeah son, I do. And I hope I always do."* If you are a hunter, I know you feel the same way. We love that feeling, and it is what keeps us coming back for more. We hope that feeling never fades away.

Pete Alfano of Whitetail Properties expresses it well when he says, *"Hands down, the white-tailed deer is the most majestic, most rewarding animal to hunt. There's nothing in this world that can shake me up physically and mentally like an old white-tailed buck can."*

The reading and study of God's word does the same thing. Take time to read it. Understand its incredible message of God's desire to change your life for the better, to save you, and pour out all His kindness on you forever (Ephesians 2:4-7). It's a thrilling message capable of stirring great emotions within us.

BURNING HEARTS

After Jesus came forth from the dead, He appeared to two disciples and walked a trail with them through the scriptures helping them to see Him and know Him. Listen to their reaction. They said, *"Did not our heart burn within us while He talked with us on the road, and while He opened the scriptures to us?"* (Luke 24:32). That's a spiritual adrenaline rush!

I keep paper and pencil on my nightstand because sometimes I am suddenly awakened in the night by an exciting thought about something in God's word. Bing! A light has come on. I sometimes want so badly to wake up my wife and share it with her, but instead, I write it down and save it 'til daybreak. Some of my favorite sermons have been produced between 2:00 a.m. and 5:00 a.m. because I was so excited I couldn't go back to sleep. I had to get up!

The prophet Jeremiah also had such a surge. Because people were rebelling against God and rejecting all his efforts to teach them, he decided he would just quit trying. He decided to squash the word inside his heart and not share it with anyone, ever again. It didn't work. He said, *"But His word was in my heart like a burning fire shut up in my bones. I was weary of holding it back and I could not"* (Jeremiah 20:9). That's contents under pressure.

THE BUCK AND THE BOOK

The God who made the whitetail that stirs you up as a hunter, wrote a book that will turn your heart inside out. If you are looking for an adventure, you will find no greater one than traveling the pages of the Bible. More than once while reading the Bible, tears have come to my eyes. I've even gotten chill bumps. And it seems that my best friends have become the men and women on its pages. I feel like I know them. I look forward to seeing them. Now, I'm not into religious emotionalism, but I am saying that when God's message is read and understood, it will naturally bring the emotions. The greatest joy comes when the message is believed and obeyed. I remember well how wonderful I felt when I was baptized into Christ for the remission of my sins (Acts 2:38; 22:16).

Much like that professional hunter, I hope my spiritual juices never run dry. To keep that from happening, you and I have to keep coming to its pages. The beautiful thing is the Bible never becomes stale. It keeps showing you something each time that you failed to see before. I call these new discoveries "nuggets" and encourage Bible students to "covet the nugget." It's a good kind of lust. Someone once said, *"The Bible is shallow enough a baby can drink from it, but it's deep enough a diver can never plumb its depths."* I've found it so. It's a mine full of treasures (Proverbs 2:1-5). Its stories have thrilled my heart since I was a little boy, and its message challenges me to this day.

So, if a little boy ever asks me, "Mister, do you still get excited when you read the Bible?", I think I'll say, "Yeah, son, I do. And I hope I always do."

THE ARROW STRIKES Have I been surprised that "buck fever" is such an exciting thing for me? Would I be disappointed if I never again felt adrenaline rushes while hunting? At the present, do I have any excitement about the Bible — God's plan for *me*? If I spent more time in the Bible, could I also come to love it and its Author even more?

Talk Yourself Down

Take passion, excitement, nervousness, and a pounding heart, and multiply by 10 (or more), and you have a tally of what buck fever is all about. It's what some call the FULL DRAW EFFECT, which is defined as "that moment when your heart is pounding and a concoction of adrenaline and concentration flood your body."

It is fuel in a whitetail hunter's tank. I live for the next moment it happens. May it never go away! But it has to be managed, or you'll spend most of your days in the woods watching white flags speeding away from you.

To master buck fever, you have to learn to "talk yourself down" so that you don't blow it in the "moment of truth." I just looked up that phrase on the web, and it means: 1. A critical or decisive time on which much depends; a crucial moment 2. The point in a bullfight at which the matador makes the kill.

In the moment, it's easy to lose focus and forget important things. Not too long ago, a brother in Christ told me of a great buck that eluded him, all because of the fever. He was rifle hunting in a ground blind, and the brute caught him off guard. He just suddenly appeared. Whitetails do that! I sometimes think they pop out of the ground! The only chance he had was to try and take a left-handed shot at a little over ten yards. That shouldn't be too hard, even left-handed. He got down on the scope, and everything went black. **Somebody turned out the lights!** He nervously tried again and again, but with all this movement, his dream buck shot out of there! What in the world happened? Here's what his investigation concluded. Not being accustomed to shooting left-handed, he closed the wrong eye when he looked into the scope! He closed the one that counted. Aww man, that hurts, doesn't it?

Now, let me tell you, I too have had my share of opportunities where I blew it. And I will again. That's hunting for you. However, there are a few things I do that seem to help me in that crucial moment.

DEER HUNTING 101

First, I try to envision possible scenarios I can get into *before* **they happen.** It's like a shortstop thinking about what he will do before the ball is hit. You can't wait 'til the moment. You bobble if you do! I use time in the stand to imagine the big one coming. I ask myself, "What should I do if he stops right there? Or if he comes this direction, when should I stop him?" I also range a few objects with my range finder so that, when a deer arrives, I can already know my distance.

At home, I sometimes watch deer shows on TV with my bow in hand. When the big one comes on the screen, I come to full draw and get him in my sights. It sounds silly I know, but I am getting use to seeing big bucks with my sight pin on them. I've killed a lot of nice bucks during prime-time TV!

Then, I literally talk to myself to get my emotions under control. This is one of the great things about the way God made us. In one of the greatest books in the Bible on leadership, Nehemiah said, "I consulted with myself" (Nehemiah 5:7). This means we can preach to ourselves in order to do the right thing. We can rebuke ourselves when we don't. *"Jeff, that was so stupid! Why in the world did you do that? Don't ever do that again!"* I also have added in some breathing and muscle relaxing techniques. It doesn't take away all the fever, but it absorbs a lot of it.

My last safeguard is a big sticker on the riser of my bow positioned next to my sights. It has four BIG letters typed on it. They are F-O-R-M. It's a silent reminder, *"Jeff, don't lose form, anchor properly, gently press your nose to the string, pick a small spot, rest the sight there, and don't punch the release."* These are PRINCIPLES a bowhunter lives by. They cannot be forgotten without it costing you — big time!

"Talking yourself down" has to be done in everyday life too. I know it is true with anger. It's a major problem among men and women. That's why we hear so much these days about someone being ordered by a judge to enroll in anger-management courses.

LEARNING FROM A MAD MESSIAH

The Bible is the book on anger management (and everything else for that matter). God made us so that we can get angry. Sometimes it is exactly what we should do. On one occasion, Jesus saw people disrespecting God's temple, and He made a whip of cords and began cracking it at the blasphemous bunch (Kpow!). He overturned tables and drove out the dove, the sheep, and the oxen.

Now, deer hunters...picture that. You've seen what happens when several deer are spooked all at once. They tear the woods up stampeding away, breaking things as they go. I remember a day when I sent fifteen deer fleeing into a waist high creek. Talk about an aquatic explosion!

Here then was a tumultuous scene caused by Jesus with a thunderous, angry message: *"Do not make my Father's house a house of merchandise!"* (John 2:16). Remember, this is not sin, for Jesus never sinned (1 Peter 2:22). It was an "outburst of goodness!" When good or God is being trampled on, it's time to get our dander up. We can be angry and not sin.

> *"'Be angry and do not sin';*
> *do not let the sun go down*
> *on your wrath."*
> Ephesians 4:26

The second part of the above passage is a great lesson for husbands and wives. Don't go to bed angry with one another. Try to settle things quickly. It reminds me of a funny story from a woman named Martha who went to bed so angry at her husband. The next morning, while the coffee percolated, she had multiple feelings brewing in her heart. There was guilt for not settling things the night before. There were left-over hurts. There was a feeling of not wanting him to leave the house without him knowing how she truly felt toward him. So, she left a note where he would be sure to see it. It said...

Charlie,
I hate you.

Love,
Martha

That's hilarious! Why do we say and do things to hurt people whom deep down we love so much?

THE STUFF FOOLS ARE MADE OF

In First Samuel 25, we are told about a time when David, the man "after God's own heart" lost his cool. He had been running from an assassin, King Saul, who was trying to kill him because he was jealous of him. So, he's out in the wilderness with his men, and he's hungry. While out there, he guards the shepherds of a man named Nabal. Thinking Nabal will gladly return the favor in some way, he asks Nabal for food for himself and his men. Nabal refused. David came unglued and beckoned to his men, *"Every man gird on his sword,"* and he took four hundred of his men with him. Someone once wrote, "This is like a man killing a cockroach with a sledge hammer." That's what uncontrolled anger does. It overreacts and often leaves a swath of steaming lava and destruction behind it.

Fortunately, Nabal's wife ran interference and turned his thermostat down. She met him with food. It calms the savage beast, you know. She tells David to disregard Nabal, for his name fits him; it means "fool." She reminds this man of God that if he follows through with his plan, he will regret it later. His conscience will hurt him. And she reminds him of the great things God has in store for him if he is faithful. I love the words she chose to capture his attention. It was hunter language this shepherd boy understood. It was balm to his ego!

"Your enemies He shall sling out,
as from the pocket of a sling."
1 Samuel 25:29

In other words, you don't have to retaliate. God will deal with the people who wrong you in His own time. God later struck Nabal, and he died. We must still pray for our enemies (and mean it), but isn't it comforting to know that the God who sees all is a God of justice, and always settles His accounts?

PRESS THE PAUSE BUTTON

Men and women, talk yourself down. Think before you act. Steven Covey, the renowned author of the *7 Habits of Highly Effective People* says there is always a space between S & R (stimulus and response). We can choose our responses. We can press the "pause" button. That principle first came from God when He warned Cain of what he might do if he didn't control his anger toward his brother. His words were, "You should rule over it" (Genesis 4:6-7).

Recently, a camp director told me of a teen who horribly mistreated another teen at camp. He said, "I was so angry I told the kid, 'You sit right here under this tree and don't move. I am so mad at you right now that you are in danger. I am going away for a minute to cool down, and then I will come back and deal with you. And you had better not move.'" He walked away, simmered down a bit, and was able to deal with the situation more effectively. The teen apologized to the one he hurt, and all was well again.

We are humans made in God's image. We are not mere animals, and we don't have to act like it. In every situation ask yourself what the Lord would want you to do. Think of His great composure on the cross when hostilities were being shouted at Him (1 Peter 2:23). Psalm 22 says they shot out the lip at Him (vs. 7). Sticks, stones, and words do hurt, no matter what is said to the contrary. Jesus refused to fire comebacks at them to harm them. And yet as one preacher put it, *"He had the power to annihilate the whole world and be done before supper"* (Paul Earnhart). And let me tell you, that is STRENGTH UNDER CONTROL. It's meekness: not weakness. Jesus was a man if there ever was one.

> *"He who is slow to anger*
> *is better than the mighty,*
> *And he who **rules his spirit***
> *than he who takes a city."*
> Proverbs 16:32

ONE T-BONE SMOOTHIE PLEASE

While discussing this piece with a friend, he said, "Jeff, let me tell you, you can be talked UP too." He told the funniest story of a time when he was in conflict with his brother. I'll change the name to protect the "not so innocent." We will call him John. His brother, in anger, did "doughnuts" in John's front yard. Well, John was fuming but was getting things in check. Just as the needle was coming back down below the boiling point, John's wife said, "Are you just gonna stand there and do nothing?!" By the way, her name *was not* Abigail! At that moment she felt more like Cruella Deville...with the emphasis on *cruel* and *devil*! She wanted her some revenge.

Well, that's all it took. Her perfectly chosen words sent him into orbit. Combining his anger with the intent not to look like a weakling to his wife, he stormed over to his brother's place and...got his jaw jacked! The next time I saw John, he was sipping a T-Bone through a straw! Actually, I saw him in church feeding on the preachin'. I'll never forget him trying to greet me with his upper and lower jaw wired together. *"Good Mawnin bruvver."*

So, the next time you talk yourself down with a whitetail approaching, remember if you can do it in the *woods*, you can do it in the *world*. Here is true strength.

THE ARROW STRIKES Have I ever "blown it" while hunting because of buck fever? In what ways have I learned to manage the effects of the fever? In my personal life, does anger ever get the best of me? Have I left others wounded? What steps can I take to do better? Do I understand from Jesus' outburst in the temple that there are some things that *should* make me angry? What are some things that should "raise my dander"?

Signs

When a deer hunter enters property he has never hunted, he scouts for signs of deer activity: anything that says, "We have been here." It might be fresh imprints of hooves in a muddy spot or bark shaved off a tree where a deer has rubbed his antlers marking his turf. He may also find a place along a tree line where a buck has scraped down to the fresh dirt. Or it may be a bedding area where the foliage is pressed flat. These signs are all the evidence he needs to set up his stand and get in the game. But it's not the *signs* he's focused upon. He is searching and pursuing the *deer* that made the signs.

Likewise, the Son of God once walked among us. I know He did. He left prints behind everywhere that proves He was here. He left them in abundance (John 7:31; 21:25). Having seen the signs, we need then to pursue Him.

Some of these signs are the many **prophecies** Jesus fulfilled concerning Himself. For example, He was born in Bethlehem (Micah 5:2), born of a virgin (Isa. 7:14), had no bones broken at His crucifixion (Exodus 12:46), and on we could go.

Other irrefutable signs are all the **miracles** He performed which left people saying, *"We never saw anything like this"* (Mark 2:12). Even a blind man easily put the pieces together. To paraphrase, "I was blind...now I see. And Jesus was in between. Go figure. It's not difficult to know who He is" (John 9:25). His conclusion was *"If this Man were not from God, He could do nothing"* (John 9:33).

The Pharisees were the only blind ones in the chapter. It reminds me of a blind sister in Christ who once said to me on the way to worship, "Jeff, people say I am blind, but I can see things a lot of people can't." She had eyes to see the unseen, the invisible, and the eternal things (2 Corinthians 4:18).

A chill-bump moment to me in John 9 is the moment the blind man is told by Jesus, *"You have both seen Him and it is He who is talking to you"* (9:37). If we will just be honest with the evidence, the signs will lead us to Him. The blind man progressed in his understanding. He first saw Jesus as a ***man*** (9:11), then a ***prophet*** (9:17), then ***"from God"*** (9:33), and at last the ***"Son of God"*** (9:35). And if you are still struggling to believe in Him, just keep scouting and tracking Him on the pages of Matthew, Mark, Luke and John. I've only given you a thimble full of the evidence. There is much more.

It's flawed logic to say, "Oh, the Gospels were written by His very own disciples who were prejudiced. They wanted to keep the cause alive so they wrote whatever they wanted to write." The truth is they had nothing earthly to gain for their message. They didn't get rich. They were hated. They were persecuted. And even with their lives on the line, they never recanted their story because they knew it was true. They saw Him. They heard Him. They touched Him (1 John 1:1-4). Their enemies may have fought against them, but they never tried to say the miracles never occurred. The signs had been done in the midst of the enemies, and they knew it (Acts 2:22). The apostles went to their graves placing all their faith in the return of the resurrected Lord. I plan to do the same.

Once again, it is not so much the *signs* God wants us to see. He wants us to see *what they point to*…Jesus is the Christ, the Son of God! It is very much like driving a car. It is not the black arrow on the yellow sign we need to see the most; it is the curve!

Can you see what these signs point toward?

"And many other signs did Jesus in the presence of His disciples, which are not written in this book. But these are written that you might believe Jesus is the Christ, the Son of God, and that believing you may have life in His name."
John 20:30-31

Evidence for Jesus is similar to fingerprint evidence. Every person has unique ridges on his or her fingers. When a print that is found on an object matches the pattern of the ridges on a person's finger, investigators can conclude with scientific certainty that **this specific individual** touched that object. Only one person can be a match.

Think with me about the prophecies concerning Jesus recorded many years before His birth. There are many of them, but someone has done the math on the chances of one man fulfilling just eight of them. It's one chance in one hundred million, billion.

Here's another way to express it. If you took that number of silver dollars, they would cover the state of Texas to a depth of two feet. Now, if you marked one silver dollar, mixed it in the pile, and then had someone to walk across Texas blindfolded, the odds of him finding the coin is the same odds of one person fulfilling just eight prophecies. To fulfill forty-eight of them would be one chance in a trillion, trillion, trillion, trillion, trillion, trillion, trillion, trillion, trillion, trillion, trillion, trillion, trillion.

The odds are that it would be impossible for *anyone* to fulfill all of those Old Testament prophecies. But Jesus fulfilled them all (Acts 3:18). The evidence points conclusively to Jesus! He is the only match.

See how simple this is? If signs in the woods can point to deer, so can signs point to the Christ. Christians can be certain their faith is on solid ground. Jesus is who He claimed to be. He is the Son of God. Indeed, He was here! He came to *your* home, to make it possible for you to go to *His*. And He is the only way there (John 14:1-6). Follow Him.

THE ARROW STRIKES In the woods, can I read the signs and draw conclusions about deer in the area? Am I able to see that Jesus actually lived here on earth and left many signs to prove He was God's Son? If I had lived in the first century and seen His miracles and heard His teaching, what would I have concluded about Him? Would I have been against Him? Since His claims are true, should they affect my life in any way? How?

"Did That Arrow Hit Where I Think It Did?"

My very first harvest with a bow will be long remembered for a couple of reasons: it was my *first*, and it was a *terrible* shot—just pure ole plain awful!

The morning had been a bust. I had not seen anything. I finally descended from the stand and began to make my way out of the woods. However, I knew I might still have an opportunity because the ground was wet with no crunch to the leaves. I thought, "I just may be able to sneak up on one undetected." Below the hill, there was a dirt road cutting into the hardwoods. I knew that sometimes a deer would stop in the road to munch on a few acorns.

Just as I had hoped, as I eased down the hill, there was a deer in the road at about forty yards. Its head was concealed by saplings, but the rest was open to sight. I didn't know if it was a buck or a doe, but for a first bow harvest, either was okay with me. Since I was a beginner, I considered anything with a bow a good deal and something of which to be very proud!

RUMP-EL-STILT-SKIN!!

I had just gotten the bow. It had been a long time since I had practiced, and I suppose I had a brain cramp and forgot how it worked. It had a fiber optic that looped around and actually gave you two dots, side by side, about a half-inch apart. Well, the outer dot is the one that you are supposed to place on the deer. For some reason, my brain said to place the deer's vitals between the two dots. So, I thought I had the vitals bracketed in the sweet spot, but actually the dot that counted was...well...on his rear end. I let her rip, hoping to stick the vitals, but when the deer ran off, he had something like a peacock feather attached to his derriere. That's French, I think, for what my granny always called the "tee-hiney." I shook my head and said to myself, *"Did that arrow hit where I think it did?"* Yep, I had launched a missile from forty yards right into the "ole gluteus maximus."

Boy, was I ever excited, but what hope could I really have? It was the worst shot ever! I went down to the road where the deer had stood, and there was no blood. I was so disappointed, but I refused to quit looking. And then, I saw it. There was a dime-size drop of blood. It pointed me in the direction of another and another.

About seventy yards away I came upon my arrow lying in a massive amount of the crimson stuff, but no deer. What in the world? Where did he go? I kept turning about in a circle, and then I saw him fifteen yards further away. Somehow his rack had gotten all broken up before this day, but he was a six-point, and perhaps an eight depending on how much was missing. I have concluded that he probably stopped along the way, reached back, and pulled the arrow out with his teeth. That hastened the end of his run because the arrow was working like a stopper in a sink until he pulled it out. The arrow had found the only lethal spot in his rump. I think it is called the femoral artery. It carries a lot of blood into the thighs and legs.

NOT EVERYTHING IS RANDOM

All of this reminded me of a battle in the Old Testament. King Ahab was a very wicked king, and God was ready to be done with him. God has His limits when hard-core rebellion sets in. Ahab goes into a battle hoping to conquer yet another city. He is warned that if he goes, he will die. He goes anyway. That's Ahab for you: stubborn and self-willed to the last. The Bible says, *"Now a certain man drew a bow at random, and struck the king of Israel between the joints of his armor. So he said to the driver of his chariot, 'Turn around and take me out of battle, for I am wounded.' The battle increased that day, and the king of Israel propped himself up in his chariot, facing the Syrians until evening; and about the time of sunset he died"* (2 Chronicles 18:33-34).

Even the Bible called that shot a random thing, yet it found a crack in the armor of Ahab, a small unguarded place. That's all it took. Since God was so displeased with Ahab, I think God made sure that arrow hit the spot. Don't you?

Now, this leads me to think about myself in battle. All Christians are at war with the devil every day. He patterns you. He looks for the best time, place, and opportunity to take you out (Luke 4:13; Ephesians 6:13). He will look for an unguarded place and attack our weak spot. We cannot be careless. We must guard every area of our lives. The area where we are the most vulnerable may also be the area we have given the least thought.

We are not alone in this battle. God has given us plenty of armor to fight Satan. But we must be sure to take up every part. Don't leave off any piece. The armor is listed in Ephesians 6, and the warning is clear. *"Therefore **take up the whole armor** of God that you may be able to withstand in the evil day, and having done all to stand"* (Ephesians 6:13). We can be shielded well to *"quench all the fiery darts of the wicked one"* (6:16).

LEAVE NO UNGUARDED PLACE

When I first began preaching in Athens, there was a young man in the church who was bitten by a copperhead snake. He and a friend were checking field cameras, and for most of the checks they were armored well with good boots. When they were done, Barrett took off his boots and put on his sandals. Some changes we don't need to make. That flip was soon to flop.

On the way out, they remembered one more camera. Barrett thought it would be okay to walk in the sandals as long as he was careful to step where his friend stepped. He was wrong. Along the way, he felt a sting on his foot that felt like he had been snagged by a brier. It wasn't. He looked back, only to see the biggest copperhead he had ever seen. It had fanged his foot, the only uncovered spot. Even a foot matters in battle. You can't do war barefooted. God says. *"...shod your feet with the preparation of the gospel of peace"* (Ephesians 6:15).

So, dress in all the armor. Don't ever forget that Satan is crafty. He will be lurking in the shadows looking for even a small opening. Be wise. Be watchful. Be strong and victorious through the Lord.

Oh yeah…Barrett is okay. He made it to the hospital and they nursed him back to health. Antivenin was not needed but was available just as the Lord's blood is our antivenin against the devil's successful bites upon us (John 3:14-15). Christians can plead for God's forgiveness when they sin (1 John 1:7-9). Barrett was told he was fortunate the snake was very large because the big ones are experienced hunters and can control the amount of venom they inject. The smaller ones do not. This one was simply saying, "Get out of here and leave me alone." Lesson learned? Flip-flops will not do. Armor up!

THE ARROW STRIKES Do I watch over my life very carefully, leaving no unguarded place? Since the devil loves to attack a weak spot in my life, what would my weak spot be? How can the Lord and I eliminate this weakness from my life?

"I Think I Know What the Army is Like"

As he slid his body over into the tub to begin scraping away layers of mud from his body, my triumphant little soldier said, *"Daddy, that was so much fun. I'm gonna tell my teacher, 'I think I know what the army is like.' "* As I wiped trickles of blood off my arms, his words exploded within my heart. They will forever be etched on "the wall" of my deer hunting memories.

We had just returned from a search and recovery mission on my first good buck. His wound was lethal, but his brain must have flipped the survival switch on his adrenal glands. Tremendous aid was sent to his muscles to put as much distance between us and him as possible.

This whitetail headed for the nastiest section of woods as late afternoon faded into night. His escape route was layered with booby traps designed to discourage our efforts to locate him. First, we had to crouch low to the ground to maneuver through a thicket of entangling and piercing briers. Next we sloshed through a creek, tripping and slipping here and there on moving rocks and slime . All the while, all our senses were on heightened alert. Every time we inched closer to him, we would hear the pounding of hooves against the ground as he strove to push himself closer to his fortress. At the last, we went into a bog where the mud was so thick it strained our muscles. Henderson was wearing tennis shoes, since he never anticipated the war ahead. More than once we would hear a sucking sound come from the ground. "Hen's" foot would emerge shoeless with a sock flapping four inches past his toes. His shoes were being swallowed up by the mud monster! We kept having to find his shoes. It was a real bother but a lasting reminder that every piece of armor is important in battle (Ephesians 6:15).

I was almost ready to back out, gather additional forces, and try again in the morning. But then Eddie, who never gives up, said, *"There he is!"* He had collapsed far out in the quagmire, and it was there he gave it up.

My imaginative juices flow as I wonder exactly what this evening felt like to my son. I wish I could have hopped on a miniature four-wheeler and driven around in his head for a while. No wonder he said, *"I think I know what the army is like."* I wouldn't take anything for the masculine trek he was forced to make this evening.

LET 'EM ROAR!!

I fear we live in a society where little boys are being feminized. Moms, please don't do that to your boys. Let them be daring. Let them have man-sized adventures. Let them ride the roller coasters. Let them get that first BB gun. I greatly appreciate the words of John Eldridge who eloquently says, *"How many parents have tried in vain to prevent little Timmy from playing with guns. Give it up. If you do not supply a boy with weapons, he will make them from whatever materials are at hand. My boys chew their graham crackers into the shape of hand guns at the breakfast table. Every stick or fallen branch is a spear, or better, a bazooka"* (John Eldridge, *Wild at Heart*, pg. 10).

Don't take the roar out of your little lion. Men were made to fight valiantly for the things that matter. If they don't, we will not have those things very long. Anything beautiful has to be fought for to be preserved. Just ask Jesus. Now, there's a warrior for you! He fought for you!

Yes, there are times when men must be tender at heart. I'll talk about that later in the piece on *Velvet and Steel* but men are made in the "image of God." Women are also made in that image, and they have strength indeed, but God also measured out His more tender traits for them. My wife has brought a tender calmness to my home but has also been a rock when I most needed it. For sure, don't tell a woman who just had a baby she is not strong. But, in contrast, just watch her special touch when she holds that baby for the first time!

When it comes to a man, I'm convinced God took a powder measure, filled it full of masculinity, and then loaded the man with it. That's why so many men feel like something is missing. God gave them something special within, but somewhere along the way they got robbed. Maybe they robbed themselves. I'm convinced much of mine had been suppressed for a long time, but it has become unleashed now. I feel more alive at this time in my life than ever before. I have great purpose and drive and determination.

I love Eldridge's premise in his book. He argues that every man needs *a battle to fight, an adventure to live, and a beauty to fight for.* That was the life of Jesus and should be the life of every man. I pray my son will have all three. He had two of the three on this hunt. I'm confident some young girl has a warrior in her future.

All of this masculinity comes from the God who made the man. He's the same God who made the thunderous Niagara falls, the tornado, the hurricane, lightning, thunder, Cape buffalo, grizzly bears, mountain lions, coyotes, bobcats, and on we could go. He is strong and fierce and is to be *feared.* That's another word in the Bible that sweet theologians have tamed too much. Just read the Bible from cover to cover and see if you get the idea that it only means that God is to be held in awe and reverence (Hebrews 10:31). I love Him, but I also maintain a healthy fear of Him. I know His power, and I know what He has the power to do at judgment day.

But have you ever noticed that so often we want to be close to what we fear? It's why we go right up to the edge of canyons and look over. We fear it but we are drawn to it because of its beauty and majesty. That's the mix I get with the God of both *wrath and justice,* but also *love and mercy.* Please, let us be what He made us to be. He is in us. Wrap your mind around that.

THE WALL

Let us be men. Let us fight for those we love. Let us be the hero in the story. Let us be rescuers. My son has heard me say to him many times along the way when something hard was in front of him, *"A boy is gonna do what a boy is gonna do. But a man has got to do what a man has got to do."* On this day, he felt like a man. He felt like a soldier. I would not surrender that for all the money in the world.

Now, let me come off my high, and back to reality. I have to say something to you, my son. *"Neither you nor I really know what the army is like."* In some ways, I feel very uncomfortable even making the comparisons. There are men and women who know all too well what the army is like. It may be that even a piece like this causes them to have unwanted flashbacks to scenes of horror they have lived through. If it does, I am very sorry, but I am trying to lay the groundwork for giving honor to whom honor is due (Romans 13:7). Soldiers, you did know that Romans 13:1-7 is about you, didn't you? God gave governments to us because we do a terrible job governing our individual lives. But a nation with no army will soon be obliterated! I am thankful to God for His plan. Soldiers, forgive us for every moment when we have treated you with contempt.

And then I wonder if my words unavoidably wound the heart of a mother who visits "the wall" looking for her boy's name. Of all the songs that have been written about our war heroes, I think I like "The Wall" by the Statler Brothers the most. I have to swallow a big lump on the "little boy" part.

I saw her from a distance
as she walked up to the wall.
In her hand she held some flowers
as her tears began to fall.
She took out pen and paper
as to trace her memories.
She looked up to heaven
and the words she said were these...

She said, "Lord my boy was special,
and he meant so much to me,
and Oh I'd love to see him
just one more time you see.
All I have are the memories
and the moments to recall...

So Lord could you tell him,
he's more than a name on a wall?"

She said, "He really missed the family
and being home on Christmas day

*and he died for God and country
in a place so far away.*

*I remember just a little boy
playing war since he was three.
But Lord this time I know,
He's not coming home to me."*

*She said, "Lord my boy was special,
and he meant so much to me,
and Oh I'd love to see him
But I know it just can't be.
So I thank you for my memories
and the moments to recall...*

*But Lord could you tell him,
he's more than a name on a wall?*

*Lord could you tell him,
He's more than a name on a wall?"*

I hope you read all of that, because if you did, you will understand why I almost had a "come apart" in the heart of our nation on another night. I stood at the Women's Vietnam Memorial in Washington, D.C. with my daughter and her high school class. Moonlight streamed across the statue of a female nurse holding a dying soldier, applying force to the gaping wound in his chest. Compassion flowed from her eyes like a mighty stream. In that era, she may not have been allowed to fight, but she was fighting her own kind of battle— for his life!

I was lost in thought until some female teacher with a handful of children said, *"Look at that, boys and girls. Another case of male chauvinism."* I thought I was going to "blow a gasket" and probably should have in "righteous indignation!" Is that all she saw? Did the real nurse feel that way as she felt the last heartbeat? Did Glenna Goodacre, the creator of the memorial, feel that way in 1993, when the monument was dedicated? I know that some women have not been given proper respect and appreciation, but come on. Is this the message these boys and girls needed to get? Dear teacher, I give you an "F" for your day's work with these little impressionable minds. Okay Jeff, simmer down now.

I know that my son's words claiming to know what the army is like were spoken innocently. He was just saying what his heart moved him to say. He's not the first kid to be fascinated with the army. Just look in Tom Brokaw's book, *The Greatest Generation*, and look at little Tom on an army base wearing a soldier's helmet getting ready to fight Hitler and the Germans!

If this afternoon's deer hunt burns a war mentality in my son's heart, I'll take it. He must know that life is war! There is one army he must enlist in. He has sung about it since he was old enough to sing.

"I may never march in the infantry.
Ride in the cavalry. Shoot the artillery.
I may never zoom o'er the enemy.
But I'm in the Lord's army.
Yes sir!"

ENTER BOOT CAMP

There will be many mentions of spiritual warfare in this book. For now, I hope my children will take a few points back to the spiritual barracks with them.

You do not have to find a war. One has come to you. I'm disturbed by the number of people who move about not even realizing there is war. They are already casualties. This is not a walk in the park. You must engage in this war against evil forces. Enlist in the Lord's army. He is ever stronger than the enemy. *"You are of God, little children, and have overcome them, because He who is in you is greater than he who is in the world"* (1 John 4:4).

Do not let any amount of obstacles deter you from finishing! Life will be full of thickets, bogs, and briers. Do not get entangled. Cut through it. *"No one engaged in warfare entangles himself with the affairs of this life, that he may please him who enlisted him as a soldier"* (2 Timothy 2:4).

Let the Lord teach you how to fight. Those who stay with the Captain never lose the war. *"Blessed be the Lord my Rock, who trains my hands for war, and my fingers for battle —my lovingkindness and my fortress, my high tower and my deliverer, my* *shield and the One in whom I take refuge, Who subdues my people under me"* (Psalm 144:1-2). When all the dust settles, be left standing! The victory is ours (1 Corinthians 15:50-58).

At last you will be awarded a spiritual medal of honor. *"Be thou faithful until death, and I will give you the crown of life"* (Revelation 2:10).

You were a fighter tonight, little man! I hope you smile in your dreams. I know I will. I saw in you tonight the attitude and spirit a soldier needs. I believe in you. Take your memories from the woods that *"by them you may wage the good warfare"* (1 Timothy 1:18). And boy, whatever you do, don't forget your boots!

THE ARROW STRIKES What has been my most difficult and challenging hunt requiring either physical or mental strength? Do I agree that we need to train our little boys to be men and fight for what matters? Can I look around me and inside of me and realize there is truly a spiritual war going on? Do I live each day with a battlefield mentality? How might it help me if I had a soldier's mindset?

I Am a Soldier in the Lord's Army

I am a soldier in the army of my God.
The Lord Jesus Christ is my Commanding Officer.
The Holy Scripture is my code of conduct.
Faith, prayer, and the Word are my weapons of warfare.

I have been taught by the Holy Spirit, trained by experience,
tried by adversity, and tested by fire.

I am a volunteer in this army, and I am enlisted for eternity.
I will not get out, sell out, be talked out, or pushed out.
I am faithful, reliable, capable, and dependable.
If my God needs me, I am there. I am a soldier.

I am not a baby. I do not need to be pampered, petted,
primed up, pumped up, picked up, or pepped up. I am a soldier.
No one has to call me, remind me,

write me, visit me, entice me, or lure me.
I am a soldier. I am not a wimp.
I am in place, saluting my King, obeying His orders,
praising His name, and building His kingdom!
No one has to send me flowers, gifts, food, cards, or
candy, or give me handouts. I do not need to be
cuddled, cradled, cared for, or catered to.
I am committed. I cannot have my feelings hurt bad
enough to turn me around. I cannot be discouraged enough to
turn me aside. I cannot lose enough to cause me to quit.

When Jesus called me into this army, I had nothing.
If I end up with nothing, I will still come out ahead.
I will win. My God has and will continue to supply all of my need.
I am more than a conqueror. I will always triumph.
I can do all things through Christ.
The devil cannot defeat me. People cannot disillusion me.
Weather cannot weary me. Sickness cannot stop me.
Battles cannot beat me. Even death cannot destroy me.
For when my Commander calls me from His battlefield,
He will promote me to captain and then allow me to rule with Him.
I am a soldier in the army, and I'm marching claiming victory.
I will not give up. I will not turn around.

I am a soldier, marching heaven-bound.
Here I Stand! Will you stand with me?

- Unknown Author

I Wanted You to Be Mounted

(An Emotional Hunter Agonizes
Over His First Good Buck)

I wanted to have you mounted, and lifted to the wall above where I work every day. But I didn't — probably because it costs lots, and I hope for one even bigger some day. This is not to bring you down in any way, for you were majestic in your own right. I can still see you walking so stately across the field toward me. I remember the rush you sent through my flesh and bones. You deserve to be displayed so that others can continue to admire you.

I wanted you to be mounted because I have sought you for years. I began pursuing you before my son was born and when my daughter was a child. I wanted a way to nurture my son to be masculine and wild at heart. I wanted him to love the outdoors and God's beautiful creation. I wanted him to be a spiritual fighter through life and escape the lion's stalking of him (1 Peter 5:8). You represent this manhood. How many fights and battles have you taken on and won? Perhaps there was one you backed away from, but your day came when you could stand your ground.

I wanted you to be mounted because the Lord used you to give me some of the greatest years of my life. All those who hunt have trials, burdens, cares, and disappointments in life. You draw us into your world, the serene one where a man can pray to his Maker without interruption, get his head together, recalibrate, and once again get ready to come at his challenges. You know...a woods fix.

While you stayed tucked away in your secret place, I sat high above in the limbs recovering in the quietness. While I never saw you, I saw God. I saw His beauty in the falling leaves, the chirping birds, the hooting owl, the hammering woodpecker, the rustling squirrels, the stalking coyote, the sunrises and sunsets, and the moonlit paths. More than that, I saw His great love for me and wondered if in His providence He set me right in the heart of deer country for therapy. Oh, what a joyous purpose you have played in my life. If you had come my way sooner, the sweetness of this moment would not be as great. I suspect I needed the wait.

I wanted you to be mounted for what you represent. You are the Great American Whitetail. You have been graced by God to be one of the smartest and wisest animals on earth. You have only survived because of your wisdom. God did not give every creature what He gave you.

*"The wings of the ostrich wave proudly, but are her wings and pinions like the kindly storks? For she leaves her eggs on the ground, and warms them in the dust; She forgets that a foot may crush them, or that a wild beast may break them. She treats her young harshly, as though they were not hers; Her labor is in vain, without concern. Because **God deprived her of wisdom, and did not endow her with understanding.** "*
Job 39:13-17

You probably lived to be almost four years old. Many of your comrades did not. You must have been given something extra. I have seen a myriad of scrubs who had great ambition and I passed on them all. You are rare. Your kind doesn't come along very often and there is a possibility I will never get a chance to connect on another like you. Was it my rattling or estrous bleats that caused you to slip a little in judgment? We hunters know it is about the only time you let up and get careless. But hey, you teach us men some vital lessons.

Many men have lost it all because they lost all good sense, did not harness their desires, and keep them where they belonged (Proverbs 7:21-27). Every man should read those verses. God has told every married man to be as a loving deer and graceful doe—to always be satisfied and enraptured with the love of his wife (Proverbs 5:15-20). My wife is so special to me. She has blessed my life so wonderfully and will be a reason I make it to heaven. She understands this whitetail addiction of mine, and it was only through her patience that I increased the chances of meeting you on the field of life.

Yes, I wanted to have you mounted. If I had let you go, I probably would have only seen you once. By placing you on my wall, I can admire you by sight for many days and maybe even pass you on to my son or daughter when I lie down to rest. You were a great fighter. You challenged me greatly. While sitting on that moonlit field, giving you time, I even prayed to God not to let me lose you. I called Eddie to help me. Without him, I probably would not have found you.

After we returned home, my son, Henderson, said, "*Dad, that was so much fun! I wish I could do it every evening.*" Thank you for the joy forever engraved on his heart. He also said, *"I am gonna tell my teacher, 'I think I know what the army is like.' "* You sent us through the briers, through the creek, and into the swampy bog. Adrenaline raged!! We panted for you, just as you have panted for the water brooks (Psalm 42:1).

I want you to know that while I decided not to mount you on the wall, you will forever be mounted in the elevated thoughts of my mind. You were special. I want you to know it. I will encounter many whitetails, if God wills, in the future but never another you. You will hold your place forever in my heart and soul, for you were the first. There can never be another to hold that "first" spot. I met you within walking distance of my country home, and I couldn't be happier about that. Eddie called you my "back-door buck!" I will see you in my mind every time I ride by that field. So, don't feel inferior because I did not give you a special spot on the wall. I would have chosen one of the best to perform his artistry on you...for he admires you as I do. You will always be a giant in my mind. People with lots of money may pay thousands for another, but...you are worth more than them all.

Author Note:

Yes, I initially decided not to mount this buck, but in the end my heart would not let me say "No" to it. *"Recovery,"* as I named him, is proudly postured just above my computer screen. I'll never forget all this deer represents, and I praise God for all the good the pursuit did for me.

THE ARROW STRIKES Have I found that time in the woods or any nature scene is good therapy for me? Trophy bucks are usually taken when they slip in using good judgment. Am I currently using good judgment and making good decisions in my life? Can the God who gave the whitetail such wisdom also give *me* wisdom for daily living?

What Makes a Trophy?

Should I mount this deer? Is it big enough? Should I hold out for one a little more impressive?

Have you ever run these and other questions through your mind when trying to decide if your harvested buck is really a trophy? What makes a trophy anyway?

Some might answer, *"Only those bucks that will qualify on the Boone and Crockett or Pope and Young scale of measurement."* I disagree. My answer? **A trophy is any deer that for whatever reason holds a special place in your heart. All that matters is that he matters to you.** To this day, even seasoned, veteran hunters will tell you that one of their favorite mounts is their first buck. There can never be another first. Remember your first date? Your first kiss? Your first love?

I understand. When a hunter looks at his trophy on the wall, his mind is filled with memories and even emotion. He never forgets the landscape, the weather conditions, the posture of the deer, the circumstances, the buck fever, and even what might have been going on in his life at the time. My eyes filled with tears as I contemplated **not** mounting my first good buck. I wondered if it was just too much money to pour into it. But my heart would not let this deer go! I know it sounds strange, maybe even weird, but I had bonded with this buck. In the end, I knew I would make a mistake and always have regrets if I didn't get this buck on the wall. If you are a hunter, I imagine you understand my feelings.

Hunters carry whatever is going on in life into the woods with them. It's the reason many of them go in the first place. It may be that the pursuit took place after disease, death, divorce, or some other difficult or devastating circumstance of life. Life brings plenty of trials, obstacles, and hurts. The Father doesn't shelter us from them, but *saves us through them.* The trophy buck can be a reminder of a meaningful milestone in a hunter's life in the woods and the world.

My first trophy buck was so meaningful to me because of the little spot in the world where I took him. He was taken in my convenience stand less than five minutes from the door of my country home. It is here that I am allowed to raise my son "country style" – complete with cotton, soybean, and wheat fields, farm ponds, and biscuits and gravy. I get to fulfill the words of a song.

> *"I'm gonna live where the green grass grows.*
> *Watch my corn pop up in rows.*
> *Every night be tucked in close to you.*
> *Raise our kids where the good Lord is blessed.*
> *Point our rocking chairs toward the west.*
> *Plant our dreams where peaceful river flows*
> *and the green grass grows."*
> (Tim McGraw)

WILL THE MOMENT EVER COME?

I considered calling this mount, "Coming of Age," because it marked a milestone in my journey as a deer hunter. For so many seasons, I have had to say, *"Maybe this will be the year,"* only to see the season end with nothing worthy of mounting. I was excited for others who would get their buck, but always wondering when mine was going to come. One of the most difficult pills to swallow was the day a young kid got an impressive, mount-worthy buck I had never even seen on my hunting property. He must have been covering a lot of ground during the rut. My hunting buddy called me and gave me the news. I was happy for the young man, but it was like a dagger in my heart. I can't say that the green-eyed monster of envy had total hold of me. It was truly okay that he had *his* deer. I just wanted *mine.*

I call the taking of my buck, "coming of age," because finally I had joined the league of hunters who had already done the same. Of course, I'm still learning, but gone are the days when I was a babe in the hunting world, hardly knowing what I was doing. And I was so happy and surprised with the composure I had in the "moment of truth." I wasn't torn to pieces with buck fever.

When I saw my trophy walking across the field like a piece out of an old Hartford commercial, I immediately knew it was a shooter. I spoke to myself saying, *"Jeff, this is it. Take your time. Make the shot good."* The deer also had "come of age" himself. He was tapping on four years old. If a buck reaches even three years old in our pressure-filled county, he is eligible for social security benefits! He is not taken easily. He has to mess up somehow.

I read with delight recently, *"If a buck reaches the ripe old age of three-and-a-half, his behavior is so out of the norm that he could almost be considered a different breed of animal. He leaves sign, but he is rarely seen during shooting hours. You will seldom kill one of these bucks by employing typical hunting practices"* (John Eberhart, pg. 30, June 2012, Deer and Deer Hunting Magazine). See why I am mounting this one? The monkey is off my back now, and I can wait relaxed and contented for whatever else comes down the line.

What are the spiritual lessons connected with my first mount? Well, for one, we treasure what we have to wait for (Galatians 5:5). Heaven will surely be worth it all. And then, we need to come of age spiritually. We need to grow as students of the Word and no longer be babies (Hebrews 5:12-14). We surely must add that persistence is major in our journey toward heaven (Hebrews 10:36). Slow and steady wins the race. Do the time. Stay at it. The day will come. It may not seem like it, but it will (2 Peter 3:1-13).

So, if it means something special to you, mount it. You won't regret it. But above all, never let your earthly trophies hinder you from the pursuing the most important things: your relationship with Jesus and heaven as your home.

> *"So, I'll cherish the old rugged cross.*
> *Til my trophies at last I lay down.*
> *I will cling to the old rugged cross.*
> *And exchange it someday for a crown."*

 What is my favorite trophy from time I have

spent in the woods? Do I tend to remember the details from all my hunts: time, place, weather conditions, circumstances in life, mood, etc.? Have I appreciated things more when I have had to wait for them? How can my time in the woods teach me patience in my spiritual journey? Can I see that the reward will be worth all the sacrifice?

"Daddy, I Feel Like I Did Something Wrong"

If you really want to have a blast while deer hunting, take my daughter with you. Bethany's idea of hunting is to sit in the stand, read a book, send text messages, and plan on saying something to get dad "tickled," knowing I can't laugh. Why are things so much funnier then? The tree shakes from the motion of two people belly-laughing while trying to hold it in. Like the day we were laughing and looked up and a pretty good six-point was fifteen yards away looking at us like we were crazy. He had that "who are you laughing at" look in his eyes, and then shot out of there.

My most memorable day with her was when she took two deer in about thirty minutes. Alabama is very generous in what you are allowed to harvest. About midmorning a doe came within range. Bethany fired the high-powered cannon (which is how a 30-06 must feel to a young lady), and the deer bolted away like greased lightning.

"I missed," she exclaimed.

I said, "No, baby girl, I don't think you did."

We were waiting a few minutes before we went to check on things, when all of a sudden— here came another one. Because she was unsure of her first shot, Bethany asked if she could take this one. "Go for it," I said. She shot again. This one fell on the spot. After a short walk, we also found the first one. Two!! This particular year, she took more in thirty minutes than I did all year. My hunting buddies made sure I never forgot that!

Bethany was so excited about her accomplishment, but I noticed she was getting quieter as we worked on loading them on the...uhh...minivan. Yep, I really did go hunting with it before I got my truck. A hunter has to do what he has to do. Did I really just admit that? Oh well, I've seen worse in Alabama!

On the way out, with two deer strapped to the rear bumper cargo rack, she broke her silence and said, *"Daddy, I feel like I did something wrong."* I understood. She was struggling with the kill. I said, "I understand baby. But you didn't do anything wrong. God gave us these animals to eat. He let you bring in some good food today." I don't know if that helped her much. She will still go hunting but is very tender-hearted about it. I want her to be. Even yet, she rides around with a little pink-deer decal on her rear window.

I cannot speak for every hunter, but the men I share hunting with are men who respect the deer. They are selective in what they take and do much in the way of advancing a great wildlife heritage in our state. It's very common for them after taking a doe to pat her on the side and say, "Thank you, girl," followed by a look up to heaven and a "Thank you, Lord." They know where these gifts come from. *"Every good gift and every perfect gift is from above and comes down from the Father of lights..."* (James 1:17).

I once saw a painting by Nicholas Rosato of an Indian lifting his arms toward heaven, expressing thanks for his harvest. His god was not the true God, but at least he knew to give thanks. God says it is okay to eat them and enjoy it as long as we receive it with thanksgiving. *"For every creature of God is good, and nothing is to be refused if it is received with thanksgiving; for it is sanctified by the word of God and prayer"* (1 Timothy 4:3-4). It is not wrong. He said so.

VEGGIE TALES

I hunt following the rules of fair chase, and I eat everything I take. If my freezer is full, I know people who are always ready for some venison. And as to eating it, at least the food I go after has a fighting chance! A head of lettuce is a living thing too, and it can't get away. Poor thing! My children and I take our hats off after every harvest, and there, on the spot, offer thanks to God.

There's much information out there these days that isn't correct and so many efforts afoot to take away our second amendment rights which affect hunters. Someone told me of one animal activist group that even placed a sign off the highway with Moses holding the Ten Commandments. The sign said, "What part of 'Thou shalt not kill' do you not understand?" Two things come to my mind. One: God was speaking of the murder of humans. Second: Do we recall how many animals were sacrificed and eaten in the days of Moses and thereafter? Sometimes, more were offered than could be counted (2 Chronicles 5:6).

Good hunters are ethical. They regard the life of their animals (Proverbs 12:10). They have respect for life because they honor the One who gives it. For those who know God, the shedding of blood is a most solemn moment. God teaches us to be reverent about it knowing that ***"the life of the flesh is in the blood"*** and *"...it is the blood that makes atonement for the soul"* (Leviticus 17:11; Hebrews 9:22). There's a message about Christ in every animal that has blood circulating through it (1 Peter 1:18-19). Simply put...something sacrificed to feed me and give me life.

IT'S FOR GIRLS TOO

A lot of girls have been surprised to discover they love to hunt. Their numbers are increasing. One of America's favorite hunting couples is Lee and Tiffany Lakosky. Tiffany says that when she was dating Lee and first tried hunting with him she didn't know if emotionally she could shoot anything and was afraid Lee wouldn't still like her. But Lee said, "That's OK. If you can't, it's no big deal."

Tiffany's first harvest was a beautiful 6-pointer and she was thrilled. I love what she says about it. *"There was no better feeling in the world.* ***I had no idea how much my life was about to change with the release of that arrow. All of a sudden, my life seemed to be so much more fulfilled.*** *I had no idea how empty my life had really been before I started hunting"* (pg. 59-60, Hunting Mature Whitetails).

Those words say exactly what whitetail hunting does for me. Hunting gives me so much joy. It is an awesome moment of time in God's creation, seeing His power and creativity and meditating on where life really is—in the Son who shed His life-giving blood for me.

So, get a kid off the couch, away from the video games and cell phones for a little while and head to the woods. Giggle if you want to. You might miss out on a nice buck but you'll take home a great memory.

"Thank you Lord for every
privilege to see the deer woods,
to relish in all of Your creation,
and to fill my table with great food.
You are truly so good to me and my family.
Through your greatest gift,
Jesus our Lord, I pray. Amen."

Have I ever felt what Bethany felt when I harvested a deer? Do I agree that hunters can be proud of their skill but should also be both reverent and thankful after a harvest? Do I take simple things like food, clothing, and shelter for granted? Can I see that God will always give me the essentials if I seek Him first in my life (Matthew 6:33)? Do I express my gratitude enough to God?

Don't Cry Son; We Are Still Huntin'!

If there is anything a hunter loves more than harvesting a deer of his own, it is seeing his children do it. I'll never forget opening day of gun season 2009. Henderson got his first deer!

The boy slept most of the morning. That's Cadillac-style hunting. It works like this:

1) Son sleeps until dad sees something.
2) Dad wakes up son.
3) Son shoots deer.

Not a bad arrangement, huh?

About 8:30 that morning, a buck eased into a small food plot. I whispered ever so carefully, *"Henderson, Henderson, wake up, wake up. He's here buddy. He's here."* He went from being sound asleep to being in the game! He worked to get in position but must have had trouble getting the deer in the scope. I waited and waited and...nothing ever happened. The deer eased on off and out of sight.

Henderson began to cry. "I pulled the trigger," he said. I'm not sure what happened. Maybe his nine-year-old finger wasn't pulling hard enough. All I know is that there was now a wailing son in a tree stand howling louder than a hungry coyote! *"Ssshhh, Henderson. Don't cry son; we are still huntin'. He's not the only deer in the woods,"* I said. I finally calmed him down but wondered what his carrying on had done to the hunt. But again, I remembered the importance of not showing a lot of frustration. "Make it fun," my late friend, Odell Wilson always said. I'm listening, Odell.

Sure enough, just a few minutes later, another deer sauntered through the thicket and into the field. It was a nice, big-bodied six-point. Henderson's developing arms could not yet handle the weight of a gun very long without getting tired. So, I eased a shooting stick under his rifle. He whispered, "That's good."

I waited anxiously. The buck was not on alert. His nose was down, and his white flag was relaxed. BOOM! The rifle fired and that nice buck kicked his back legs high in the air like a bucking bronco. It was a sight Henderson had seen on TV and most always means a great shot. "Got him!" he exclaimed. He knew the shot was good.

In the Bible, Moses knew all about crying children too. In his days, the children of Israel had the task of traveling out from their Egyptian bondage toward the promised land. However, it was easier for God to get them out of Egypt than it was for Him to get Egypt out of them. They cried all over Moses as they remembered the food they ate in Egypt. They begged for a return to those days. Moses said, *"Where am I to get meat to give to all these people? For they weep all over me, saying, 'Give us meat, that we may eat' "* (Numbers 11:13). Their complaining and crying was beginning to wear on him. He even asked God to take his life if this was the way life was going to be.

Murmur, mumble, mope and moan: that was the spirit of most of the Israelites. Later, the so-called warriors who faithlessly whined about their inability to conquer the Promised Land were not allowed to enter. It is true that *they* could not. But *God* could. A new group of faithful conquerers took Canaan.

BIG BOYS DO CRY

Let me be clear here. It's alright for men to cry at times. We have unfairly taught through the years, "Hush now. Big boys don't cry." Does this mean that Jesus wasn't a big boy? He was the strongest man who ever lived! What about the other great men in the Bible who cried? Not only did they cry, they should have. They had good reason. *You can judge the character of a man by the things that make him cry.*

- Jesus cried at the tomb of Lazarus (John 11:35).

- Jesus wept over the lost souls in Jerusalem who rejected Him (Luke 19:41-44).
- Peter "wept bitterly" after his denial of Jesus (Luke 22:62).
- Paul wept over sin in a local church (2 Corinthians 2:4).
- Joseph wept upon seeing his brothers again and their repentance (Genesis 45:1-5).

I appreciate our intent to try to nurture brave and courageous hearts in our little men. I really do. I strive to do it too. But just because a man cries, it doesn't mean he isn't strong. Even a modern-day soldier has an element of fear, but he manages it. I read a sign once that said, *"Courage is fear that has said its prayers."* We bring our emotions to God who settles them and then puts them to use for His glory.

I wasn't bothered that Henderson was crying. I just wanted him to know that we were still in the game! I didn't want him to quit. This is the one thing that stands out about all the people of faith in the Bible. They never quit. Disappointed? Yes. Discouraged? Yes. Losing a battle here and there? Yes. But never quitting. I had to seize the moment with Henderson. His hunting of this whitetail was good training ground for the challenging setbacks in the world we live in outside of the woods.

We are more than conquerors through Him who loved us (Romans 8:37). We don't draw back. We continue to believe to the saving of the soul (Hebrews 10:38-39). Through faith and patience, we can inherit the promises of God (Hebrews 6:12).

My little man-cub proved himself a conqueror on this day. He wiped his tears and got back to the task at hand. As a result, he has three big pictures and a rack mounted on his wall! We see it every night at bedtime. I usually look at it and with a tone of amazement ask, *"Who shot that nice buck?"* He smiles and triumphantly says, *"I did."* That's the reward for not giving up and for pressing on. Maybe big guys need to take that point to heart too.

THE ARROW STRIKES Do I believe it is okay for a man to cry? What things have I cried about, and what do those moments reveal about my character? What can I learn from my setbacks in the woods to apply to everyday life? Am I a whiner? Do I complain too often? Do others see me as tenderhearted but also strong and resilient?

Velvet and Steel

Velvet and steel. Those are what make whitetail deer. It is another reason why they hold such a fascination to me. I can see how God embedded these two qualities into them when He made them. But I also believe God wants these two things in us, so we can put them to work where they are needed in our lives.

DEER IN VELVET

No doubt, you have heard the phrase "deer in velvet." It's that time of year when a buck's antlers are developing. They are covered with a soft and very sensitive material called "velvet." This sensitivity helps the deer to be careful not to bump his antlers while they are growing. It hurts!

This soft velvet is made of nerves and blood vessels that supply nutrients to the growing antlers. When the antlers have grown as large as they will be, blood flow shuts off, and the antler gradually dies and sheds the velvet. What's left is very strong, solid bone! It's hunter's hardware! The buck will proudly use his antlers in a contest of strength (otherwise known as a fight) against other bucks. I love the concept. **Something soft...building something strong!**

THE SENSITIVE SIDE

The whitetail's soft quality is displayed so beautifully by the female: the graceful doe. Those who study whitetails say that after a gestation period of about 7 months, a doe will go off alone to a place she has selected to have her baby, called the nursery area. She will chase other deer away that try to follow her. What could be more tender than a mother deer nursing that spotted little fawn in a quiet, private place? Nothing is more intimate than a mother nursing her baby. The apostle Paul says that he even used this approach with newborn Christians. There are simply times we need to be tender, just like velvet.

*"But we were **gentle among you,**
just as a nursing mother
cherishes her own children.
So, affectionately longing for you,
we were well pleased to impart to
you not only the gospel of God,
but also our own lives
because you had become dear to us."*
1 Thessalonians 2:7-8

One of my favorite deer pictures hangs in my "man cave." It is a picture of me with a live doe at a deer farm. I am crouched down beside her. She stayed with me, letting me rub her across her back, and she sniffed at my cheek. She was so close to me her breath fogged my glasses! I loved that wonderfully tender moment. How can you not fall in love with something so tender and delicate?

I am told by those who operate deer farms that the deer are so delicate. If anything gets out of balance they will get sick. Someone must care for them.

MEN OF STEEL

One of the elders where I preach shared with me the most fascinating deer story I have ever heard to also demonstrate what I mean about their "steely" side.

He had stopped along a road where a bridge crossed the creek. He heard dogs barking in the distance. It sounded like they were hot on the trail of something. Suddenly a buck emerged from the woods! You are not going to believe this next part! I once heard of a buck crawling backwards to inch his way to safety, but this takes the cake!

The buck walked into the water, and headed upstream about fifty yards. He then sat down to totally submerge everything except his antlers, ears, nose, and eyes. It looked like nothing more than reeds in the water. And there he stayed, cooling off, and not moving. The dogs tracked him to the water but lost him. No scent and no sight! They barked frantically but moved on. Can you see why these awesome works of God continually fill me with wonder and amazement?

These creatures have nerves of steel! Don't you know it took everything that buck had within him to sit perfectly still when dogs were right upon him! And I am persuaded that many times hunters have walked right past a monster buck, who refused to move even a millimeter. How well would you do holding your composure with a stalker five feet away from you? Strong, I tell you! That's what these masterpieces of God are!

Bucks are fighters too. Once, during the rut, I was rattling horns together, and a buck charged right up to my stand. He stood less than ten yards from the base of the tree. His neck was punctured and bloody from a previous fight, and he was looking for some more action! I watched him bellow steam from his nostrils like a dragon. To this day it is one of my favorite whitetail memories.

I recently read of a man who was raising a buck as a pet. He lived to regret it. He took some acorns into the pen, and the buck attacked him. He says, "That deer picked me up, and I weigh 260 pounds, and carried me 30 or 40 feet in the air, never put me down. I was just like a rag doll. I was on top of his horns, and my feet were off the ground. I was in the cradle and couldn't do anything about it." When he finally put the man down, he dug in with his antlers which went through the man's sinuses, through his optic nerve, and stuck into the edge of his brain.

Alabama Wildlife and Freshwater Fisheries Director, Chuck Sykes, said of the attack, "In the summer and early fall, the bucks are in bachelor groups. All the boys are hanging out, and everybody is friendly, and everybody is happy. When the weather gets cold, that testosterone increases as breeding season is coming in. Then nobody is a buddy. Everybody fights. If they are used to a human as their buddy during the summer, they don't care that you were their best friend then. It's 'all about me' when rutting season comes about. They defend their territory and assert their dominance. Period." (Alabama Hunting & Fishing Digest 2014-2015, pg. 30).

When testosterone begins to flow in the woods, the most threatening of all vocalizations made by bucks is the "snort-wheeze." If that one catches you off guard, it will scare you right out of the stand or at least make the hair stand up on your arms. It sounds something like *"phiit, phitt, phiiiiiiiiiiiiiiii."* A buck makes this intimidating sound by blasting air through his pinched nostrils. It's easy to picture snot and hot steam erupting! When made by a dominant buck, this sound says to an underling buck, *"Back off, Jack, before I give you a whippin' you will never forget."* He's warning of a real "slobber knocker" of a fight. He has every intention to protect both his doe and his territory. If a hunter tries to imitate a snort-wheeze to attract a buck, he should use it only on a very mature one. Most of the time only the big buck will risk it in hopes of finding a doe in estrus. A smaller buck is likely to hear it, tuck his tail, and "get out of Dodge."

BUCKS AND MEN: A LOT IN COMMON

The Creator not only gave these "boys of winter" the steel within them; He expects them to use it. He did the same with men, husbands, and fathers. At times, we have to be stern, even commanding and charging our children to do right. Abraham did with his children (Genesis 18:19). Paul also saw the value and the need to sometimes help others with these more fatherly traits.

> *"As you know how we **exhorted**, and **comforted**,*
> *and **charged** every one of you,*
> ***as a father does his own children,***
> *that you would have a walk worthy of God*
> *who calls you into His own kingdom and glory."*
> 1 Thessalonians 2:11-12

JESUS: A MIXTURE OF BOTH

Can we not see these contrasting qualities in Jesus? How tender He was dealing with those who were truly seeking to overcome their sinful lives like the woman caught in adultery in John 9. But this same Jesus stood up to the hard-hearted Pharisees calling them hypocrites and comparing them to graves or tombs that are so beautiful on the outside but inside are full of dead men's bones (Matthew 23:27).

And what nerves of steel He manifested when soldiers came to arrest Him in the garden of Gethsemane. No shrinking back. He went forward and said to them, *"Whom are you seeking?"* When they said "Jesus of Nazareth," He said, *"I am He"* (John 18:3-6). *They* were the ones who drew back and fell to the ground!

But don't forget that He also wept before and after those moments (Hebrews 5:7; Mark 14:34-35; Luke 19:41). Again, the character of a man is seen in the things that make him weep.

Velvet and steel. That was Jesus. And it should be every man. I must credit author, Aubrey Andeline, for first using these two words to describe manhood in his book on masculine development.

THE NEED FOR VELVET AND STEEL

We need velvet and steel in our marriages. We need husbands who can wear two hats. They can be tough, daily warriors against the world, but they can also be lovers with a tender touch. Deuteronomy 24:5 teaches this beautifully. God mandated that a man who had taken a wife was not to be charged with war duty or other responsibility for the first year of his marriage. What in the world did God want him to do? *"Be free at home...and bring happiness to his wife, whom he has taken."* Steel and velvet.

Do you remember General Norman Schwarzkopf, commander of Operation Desert Storm in the Persian Gulf? Americans affectionately called him *"Stormin' Norman."* But guess what his wife called him? I read somewhere that she called him *"Pookie Bear."* It sounds as if he understood when to be a man of velvet and when to be a man of steel.

Spiritually, a man is to be the wife's leader...protecting her. But he is to also be her velvet, covering her with love and sharing spiritual nutrients from the word of God for her to grow. Ephesians 5:25-29 shows what Jesus does for His bride, the church.

*"Husbands, love your wives, as Christ loved the church
and gave Himself up for her, that He might sanctify her,
having cleansed her by the washing of water with the word,
so that He might present the church to Himself in splendor,*

without spot or wrinkle or any such thing,
that she might be holy and without blemish.
In the same way husbands should love their wives
as their own bodies. He who loves his wife loves himself.
For no one ever hated his own flesh,
but nourishes and cherishes it,
just as Christ does the church." (ESV)

So, a real man will battle for her daily, working hard to provide for her physically, but he will also be "a man of the book," nourishing his wife with it. The Bible is the center of their home.

I have also tried to stress that Ephesians 5 shows that a man's major need is to be **respected**. And a wife's major need is to be **loved**. Verse 33 is really clear.

"Nevertheless, let each one of you in particular
*so **love his own wife** as himself,*
and let the wife see that she
respects her husband."

Wives need to show reverence and respect for their husbands. Express appreciation for his leadership. Make him feel admired. Submit to his Christ-like leadership. Husbands must let themselves be tender, loving, and romantic. Tell her you love her, send flowers, leave loving things on sticky notes, call her to see how her day is going, etc. It is a beautiful cycle. *Her making him feel like a man, like steel. Him making her feel like a woman, like velvet.* It works. Well, of course it does. It's the way the Creator made us.

Velvet and steel is needed with children. They need a mom who says to the child on the swing, *"Be careful. Be careful."* But they also need the dad who says *"Go higher. Go higher."*

I mainly believe children need to be dealt with tenderly. Every step of the way they need to be praised for the good things we see in them. We need to catch them doing right and tell them how proud we are of them. More than once, with Jesus listening, His Father said, *"This is my beloved Son, in whom I am well pleased"* (Matthew 3:17; 17:5). How good that must have felt to Jesus. I am sad for children who never hear such words. But there will be times when our children must be rebuked and disciplined. The Bible plainly says, *"The rod and reproof give wisdom, but a child left to himself brings shame to his mother"* (Proverbs 29:15). Maybe the words of Holly Dunn's song say it best. She clearly appreciated both velvet and steel in her childhood home.

> *"Daddy's hands were soft and kind when I was crying.*
> *Daddy's hands were hard as steel when I'd done wrong.*
> *Daddy's hands weren't always gentle*
> *But I've come to understand.*
> *There was always love in Daddy's hands."*

Velvet and steel are needed in the church. The Bible teaches us to tailor our efforts to correct brothers and sisters in Christ. Every person doesn't need the same thing. One may need velvet. Another may need steel. First Thessalonians 5:14 says, *"Now we exhort you brethren, warn those who are unruly, comfort the fainthearted, uphold the weak, be patient with all."* Can you see both velvet and steel?

First Corinthians 5 calls for an action of steel against a brother in the church having sexual relations with his father's wife and evidently refusing to repent. The church was told to withdraw from such a man. When we dig our heals in the sand of sin, God calls for steely discipline. Yet, even this is intended to save our spirits on the day Jesus comes again (5:5). Love must sometimes be tough love.

Velvet and steel are needed in this country of ours. Folks, America is in trouble. We are literally in a leadership crisis in high places. While we appreciate those who still lead according to the Biblical principles...they are few. I long for a return to a better America.

Alexis DeToqueville is credited with the following words. There is some debate as to whether he is the author. But whoever is the author, he is right on track. His findings match Proverbs 14:34, which says it is righteousness that makes a nation great!

> *I sought for the greatness and genius of America*
> *in her commodious harbors and her ample rivers -*
> *and it was not there . . .*
> *in her fertile fields and boundless forests*

and it was not there . . .
in her rich mines and her vast world commerce
and it was not there . . .
in her democratic Congress and her matchless Constitution -
and it was not there.
Not until I went into the churches of America
and heard her pulpits flame with righteousness
did I understand the secret of her genius and power.
America is great because she is good,
and if America ever ceases to be good,
she will cease to be great.

God's nation of Israel faced the same problem in the Old Testament. God looked for strong, righteous men and they couldn't be found. God says, *"So I sought for a man among them who would make a wall, and stand in the gap before Me on behalf of the land, that I should not destroy it, but I found no one"* (Ezekiel 22:30).

Recently, I learned of Gianna Jessen. She is a survivor of a late-term saline abortion. I got on the internet and listened to her speak to a group of men in the Parliament house of Australia. She pleads for men to step up. Gianna doesn't really want to be in the role she is in, but in the absence of strong male leaders, she feels she has no choice. Listen...

"For just a brief moment,
I would like to speak directly to the men
in this room and do something that is never done.
Men, you are made for greatness.
You are made to stand up and be men.
You are made to defend women and children.
Not stand by and turn your head when you
know murder is occurring and do nothing about it.
You are not made to use women and leave us alone.
*You are made to be **kind and great and gracious and strong***
***and stand for something** because men, listen to me,*
***I am too tired to do your job**...*
You are made to defend what is right and good.
This fiery young girl will stand here and say,
'Now is your moment.'
What sort of man do you want to be;

a man obsessed with your own glory,
or a man obsessed with the glory of God?"

May God give us great wisdom to see the value of both velvet and steel and to know when to use each.

THE ARROW STRIKES Do I bring the qualities of velvet and steel into my relationships? Of these two, which do I need to develop more? Am I a good model of a godly man or godly woman? Have I thought of God and Jesus being more like velvet or steel? Why is it important for me to know both the "goodness and severity of God" (Romans 11:22)?

The Bridge

I am blessed abundantly by God to have places to hunt in Alabama and Tennessee. People with very generous hearts have given me a gift.

There's a fair amount of travel to these places of beauty. As I travel, I cross many bridges. Just today I crossed twenty-four of them. Yes, I counted them. Some are small. Some are big. Some are really, really big. But all of them are essential. Without them I could never be where I want to be.

There's even a bridge in the heart of the woods on one property. It lies across a creek heading toward one of my all-time favorite hunting spots. There is good deer movement there and a lofty view from which to hunt and be alone—just me and God.

Without this bridge, I am stuck. The span is too wide. The water is too deep. It would be silly to attempt to jump. I don't have enough strength. I would fall short. And freezing water doth cause much pain! I'm not a fan of hypothermia. It is a sure way to become disoriented, lose all sense of direction, and even die.

But someone built a bridge. Someone took large beams and laid them across that span. I don't know who did it, but I am so thankful they did. There's no fun on this side. But on the other side there is joy and happiness, and I surely don't want to miss out on any of it.

LISTEN...

If at all possible, please find the quietest place you can to continue reading what I am now writing. It is the centerpiece of this book. I want to talk with you about **the greatest bridge ever built—the cross of Jesus**. I do know Who built that one, and we are about to cross deep water indeed!

We need to know what the cross of Jesus was all about. I didn't for the longest. And I'm certain that I can never fully comprehend all that happened there. It's too wide, too long, too deep, and too high (Ephesians 3:18-19). Why did Jesus have to die? Why was it such a horrible death? What was the purpose of it all? God wants us to know the answers to these questions. Here it is in five points:

1. **Our sin separates us from God and makes us His enemy** (Isaiah 59:1-2). What a chasm sin creates between us and Him! This holy God is on one side and we, the sinners, are far away on the other. We need to be reconciled to Him, but there is no way for us to cross back over. We are powerless to do anything.

2. **We are under a death penalty. Death means "separation."** The Bible says, *"The wages of sin is death"* (Romans 6:23). It's not just physical death but also what the Bible calls the *"second death."* It's eternal punishment (Revelation 21:8). The book of Romans teaches that all are guilty of sin. All have fallen short (Romans 3:23), and are facing the wrath of God if something isn't done (Romans 2:4-9). I know this is bad news. But we will never fully appreciate the "good news" until we get a grasp on the bad. Everyone speaks freely about salvation, but salvation *from what*? We are saved from *something*. That something is hell, and Jesus talked about it more than any other person. He ought to know.

3. **God has to punish sin with death (that's justice). But God doesn't want us to have to pay the penalty (that's justification).** God had three choices:

a. *Ignore our sin* (but that gets in the way of His justice).
b. *Make us pay the penalty* (but His heart of love doesn't want that).
c. *Pay the penalty Himself* (and that's what He did)! Amazing love. (Romans 3:25-26; 1 Peter 3:18; 2:24; 2 Corinthians 5:19-21).

4. **God built a bridge with a hammer and nails.** It's the cross of Jesus. Thanks to the Builder! We can cross with the CROSS! This is the Gospel— the "good news." Jesus paid *our* penalty on the cross and appeased the wrath of God. He took what was due us. This is the meaning of Romans 3:25. The cross, with Jesus on it, was put on public display for all the world to see that God never lets sin go unpunished. The penalty was paid. God was satisfied (Isaiah 53:10-11). There is now a way to cross the gorge and be friends with God again. And it was planned before we ever sinned (Revelation 13:8). For illustration, look at my sketch below. Notice what the Holy Spirit teaches in Romans 5:6-11. I have highlighted some key phrases.

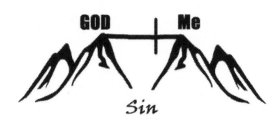

[6] *For when **we were still without strength**, in due time Christ died for the ungodly.* [7] *For scarcely for a righteous man will one die; yet perhaps for a good man someone would even dare to die.* [8] *But God demonstrates His own love toward us, in that **while we were still sinners, Christ died for us.*** [9] *Much more then, having now been justified by His blood, we shall be **saved from wrath** through Him.* [10] *For if when we were enemies **we were reconciled to God** through the death of His Son, much more, having*

*been reconciled, we shall be **saved by His life**. [11] And not only that, but **we also rejoice in God** through our Lord Jesus Christ, through whom we have now received the reconciliation.*

5. **The bridge (cross) doesn't automatically save everyone. We must <u>obey</u> the gospel (2 Thessalonians 1:8).** The core of the Gospel is that Jesus died, was buried, and then rose to eternal life (1 Corinthians 15:1-4). To obey the gospel, we do the same. We die to sin. We are buried in baptism. We rise to walk in newness of life (Romans 6:1-7). Our sins are washed away (Acts 22:16).

THE GOSPEL → Jesus died. / Jesus was buried. / Jesus was raised.

OBEY THE GOSPEL → I die to sin. / I am buried. / I am raised.

I read once of a man who was on his way to be baptized into Christ. His brother came along to witness. But the water was a little swift. As John was entering the water, his brother cried out from the hill, *"John, don't do this! A man could die doing this."* John replied, *"Precisely! And it has taken me years to figure that out!"*

And let me add this. We must leave our old man behind in the grave. Our determination is not to continue in sin. When Pharaoh wanted Moses to compromise and leave some of Israel's livestock in Egypt, Moses boldly told the king, *"Not a hoof shall be left behind"* (Exodus 10:26). That fits well with this book, doesn't it? When we leave bondage, we leave it completely. We must not leave any part of us in slavery to sin, not even a hoof!

SEEING IT IN ACTION

Sometimes understanding the plan of salvation is made easier by simply watching what someone did to be saved. In Acts 8:26-40, we have the conversion of a man from Ethiopia. Salvation is as simple as doing what he did. Take time to read it.

- He was reading in the scriptures, but needed some guidance.
- Philip arrived to teach him.
- He saw his sin.
- He heard about the life of Jesus and His horrible death.
- He confessed his faith in Jesus, the Son of God.
- He was baptized to access what the cross offered.
- He went on his way rejoicing! He was born again (John 3:3,5).

Jesus said it a nutshell, when He said, *"Go into all the world and preach the gospel to every creature. He who believes and is baptized will be saved; but he who does not believe will be condemned"* (Mark 16:15-16).

WHAT GOOD IS A BRIDGE TO US...

...if we will not make use of it? If you have not already obeyed the gospel, will you in faith cross the bridge? If we do not, His words to us on judgment day will be *"depart from Me"* (Matthew 7:21-23). And there will be a great gulf between us and Him with no way to cross over to Him. We will forever be separated from Him (Luke 16:19-31).

When we consider the great lengths Christ went to in order to save us, wouldn't obedience be the only rational decision (2 Corinthians 5:14-15)? He died for you and me. Why not live for Him?

THE ARROW STRIKES Have I understood how repulsive sin is to a holy God? Do I tend to think that everyone goes to heaven? As I think about the chasm between God and those in sin, on which side of the chasm am I? Do I understand that Jesus had to bridge the gap? Am I thankful for His love and grace? What does it mean to obey the gospel? Have I obeyed?

Blood and Water

I have a picture saved in my files that to some might be unsightly, but to me it tells a beautiful story. It's a picture of a creek, and a large section of it is crimson-colored. Eddie harvested a doe this day and had taken his deer down to the creek and field dressed it. I would say only a pint of blood emptied into the creek. I never realized so much water could turn color from such a small amount of blood.

Deer hunting, field dressing, and the processing of meat has given me a little bit more of a feel for what the Israelites experienced when they offered animal sacrifices. Those sacrifices were a type of the Christ to come—the innocent dying in the place of the guilty. To be honest, I am thankful for the experience. Most of us are far removed from anything like that. You just can't learn as much picking your food off the meat counter at the grocery store. But now, with my senses, I can see and smell the Old Testament tabernacle when I read about it. It was a beautiful place but it was also a butcher shop, a reminder of the terrible ugliness of sin.

Do you remember the very last plague God brought upon Pharaoh before the Israelites were freed from their slavery in Egypt? It is hauntingly referred to as "The Death of the Firstborn." God was going to pass through the land at midnight, and every house where blood was not applied to the doors would lose its firstborn—whether person or livestock.

"WHEN I SEE THE BLOOD"

The Israelites obeyed. They took the blood of a lamb and smeared the blood on the doorposts and the lintel: the beam across the top of the door. God said if He saw the blood, He would pass over that house and no judgment would come to it (Exodus 12:13).

That night there was "a great cry in Egypt, for there was not a house where there was not one dead" (Exodus 12:30). There were lives lost in Pharaoh's house and at last he had enough. He told the Israelites to "be gone" from Egypt.

The Jews celebrated the Passover every year. Christians see a type of Christ in the Passover. He is our Passover (1 Corinthians 5:7). When God sees His blood applied to our lives, He can pass over us and not bring punishment to us.

I have heard it said that during the Passover in Jesus' day a massive number of lambs would be offered. What happened to all of that blood? They were supposed to pour it at the base of the altar at the temple. Some of my studies indicate there was a drainage system where water trickled through and washed the blood down below into the Kidron Valley. I don't know if it is speculation, but someone has suggested that it is altogether possible that Jesus saw a crimson-colored brook as He crossed it on the way to the garden of Gethsemane (John 18:1). I do think it is possible, but I urge caution when the Bible does not give all the details. Nevertheless, it is interesting to ponder. If He did see such a brook, can you imagine what went through His mind knowing He was the Lamb soon to be slaughtered?

I do know that the blood of all those animals, multiplied by all the years Israel was a nation, cannot cleanse us of even *one* sin. The only reason God forgave them of sin when they offered animal sacrifices is because He knew the cross of Jesus was coming. They were saved on credit. His payment was coming. Jesus is our Passover Lamb and only His blood can cleanse us (Heb. 10:1-4,11-14).

My attention is seized when the soldiers go to the crosses on Calvary intending to break the legs of those crucified (John 19:31-37). I understand that slamming a mallet into the legs and breaking them keeps the victim from lifting up in order to exhale. It hastens death. They broke the legs of the thieves, but did not break Jesus legs. Why? Well, He had already died. But there is a greater reason, and how thrilling it is. Jesus is our Passover lamb and the Old Testament had said that the lambs were not to have broken bones. Does that give you chill bumps? It does me. God saw to it that His Son's legs were not broken. And when they pierced Jesus' side, what came out? The Bible says *blood and water*.

GOD'S OPERATION

These two, blood and water, flow beautifully together as a duo in our salvation. One is the *ground* of our salvation (the blood) and the other (the water) is the *means* of contacting that saving blood. His blood doesn't automatically save anyone. We have to come to it in faith and trust.

The Holy Spirit teaches that our sins are washed away *in the blood of Jesus* (Revelation 1:5) and also says that our sins are washed away *when we are baptized* (Acts 22:16). That's blood and water. Baptism is an act of faith where we are calling upon God to cleanse us in the precious blood of His Son (Galatians 3:26-27; 1 Peter 3:20-22). When God buries us with Christ in baptism, we contact His saving blood and rise to walk a new life (Romans 6:1-7). Read the book of Acts soon, and see all the conversions of people washed from their sins in His blood. He adds all those who are blood-bought to His church (Acts 20:28; 2:47; 1 Peter 1:18-19; 1 Corinthians 6:20). The conversions are thrilling to read, and I hope you will join the obedient if you haven't already.

Now, the day you are baptized, you will not literally see the blood nor will you see God's hands at work. But both are there. It is God's operation: not ours, nor the preacher's. God buries. God raises.

> *"buried with Him in baptism,*
> *in which you were also raised with Him*
> *through faith in the working of God,*
> *who raised Him from the dead."*
> Colossians 2:12

And so, it was only a pint of blood in a creek, but it flooded my mind with many thoughts and filled me to the brim with great thanksgiving. Love like this only flows from the Lord. And seeing that creek reminded me of all the baptisms I witnessed as a little boy. It was our tradition to immediately begin to sing "Oh, Happy Day" as soon as the person rose to a new life in Christ. I leave you with some of the words.

Oh, happy day that fixed my choice,
On Thee my Savior and my God!
Well may this glowing heart rejoice,
And tell its raptures all abroad!

Happy day, happy day,
When Jesus washed my sins away.
He taught me how to watch and pray,
And live rejoicing every day.

Happy day, happy day,
When Jesus washed my sins away.

(Philip Doddridge & Edward Rimbault)

THE ARROW STRIKES What have I learned from today's devotional about blood and water? Have I tended to see baptism as a work of God (God's operation) or solely a work of man? Can I see that it is an act of faith in God's operation and an essential part of the plan of salvation? Has the blood of Christ been applied to my life in baptism? Have I understood the revolutionary change that is to occur as one dies, is buried and raised in baptism?

SUMMER

In the world: Ahh...sunshine, sandals, and flip-flops! Tire swings and shade trees. Splashing water and inner tubes. Vacations and VBS. Bobbers floating on the lake. Largemouth bass are resting under submerged logs. Cottonmouths are sunning on top and reminding us that every season of life has its *delights* and *dangers*. Baseball is in full swing. There are home-grown tomatoes, corn, peas, watermelon and homemade ice cream. Dad grills in the backyard. Summer is here and so are hummingbirds, butterflies, lightning bugs, and ugh...houseflies and "skeeters!"

In the woods: Whitetails are not seen as often. It's hot, and they rest in the shade of the woods; however, in the early morning and at sunset they will prance in the fields. God makes sure they always have the perfect coat of hair—warm in the winter and cool in the summer. Their summer coat is shorter, thinner, and more lightweight. The reddish brown color reflects the sunshine and helps to keep them from overheating.

Some of the bucks are starting to think they are "big stuff," sort of like teenagers. By late summer they will be antlered and covered with velvet. The little ones are wagging their tails and learning how to communicate. Most of the wagging simply means "I'm having fun!"

In the Word: It's summertime in your journey toward heaven. You are no longer drinking milk. You have learned how to feed yourself daily and eat more solid spiritual food just like a yearling graduates to grasses, juicy leaves, and berries.

You are understanding God's word better and better. Verses you once didn't understand are easier now. Everything is fitting together and making sense. For that matter, life makes sense. You have purpose, and it feels wonderful!

During this time you have even become a teacher of others and are leading others to the Lord. God surely is proud of your progress "by this time" (Hebrews 5:12-14). You are enjoying being in the family of God. Your progress is becoming evident to all (1 Timothy 4:15), and it feels good to know God is working within you. He loves finishing what He starts (Philippians 1:6; 2:12-13; Hebrews 12:2).

Be careful during this part of your life in Christ. It is easy to become spiritually proud and let your guard down. Remind yourself to flee youthful lusts (2 Timothy 2:22). Also, if you are bringing up children at this time, it can be a hectic time and full of distractions. You are working hard. Don't let the "cares of this world" choke the word from your life or theirs (Mark 4:19). Press on!

"But also for this very reason,
giving all diligence, add to your faith virtue,
to virtue knowledge, to knowledge self-control,
to self-control perseverance, to perseverance godliness,
to godliness brotherly kindness and to brotherly kindness love.
For if these things are yours and abound,
you will neither be barren nor unfruitful
in the knowledge of our Lord Jesus Christ."
2 Peter 1:5-8

Perfect Walkers

I am sometimes asked by other whitetail lovers, *"Why do you like deer hunting more than any other kind of hunting?"* My list of reasons keeps growing as I learn more and more.

One of my most common answers: *"I love the mystery of deer hunting."* For some reason, I get especially excited on those grey, slightly foggy mornings. In those conditions, the ground is normally wet and very quiet. Deer seem ghostly when you see them walking gently in the foggy mist.

Adding to the mystery is the moment a deer suddenly appears in a spot where there was NOTHING a moment before. You look away for one second, turn back, and there he is. It's like something magical!

A friend of mine harvested his best buck ever that way. Fog was hovering on a field, blocking his view, when all of a sudden a slight breeze blew from west to east, slowly pushing away the patch of fog, and there Goliath stood!

It's not magic. It's just that deer are *perfect* walkers, and when they need to be, they are *secret* walkers. This is possible because of the way the Creator made their legs. When a deer is on a steady gait, his back foot will always land in the same spot as the front foot. Because of this wise design from the Designer, a deer knows that **if the front hoof, which he can see, goes down quietly, the back hoof will also.** They know how to walk. It's built into them. I might add, they also know when to hold up and not take another step. When they have carelessly walked into danger, they can come to an abrupt halt and refuse to move.

Have you ever gotten into a "stare down" with a deer? If you hunt enough from tree stands, it will happen. One afternoon I heard the snap of a twig on the leafy ground behind me and foolishly jerked my head around to look. There was a small buck looking right at me trying to figure me out. The bad thing was my head was twisted around backwards, and I was stuck. I really didn't want to harvest this buck, but I did want him to settle down and move on without activating neighborhood watch. He must not head bob, rubberneck, stomp, snort, or run.

Eyeball to eyeball we locked in on each other for what felt like forever. Each of us were as unmovable as stone. My neck began to hurt really bad. I was afraid that in the cold, I might harden that way! My eyes also got very tired and dry since I was trying not to blink as often. You know how hard that is. Finally, I had done my job so well, he convinced himself it was safe. He dropped his head and continued his walk.

All of this makes me think about my walk with God.

WALKING WITH GOD

The Bible shows that we are to do the following:

- Walk **with** God (*enjoying harmony and companionship* - Amos 3:3; Genesis 5:24).
- Walk **before** God (*for His inspection* - Genesis 17:1).
- Walk **after** God (*following His lead* - Matthew 16:24).

Enoch is a great example. The Bible says, *"Enoch walked with God; and he was not, for God took him"* (Genesis 5:24). He lived a beautiful life, walking and talking to God. God loved this man so much He wanted to go ahead and bring him into Paradise (Hebrews 11:5). I don't know how it happened, but perhaps one day God said something like, "Enoch, come go home with me." Enoch wanted to go. So, God took him. I have to ask myself, "Am I the kind of person God wants to take home with Him? Is my walk pleasing to Him?"

WALKING IN THE STEPS OF JESUS

Our walk with Jesus is much like the whitetail walk. Jesus places His foot down first and we are to follow with ours, in the same spot. With a whitetail, it's almost like the front foot says to the back one, *"Follow me."*

Jesus said those words often to His disciples. He said them when He called them to be His disciples (Luke 5:27-28). He said them when He was challenging them to die to self, telling them they had crosses to carry too (Matthew 16:24). Even at the very last as He was preparing to go back to heaven, He said, *"Follow Me"* (John 21:15-25). He wants it to be "second nature" to us. He leads. We follow. And it begins with our re-birth. Our steps match His. He died. He was buried. He was resurrected. We do the same thing in obeying the gospel and please notice we do it *with Him.* Front foot and back foot together. *Crucified with Him* (Romans 6:6). *Buried with Him* (Romans 6:4). Then it says, *"Just as Christ was raised...even so we"* (Romans 6:4). Isn't that neat to see?

God made it easy. He sent Jesus and in essence is saying to us, "If you are having trouble understanding how I want you to live on earth, watch Him." Ultimately, hoof prints don't matter in the grand scheme of things. His prints do! His steps are perfect. He will never mislead. We are safe if we step where He steps. Our prayer should ever be for God to make us sure-footed like a deer so that we might not slip and fail to reach the high hills. Three verses in the Bible mention it. You can learn lots from a deer and the One who made him.

> *He makes my feet like the feet of deer,*
> *And sets me on my high places.*
> Psalm 18:33

And let's be sure to get this. **We are to strive each day to have a perfect walk.** The call is to walk in His steps, and those steps are perfect. Peter says we are to *"follow His steps: Who committed **no sin**"* (1 Peter 2:21-22).

Does this high standard bother us? It doesn't seem to bother us with our favorite ball team. We want them to go for #1. When you are on the archery or gun range, what do you do? Do you strive to hit the bull's eye every time? I do. That's my aim every time out. I strive for perfection, and I have fun doing it. I don't want to "miss the mark." By the way, that's what sin is: missing the mark. Why would we take bow practice more seriously than the calling of God to walk in His steps?

We follow Him through good times. We follow Him through bad times. We even follow Him when His instructions don't make sense to us (Luke 5:4-5). And we never quit doing it, for *"each step I take just leads me closer home."*

WALK WORTHY OF THE CALLING

The Bibles teaches that we have a high calling when we become Christians, and we are to walk worthy of it (Ephesians 4:1). We are called to walk the way disciples walk.

I love the Andy Griffith episode when Wally fires Gomer from his job at the filling station. Gomer stops by the Sheriff's office to see Andy and tells him he got fired. But all is well because Gomer is on his way to check into a butcher's job. Andy says, *"Gomer, do you know how to cut meat?"* Gomer replies, *"Do you think they will ask me that?"* Too funny! Of course they will. That's what butchers do.

And we can be sure that God is looking to see if we are doing what He designed Christians to do. It's the calling. For sure, we need *less talk* and *more walk*. Better yet, let's do both. Let's *talk the talk and walk the walk*. Jesus' most scathing words of condemnation were reserved for hypocrites who wore masks to hide who they really were. They professed one thing and did another (Matthew 23). So, let's examine ourselves. Are you walking worthy, or could God nominate you for best actor?

WALK AROUND THE WICKED

Proverbs is full of passages warning us not to walk with the wicked. *"If sinners entice you, do not consent"* (Proverbs 1:10).

"Do not enter the path of the wicked, and do not walk in the way of evil. Avoid it, do not travel on it; Turn away from it and pass on" (Proverbs 4:14-15). If you see evil, don't take another step in that direction. Pass on!

Should you ever find yourself in a bad place, get out quick. Rest assured a deer does, really fast! Wise people look for the quickest exit in every building they enter. Too many people have lost their lives trying to make it back to the door where they entered, and yet a window was right behind them.

WALK WELL IN SECRET

Occasionally, someone will ask me, "Does it ever bother you that some are looking so closely at you as a preacher?" It is true that preachers and their families sort of live in a fish bowl with big eyes peering at them through the glass.

Truthfully, it has never really bothered me. I guess that's because I realize my life is always before the eyes of God and I am more so trying to please Him, not men (Proverbs 15:3; Galatians 1:10).

And let's not confuse reputation with character. Reputation is what men *say* about you on your tombstone. Character is what God *knows* about you.

It makes me wonder how many people have had glowing and wonderful eulogies but God knew better. It reminds me of the words of a country music song called "Two Black Cadillacs." The storyline is that a man's wife and his mistress conspire to kill him, and do! I'm not endorsing that, but it happens! For the longest time the mistress hadn't known about the wife, and the wife hadn't known about the mistress. They both come to his funeral in respective black cadillacs. It was a fine funeral, I tell you. *"And the preacher said he was a good man and his brother said he was a good friend. But the women in the two black veils didn't bother to cry. They took turns laying a rose down, threw a handful of dirt into the deep ground. He's not the only one who had a secret to hide. Bye, bye. Bye, bye."* (Writers: Carrie Underwood, Hillary Lindsey, Josh Kear).

Don't work on your funeral. Work on your life. Whitetails walk in secret masterfully. I also want to strive to do that because *what I am in secret* is **what I am**!

WHAT ABOUT MISSTEPS?

The truth is I do miss on the archery range even as I strive for perfection. But that doesn't change my standard. And God doesn't change His either. What should you do when you misstep and your feet fail to land where His did?

- **Pull the foot back. Confess the wrong. Continue your walk** (1 John 1:7-9).

- **Learn from the wrong steps.** Whenever I or someone with whom I'm hunting misses a deer and he flashes away like lightning, I always say, *"You educated him!"* I believe every deer learns from his mistakes and so should we. The monster buck became a giant because he learned a lot along the way, and now he makes far less mistakes. So can you. You can "fail forward." You are not *sinless* on the journey, but you can *sin less*, and less, and less. Christians are not "sinners" in the sense that they deliberately keep on living to sin. They are to be God's workmanship: something He is proud to see and display to a lost world (Ephesians 2:10).

- **Let the Lord smooth the missteps in the sand**. Let Him wipe them clear in His forgiveness. What will you see then? A perfect walk. The missteps are not seen and will not even be remembered by Him (Hebrews 10:16-17).

FOOTPRINTS IN THE SAND

One day you will look back at the steps of your life. Some of the times will be times when you thought,"I cannot take another step." But later, you realize something interesting. You had arms underneath you (Deuteronomy 33:27). I've always loved the piece called "Footprints in the Sand." I leave it with you to ponder and rejoice in.

One night a man had a dream.
He dreamed he was walking along the beach with the Lord.
Across the sky flashed scenes from his life.
For each scene, he noticed two sets of footprints in the sand;
one belonged to him, and the other to the Lord.

When the last scene of his life flashed before him,
he looked back at the footprints in the sand.
He noticed that many times along the path of his life
there was only one set of footprints.

*He also noticed that it happened at the very
lowest and saddest times in his life.*

*This really bothered him and he
questioned the Lord about it.
"Lord, you said that once I decided to follow you,
you'd walk with me all the way.
But I have noticed that during the most
troublesome times in my life,
there is only one set of footprints.
I don't understand why when I needed
you most you would leave me."*

*The Lord replied, "My precious, precious child,
I love you and would never leave you.
During your times of trial and suffering,
when you see only one set of footprints,
it was then that I carried you."*

THE ARROW STRIKES Do I think as often as I should about making my footsteps match the steps of Jesus? Have I even begun my walk with God? Would others say that I "walk the walk" as well as "talk the talk?" What should I do with my missteps? Is there anywhere I need to quit walking?

Mentors

At the beginning of this book, you were introduced to Eddie Simmons, a friend I call my "deer mentor." In my mind a mentor is someone in addition to the Lord or your parents who makes a great difference in your life.

A mentor is defined as "a wise and trusted counselor or teacher." That's what Eddie has been to me in the woods, and it is what my Uncle Thomas has been to me in the Word. It is a great blessing to have such people in our lives and God loves them. Joshua had Moses to teach him. Samuel had Eli. Timothy had Paul.

Paul defines well the aims of a spiritual mentor. He says to the brethren at Philippi:

> *"The things which you **learned** and **received**
> and **heard** and **saw** in me, **these do**,
> and the God of peace will be with you."*
> Philippians 4:9

That says it. It's what I have done with Eddie. What I learned, received, heard and saw from him about hunting the whitetail, I now do. It's what I did with Uncle Thomas too as he taught me from the pulpit when I was young. To this day, I continue to give great consideration to his counsel. But let's be sure we add this essential element. If it is a spiritual mentor, be certain they are following Christ. The point is not to be like them but rather like the One they follow. Paul added, *"Imitate me, just as I also imitate Christ"* (1 Corinthians 11:1).

What will the results be? *"Everyone who is perfectly trained will be like his teacher"* (Luke 6:40). It's what I have wanted. My supreme aim in life is to be like Jesus.

"DID YOU USE TO BE A SIMMONS?"

It's happening in the woods too. I really do believe I have become a better hunter because of Eddie. He's a deer magnet, I tell you. It's hard to explain or understand but he just has a knack for it. He thinks like a deer. For that reason, his house is a deer museum with several beautiful mounts. And he's rubbing off on me.

I was so surprised at my composure in the "moment of truth" when I took my first trophy buck. I always thought my buck fever would be so bad that I would blow it. Instead, I talked to myself when I saw that rack bobbing across the patch of woods. I said, "Jeff, this is it. The moment you have waited for. Execute. Take your time. Pick a spot. Slowly squeeze the trigger." I credit the calmness on that day to Eddie, even though I still get the shakes most of the time. I hope I always do. Because of his sense for deer patterns and stand locations, I have become accustomed to having whitetails all around me.

I couldn't help but laugh recently when someone said, "Did you use to be a Simmons before you were a May?" My comradery with Eddie is more than about whitetails. He is also that "friend that sticks closer than a brother" (Proverbs 18:24). We are brothers in Christ who push each other onward and upward. He is so upbeat and full of life: the kind of a person I like having around me. Lead on…I'm following.

I know that my son has also profited from being with him. Every boy needs good men in his life besides dad. It reinforces what men are supposed to be. He has especially gotten pumped up about Mr. Eddie bringin' "Ole Red." "Red" is a Dodge Ram pickup truck geared really low to handle most any terrain. It's been our snowplow making it possible to hunt on days when the roads were full of snow. Ole Red has a ram mounted on the hood. Eddie often says, *"Hey Hen! Do you see the direction that goat's head is pointed? Well, hang on, that's where we are going!"*

As Henderson and I waited on that moonlit field for Eddie to help me find my first good buck, he said, "Daddy, what's Mr. Eddie coming on?" I said, "He's bringing Red." "Oh good," Henderson replied.

We still have a message on our answering machine from when Henderson harvested his first deer at age nine. On the machine Eddie recorded a crazy little song using the tune of John Denver's "Leaving On A Jet Plane." It goes like this. *"Well my bags are packed. I'm ready to go. I'm taking Henderson down to kill some mo'. I know that he'll kill all that we need to eat."* We just can't erase it. It was with Eddie's .222 that Henderson took his first deer. That too is a cherished memory. Another hunter laughed at us for hunting with such a small caliber, but Eddie said, "Put it in the gear box and it'll do the job." He was right. Henderson placed a perfect shot in the vitals, and I was so glad to make sure our skeptic knew we did it with the .222.

Only God knows whether Eddie or I will enter Paradise first. I do know this. We long to meet on that shore. I will never forget my friend and deer mentor. We have walked many miles together. How many times has he signaled me to head out of the woods with his perfect owl hoot? I will remember him and smile every time I hear an owl. I will remember him every time I eat a piece of the best deer jerky in the world. I'll remember when I put on my BDU (battle dress uniform) "rip stop" camo. I'll remember when I whittle a stick to use as a handle to drag my deer. I'll remember on the days I get an itchy trigger finger because Eddie's finger itches more than anyone I know. And I'll remember when I go to the house of the Lord. Thank you, my friend, for sharpening me in ways of the woods, but most of all, thank you for sharpening me *"as iron sharpens iron"* in my walk with God (Proverbs 27:17). I will forever be indebted to your friendship.

YOU WERE THERE WHEN...

Then there is my mentor in the Word, my uncle Thomas May. He recently celebrated his 75th birthday. That puts him in the middle of the bonus years by reason of strength (Psalm 90:10). His time is now spent caring for his precious wife who has dementia or Alzheimer's. He is modeling what true love is all about. I was touched recently by a post he put on Facebook. Let's all download it into our hearts and help those dealing with this terrible disease.

Alzheimer's Request

Do not ask me to remember,
don't try to make me understand.
Let me rest and know you're with me,
kiss my cheek and hold my hand.

I'm confused beyond your concept.
I'm sad and sick and lost.
All I know is that I need you,
to be with me at all cost.

Do not lose your patience with me,
do not scold or curse or cry.
I can't help the way I'm acting.
I can't be different though I try.

Just remember that I need you,
that the best of me is gone,
Please don't fail to stand beside me,
love me 'til my life is gone.

(Owen Darnell)

On his birthday, I wrote him to let him know what he means to me.
I said…

"Happy Birthday!!

*Where do I begin? For all my life, you have been my mentor.
You were there when I was doing little Bible talks and shaking like a
leaf. You were in the pulpit teaching me when I may have seemed
like I wasn't listening. You were there when Susan was baptized. You
were there when I asked, "Unka Tonk, should I preach?" and you
answered, "Don't do it if you can keep from it."* (He was saying that
preaching is for those who cannot keep from it - 1 Corinthians 9:16).
*You were there every time I have needed advice or a Bible question
answered. I have always been amazed at your wisdom. You were
there when I went through one of the worst times in my life as a
preacher. You've always been there!*

I simply cannot and do not want to imagine or do life without you. You are a spiritual father to me, my rock who follows the Rock. I have never once been disappointed in you or ashamed of anything you have ever done. You have modeled what CHRIST is all about. I have been so proud many times to say, "My Uncle Thomas used to say..." I have glowed with joy when someone would come up to me and say, "Guess who I met? Uncle Thomas!" And I suppose one of the greatest sermons you have ever preached is the one you are preaching now as you so tenderly care for Aunt Neal with intense love and commitment.

Nightly news will probably never have a segment about your life, but God knows, and I know He is proud. If you had lived before Hebrews 11, I believe your name would have been in there. I know this...you are forever engraved in my book. I love you more than words can ever say. I hope you know that. May God bless you in the greatest ways He can. And again, have a great birthday, Unka Tonk!

Love, Jeff

So, I beg you fellow hunters. If you get a chance to mentor someone in the woods, do it. Better yet, if you are a Christian, mentor them in the Word of God. There just might be someone near you who needs it badly.

Just recently a friend of mine who teaches a trade told of a young man in his class with whom he talked during breaktime. He said the young man's background was as bad as he had ever seen. He had just returned from rehab. His dad left this boy's mother, and him, and his sister. He said, *"I've never been hunting in all my life."* He said, *"I have only one memory of my dad. We are beside a creek bed, but I can't remember what we were doing?"* My friend said, "Do you have any kinfolk that might take you?" He said, *"Well, my mother's brother used to go, but I wouldn't call him about hunting."* Still probing, he was then asked, "What about your friends?" He said, *"I can't get with them or I'll soon be back into the things that have messed up my life."* So sad. He needs a strong man in his life.

If you know of someone like that around you, could you be a mentor to them? Would you? If they are wanting to hunt, will you introduce them to all the joys of it? We need to create more hunters. It's a treasured American privilege and blessing. But it doesn't have to be a trip to the woods. It could be lunch at a fast-food place or whatever. Start somewhere and make a difference. Invest yourself in someone else. Jesus did. And aren't you glad He did?

THE ARROW STRIKES Do I have special mentors in my life? What difference have they made in my life? Have I taken the time lately to tell them what they mean to me? Have I seen anyone around me who could use a mentor? What could I do to help them?

We Interrupt This Marriage

Have you seen any of the signs and bumper stickers hunters and fishermen display about marriage? Some of them are really funny, but I wonder if others actually hurt the heart of a good woman.

Here's one I thought was funny.

"WANTED:
Good woman.
Must be able to clean, cook, sew,
dig worms, and clean fish.
Must have boat and motor.
Send picture of boat and motor.

Then there was the one I saw on the back of a truck. And because I knew the man and his treatment of his wife, it made me both sad and angry at the same time. I couldn't help but wonder how proud his wife must have been for him to ride around town with it displayed for all to get a good laugh, at her expense. It simply said…

My wife: maybe.
My gun: NEVER

Truth be known, the wife of every avid deer hunter sacrifices much. This is well-expressed in the sign that says…

We interrupt this marriage
to bring you deer season.

Now, that one speaks the simple truth even in the home of a man who cares very much about his wife and his marriage. If the hunter is avid, like myself, it is a season where there has to be a lot of giving on his wife's part.

A slight cool "teaser" is felt in North Alabama's September air that gets everyone excited. It says that Alabama and Auburn football is headed toward kickoff, and Tennessee's opening day of bow season will soon arrive. Either way, it means that a lot of wives will be losing their husbands to the recliner or to the woods, and on most Saturdays...both!

DEER HUNTER'S WIVES: SPECIAL BREEDS

Each year in late August, I begin listening to my fall theme song. It is Steve Chapman's song called "The First Winds of Autumn." Steve hunts middle Tennessee so he feels and sees the same changes I experience. He sings about cornstalks turning brown, goldenrod beginning to bloom (ah choo!), and hummingbirds feeling that old Mexico call. Then he sings...

"And when tears touch the cheeks
of my sweetheart, she knows...
Soon it's farewell to her man
with the arrow and bow."

The heart of a hunter,
who can explain?
How the first winds of Autumn
seem to whisper my name.

And they send me to dreamin'
about the morning I'll go,
back up to the hills with
my arrow and bow."

I am fortunate to be married to a beautiful woman who is very understanding and patient when it comes to deer hunting.

Maybe that's because she grew up in the country with a daddy and a brother who both hunted. Plus, she is married to a preacher, and she knows his need sometimes to get away. One of my favorite T-shirts has a bow hunter walking into the dark morning woods, and it says, ***"Gone thinkin."***

It takes a unique kind of woman to be married to a deer hunter. She puts up with being roused from sleep as her husband gets up to go hunting. She endures all the clothes she has to wash in a special way, with no scent detergent. She sits through a lot of deer talk between hunters. She can handle the processing of a deer in her backyard. And in Susan's case, she even faces her fear of snakes in the off-season in order to help me plant food plots, adjust stands, and clear shooting lanes. Just yesterday, I stepped right over the top of a nonpoisonous one just before she saw it. It quickly slithered at my feet. And let me tell you, for a girl who doesn't dance, she was putting on some moves! Now, that's sacrifice.

So, she joins me in this whitetail pursuit. Years ago, she said to me, *"I think when you get your first good buck, I am gonna be even happier about it than you!"* And she was! Seeing me happy makes her happy.

Our text thread on my phone the final minutes of closing day this past year says it all. It was an enjoyable season but also a very sad one for us. We had to say goodbye to her dad who passed away in late December. We would never have imagined it back in October, but it just goes to show that life has seasons and we never know what they may bring. Hunting came to an abrupt stop as we devoted ourselves to caring for family (1 Timothy 5:4). To help you understand our conversation, she is the "Love of My Life" in the following text thread, and I am her "My Main Squeeze."

> My Main Squeeze: 6 more minutes
> My Main Squeeze: 5 more minutes
> Love of My Life: This is sad. I may have a moment. Don't you want to stay 'til noon?
> My Main Squeeze: 4 more minutes
> My Main Squeeze: 3 more minutes
> Love of My Life: Tears
> My Main Squeeze: 2 more minutes
> My Main Squeeze: 1 more minute

My Main Squeeze: 3,2,1...DEAR season, woo hoo. I am ready.
Love of My Life: Did you have fun Bootsy?
My Main Squeeze: I did have fun Bootsy!

"Bootsy" is a little "pet" name we sometimes use for each other. It comes from a movie where a little girl runs away from home and unknowingly hides in a car owned by some goofy criminals, one of whom is called Bootsy. They laugh and play with her, and she actually has more fun those few days with Bootsy than with her own family because they never had time for her. At last the criminals are caught and are about to be taken away to prison. With her parents watching, Savannah runs into Bootsy's arms. She asks with an adorable, appreciative smile, and the cutest little voice if Bootsy will come to see her. He promises. And once again, Savannah smiles.

Well, guess what Susan and I did the day after closing day? We spent the entire day together having fun with one another. She had so looked forward to it: **Opening Day of DEAR season!** We even plan to take more short trips together this year. Time passes quickly. I know the day can come when we may need to spend more time nursing our family members and maybe even ourselves (Proverbs 23:22; 1 Timothy 5:4). My philosophy is to *spend as much time together as you can while you can.* I've seen too many couples save up a nice nest egg with plans to get away with each other more when they retire. And then it just doesn't work out.

THE DEAR OF YOUR LIFE

Men, while we may have a season that is a little interruptive to marriage, let's make sure that we never forget what's most important. Be sure to feed your marriage during and after the season, and be willing to sacrifice time in the woods when more important things arise. Christ is very clear when he says, "Husbands, love your wives, just as Christ also loved the church and gave Himself up for her, so that He might sanctify her, having cleansed her by the washing of water with the word, that He might present to Himself the church in all her glory, having no spot or wrinkle or any such thing; but that she would be holy and blameless. So husbands ought also to love their own wives as their own bodies. He who loves his own wife loves himself; for no one ever hated his own flesh, but **nourishes and cherishes** it, just as Christ also does the church." (Ephesians 5:25-29 NASV).

Even during deer season, there are little things you can do to remind her that she is always loved deeply. Can I suggest a few?

1. Tell her you appreciate her sacrifices during the season.
2. Tell her you love her, and kiss her as you leave. Caution: This applies only if she is awake. Don't wake her up!
3. Take her to your hunting place, and show her your stand locations. When you go hunting, tell her where you will be and when to expect you home. It reduces her worry.
4. Wear a safety harness, and emphasize safety in all you do. Come home safe!
5. Send her a text message while in the stand telling her you love her.
6. When you are home, try really hard to minimize "deer talk." Be into what she is into.
7. Set aside a date night to concentrate totally on her.

These things will help her not to feel like deer hunting has become a rival. Simply put, help her to always know that she is your trophy: that you prize her above all others! That's why I have one sign placed in my man cave that says to my wife and others who see it how treasured she is. It simply says, *"A hunter lives here with the dear of his life."* Thank God for blessing me so richly with a wife who is rare (Proverbs 31:10). And may my children rise up and call her blessed (Proverbs 31:28). Thanks, Bootsy. I sure had fun!

THE ARROW STRIKES Have I allowed deer hunting or any other sport or hobby to keep me from focusing on my marriage? Am I more centered on my needs or my mate's needs? What could I do today to show my spouse my love and dedication?

Hide the Babies

It seems that no matter how much time you spend in the woods, another "first" is sure to come – something you've never seen, something that's never happened before.

I remember the day Eddie and I were scouting new property in the Middle Tennessee hills in the early fall. We were crouching and working our way through a thicket, when all of sudden, Eddie stopped and whispered, *"Jeff, there's a deer."* She stood there broadside looking our way. It was almost like she wanted to be seen. We took a step or two in her direction, and she moved away. We didn't follow.

I turned left to take a different path out of the thicket. I was a little lost in thought when all of sudden something jumped up at my feet! I almost jumped out of my skin! It was a little spotted fawn. She was beautiful! I had never before been that close to a fawn in the wild. I almost stepped on her. I figured everything that happened was pretty random. I didn't connect any dots.

Later I was doing a little reading about how a doe protects her baby. Her little one is camouflaged wonderfully by God. She lets it nestle in cover, hidden from danger. If a predator approaches, the doe will work to get its attention and then hope to lead the predator away from the fawn as it chases mama. It's what the Bible calls "natural affection" (Romans 1:31 KJV). It's the love a mother has for her baby—a love that is willing to risk and sacrifice for the safety of the little one. I now think this is exactly what was happening the day Eddie and I jumped the fawn. Its mama was probably trying to lead us away on "a wild deer chase."

This protective instinct begins early for the whitetail. Even after giving birth in the nursery area, the mother will not stay there very long. She knows that a lot of scent was dropped to the ground during the birthing. The nursery is a dangerous place to stay, so she and the baby will move soon.

HIDDEN FROM DANGER

God's people today need to stop and thank God for some mothers who hid their babies.

Moses was hidden from the wicked Pharaoh of Egypt. Paranoia set in on Pharaoh because the children of Israel were growing rapidly. Numbers were skyrocketing. He commanded for all the baby boys among the Israelites to be thrown into the Nile River. Talk about heartless!

But Moses' mother protected him. She hid him as long as she could. At three months old she made an ark of bulrushes and nestled him among the reeds at the banks of the river. This insured he would not float away. Moses' sister hid nearby to see what might happen. Then God went to work in His awesome providence.

Pharaoh's daughter came down to the river to wash herself and saw the ark. When she opened it, she saw the baby weeping. Can we imagine how little Moses melted her heart? She wanted to take him as her own. Quickly, Moses' sister seized the moment. She stepped up and asked if she could get a Hebrew woman to nurse the child. Guess who she went to get? Do you have chill bumps? I do. She went and got Moses' very own mother!

Pause and marvel here. The one who would deliver the Israelites out of Egyptian bondage was reared in the family of Pharaoh...all expenses paid. The one who would lead Israel to life came out of *a place of death*. Tuck that thought away for a moment. He was named Moses by Pharaoh's daughter because *"I drew him out of the water"* (Exodus 2:1-10).

Jesus was hidden from King Herod. Like Pharaoh, Herod also became paranoid when he heard about the birth of the king of the Jews. In Herod's mind, this so-called newborn King had to be exterminated. To be sure Jesus was killed, Herod ordered the massacre of all the male children two years old and under who were in or around Bethlehem. But Jesus' mother hid her Son in Egypt after Joseph was warned about Herod's plans in a dream. The book of Revelation reveals that it was actually the devil who was behind the scenes working to kill Jesus. He's always the enemy behind the enemy.

"...And the dragon stood before the woman
to devour her Child as soon as it was born."
Revelation 12:4

Thanks to God's warnings and Mary and Joseph's obedience Jesus did not die prematurely. And thanks to the wise men, this poor couple now had money for the trip (Matthew 2:11). Jesus died on His own timetable (John 10:17-18). He would later walk to Calvary and die there for our sins. And once again, a Deliverer came forth from *the place of death*. In both instances, with Moses and Jesus, the place intended to be their end...was the place of salvation for the people of God! No one can outwit God!

I really love Mary for what she did for Jesus. Her place in God's scheme of redemption is intriguing and amazing to me. Think about it. She *delivered* the One who would *deliver her*! I wonder if she ever taught Jesus about the creation of the world. And if she did, did He say to her, "Yes mother. I know. I was there" (John 1:1-3)? Such things make the circuits in my brain smoke. The Creator of the world allowed Himself to be cramped and formed in a woman's womb. You will never read a more thrilling story!

Thank God for mothers who hide their babies. I hurt deeply for children who have not been protected by their parents. Some of them might have been great leaders...but we will never know. They were never given the chance to enter the world. Others who have been allowed to live have been exposed to so many terrible things children should never have to witness...and much of it coming from their parents. Sad. Sad.

THE GREATEST DANGER

I can hardly believe I live in a country where children cannot roam about safely as I did when I was little. I lived in a small town, rode my bicycle all over town, and my parents never feared for my safety. There just weren't very many "boogey men" around in those days.

What a tragedy that our children cannot even go to school without being a little insecure and parents hoping and praying they will be safe all day. When I went to elementary school, one of the greatest issues was to keep *gum* out of the school and out from under the desks, not trying to keep *guns* out! It used to be that a school principal's greatest job was to make sure the children were taught. But recently one said to me, *"If I come to the end of the day, and all my children are SAFE, I feel that I have done my job."*

And of course, we are willing to stop at nothing to keep our children safe from physical harm. This we must do! I wish I would never have to see another mother grieving over the death of her child at school. My prayers are with all of them. And I rejoice that such little ones are eternally *"safe in the arms of Jesus."*

> *"But Jesus said, 'Let the little children*
> *come unto me and do not forbid them;*
> *for of such is the kingdom of heaven."*
> Matthew 19:14

As parents we must realize there is a greater danger. When we ask God to give us a child, and He does, **we now have an eternal soul for which we are responsible**. This soul will one day spend eternity somewhere…and where that is has a whole lot to do with us parents. Life has many choices: eternity has two.

The devil came after Moses. He came after Jesus. And he will come after our children, too. He is a murderer (John 8:44), but his greatest act of murder is when he keeps a soul away from God, the only source of eternal life. Simply put, the devil's greatest desire is to keep your child from knowing God and one day obeying the gospel. And he does his job well, distracting parents from their most important mission: teaching their children the Bible and God's will for their lives.

CHILDREN ARE LIKE SPONGES

Children's minds are like sponges. Their little brains are fresh, new, impressionable, and amazing! Don't underestimate what your children can learn from the Bible; they can be captivated by it.

Recently, I was preaching and mentioned some great Bible characters. I mentioned an event in Abraham's life, calling upon the audience to visualize the scene. I then said something to the audience like, "Can you see it?" And a little child spoke out and said, "YES!" She was wrapped up in the story, and she blurted out without any forethought. It just shot forth from her heart. Please, don't care more about their schoolwork or sporting activities than their knowledge of the Bible. The latter will touch eternity; the former will not. I love the following words of Daniel Webster. They are well-received, especially as I apply them to writing God's words on our children's hearts.

> *"If we work upon marble, it will perish;*
> *if we work upon brass, time will efface it;*
> *if we rear temples, they will crumble into dust;*
> *but if we work upon immortal minds*
> *and instill into them just principles,*
> *we are then engraving that upon*
> *tablets which no time will efface,*
> *but will brighten and brighten to all eternity."*

The greatest thing you can do to protect your children from Satan is to teach them God's word. If you do, when they are of age, Satan will have a hard time getting them to sin if they know what God teaches (Psalm 119:11; Matthew 4:1-11).

When do you start teaching them? When my first child was born, I asked my Uncle Thomas, *"Unka Tonk, when should I start teaching her?"* He said, *"Start right now."* I responded, *"But Uncle Thomas, she's just a baby. She will not understand a word I am saying."* I'll never forget his response. He said, *"That may be so, but if you start today reading Bible stories to her, she'll never remember a day when you weren't doing it."*

I know that I am now rejoicing to hear that my first grandchild, 6-month-old baby Garrett is being read to. He is so special to me. Psalm 78 says that when my daughter teaches Garrett the same things I taught her, she is teaching *my child* (78:4). What a great thing to realize that God's precious word can flow from me, to my child, to my grandchild. That's a three-peat! A dynasty (Deuteronomy 6:1-9)! I pray it happens! Don't you want it to happen for you?

THE GREATEST DAY IN YOUR CHILD'S LIFE...

...is not the day they get their driver's license, graduate from high school, or get married. The greatest day is the day they become a Christian.

That day will come if you have carefully nurtured their souls toward knowing Christ. It may be on a Sunday. You are worshiping, and the invitation is offered for someone to come to the Lord, and then you watch your child through blurred, teary eyes walk the aisle, take the preacher's hand, confess their faith in Jesus, and be baptized in His blood. Or it could be in the middle of the night, that child who has now reached an age of accountability (Deuteronomy 1:39) wakes you up wanting to talk about his soul and wanting to be baptized into Christ. He does not want to delay but obeys immediately as the Bible teaches one should (Acts 16:30-34). There are no delayed baptisms in the Bible.

The greatest words you will ever hear your child say precedes his/her baptism. *"I believe that Jesus Christ is the Son of God"* (Acts 8:36-38). Trust me, your heart will burst with joy when your child enters into Christ, and the angels of heaven rejoice with you. Angels pay attention to what matters (Luke 15:7,10).

After baptism, the obedient are then hidden in Christ. Satan cannot accuse them of any wrong. If they do wrong again, and they will, God will gladly cleanse them as they confess it to Him. They can stay hidden in Christ!

A FINAL PLEA

Can I make a final plea to you if you don't have a child yet? **If you don't plan to devote your life to teaching your child about God and His word, please don't have children**. I know that sounds gruff, but it is immoral to bring an eternal soul into the world with no intent to teach them what life is all about. It's the greatest crime that could ever be committed, a spiritual homicide. We are humans, not whitetails. We are made in the image of God with eternal destinies. Whitetails are not. If they can know to protect their babies, we can know to protect ours.

But if you plan to lead your children spiritually as parents should, I pray your quiver will be full of them and you will know the joys and rewards of being a parent (Psalm 127:3-5). Have the spirit and attitude expressed in these verses.

"Then Manoah prayed to the Lord, and said,
'Oh my Lord, please let the Man of God
whom you sent come to us again, and
teach us what we shall do
for the child who will be born.'
(Judges 13:8) –
The words of Samson's father

"If you will...give your maidservant a male child,
*then **I will give him to the Lord***
all the days of his life...'
(1 Samuel 1:11) –
The words of Hannah, Samuel's mother

THE ARROW STRIKES Have I tended to see the devil only as a red-bodied cartoon character with horns, a long tail, and a pitch fork, or do I know he is real and set upon destroying souls? Am I trying to hide myself and my family from him? Do I pray against the devil as often as I should? Do I rejoice in God's protection?

Tree Stands Can Seem Mighty High to a Little Boy

Okay, I admit it. When I first started hunting several years ago, walking through the woods by myself in the dark was just a little unsettling. "Boogers" are in the woods, you know. But I can't imagine what it is like for a little boy.

The day was good. Henderson was ten years old now and the walk in the dark didn't seem to bother him, especially with dad as his partner. But we were headed to "The Pod." It was a new, two-seater, tripod stand, made of solid steel but reaching up into the first heaven where nosebleeds begin. This was where he wanted to be. It never crossed my mind that we were about to have a major lesson on facing our fears.

Down the hill, across the creek bridge, and finally we were there. Daylight was slightly breaking. There stood this behemoth of a stand. Steps were ascending up into the darkness. My little man boldly took five steps upward and then came to a stop. He lifted his foot for number six but never took it. Then he took four, three, two, one, and... touchdown. He was on the ground with me again!

Fear filled his heart, and tears came to his eyes. He set out again. This time he went to about the seventh rung and then came down again. I prodded and encouraged. I knew I had to be patient and not get frustrated with him. A fisherman once told me, "If you take it too serious and get on his case the whole time, he will not want to go again. Make it fun. If slapping the water with a fishing rod is fishing to him, let him do it and you will have him for life."

Perhaps here is where I need to say that I do not believe we avid hunters should push our children to hunt. They don't have to love what we love. If they don't want to go, don't make them. If they are afraid of the larger gun, don't force them to shoot it. Let hunting come to them in their own time. It's the approach I have used with Henderson, and I've never regretted it. He loves it.

So, I offered to go to another stand. He didn't want to go. I offered to hunt on the ground. He shook his head "No" to that idea too. He had to do this. I understood. A moment more passed in silence, and then he asked, "Dad, will you go up first?" "Do you think that will help you?" I asked. "Yes sir."

I made my way on up and settled into the stand. Henderson surveyed the distance one more time and started his ascent. Again, at the halfway point, he halted. Somewhat assertively, I looked him in the eyes and whispered, "Henderson, look at me. Keep your eyes on me. Don't look down. Remember Peter walking on the water and keeping his eyes on Jesus." Henderson had recently given a five-minute talk on that in a training class at the church building. With that said, he fixed his eyes on mine and ever so carefully made each step all the way to the top. I could feel his relief when he sat down next to me.

GETTING OUT OF THE BOAT

Fear can be paralyzing. It shuts us down. It keeps us in our comfort zones. But there is never growth in the comfort zone. Who can forget Peter's seeing Jesus walking on the water and asking to go to Him? All was well as long as He stayed focused on Jesus. He was full of confidence. But then he started looking at circumstances around: him; the wind was howling, and the waves mounted. Both were shouting, "You cannot do this!" And, he sank. Jesus reached out, took him by the hand, and lifted him up. Then came words Peter didn't want to hear. *"Oh you of little faith, why did you doubt?"* (Matthew 14:31).

Peter needed those words. I do have to give him this much— **he got out of the boat!** So must we. It has been said, "You'll never walk on water unless you get out of the boat." *Fear* has to be met with *faith*. We must dare to do the scary things. Maybe this is why "Do not fear" or its equivalent is mentioned so many times in the Bible. Someone has said it is there about 366 times. If so, that's one for every day and one thrown in for leap year. Whether it is sharing the gospel with others or developing a new talent to use in the Lord's service or whatever, we must step out of the boat. I love the words I saw recently on a sign. "Courage is fear that has said its prayers." The Lord told Joshua, *"Have I not commanded you? Be strong and of good courage; do not be afraid, nor be dismayed, for the Lord your God is with you wherever you go"* (Joshua 1:9). With His commands always comes His enablement.

Ironically, once Henderson was seated in the stand, a timely message was in front of him. Eddie, the welder, had burned into the frame, "Philippians 4:13." Do you know the verse? *"I can do all things through Christ who strengthens me."* We need to burn it into our heads. Christ will help us to keep putting one foot in the front of the other.

God willing, there will be many more hunts and more ladders for my son to climb in the woods. He will climb them now with less fear. When he does, I hope he will always remember this day. The Lord never promised an easy climb, but He does promise His help. By faith we can conquer all our mountains (Matthew 17:20). And when you arrive at the top, it's worth every step you took to get there! Heaven will surely be worth it all.

THE ARROW STRIKES In what ways are my growth and development hindered by fear? Do I need to step out of the comfort zone? What is something I would love to do if I overcame my fears? What is within the realm of possibility? Do I believe God is bigger than any challenge I might face and can help me on to victory?

When Parents Need to Snort

My heart began to race a little when I heard some methodical steps in the thicket to my left. After a moment or two, a very small doe came in front of me. She was so little; there was no way I was going to take her. I simply took the time to admire how precious she was. As she mulled around in front of me, I heard some more steps in the thicket. I thought, "Here comes my chance." In my mind, I could picture a couple more does and big daddy behind them.

I readied my muzzleloader, the old smokepole! But at that very moment, a southwest wind came up and began to swirl. I thought, "No. No. No! I am going to get busted." And that's exactly what happened. Little one's mama was in the thicket, and she got a nose full of me, and let me tell you, she cut loose with the racket! "Racket" is another one of my granny's words. When we would be making a lot of noise, she would holler out "Y'all cut out all that racket." In a word…hush!

Well, mama doe would have nothing to do with being quiet. She snorted and stomped— and stomped and snorted. She was like the fire siren in my hometown that went off whenever there was a fire. It summoned all of the volunteer firemen to jump in their cars and head to the fire. One of the problems with that system was that most of the time all of us townspeople would jump in our cars too and head off trying to find the fire. It was some real action for a small town!

Little one looked around trying to figure out what the danger was, but she never did know I was anywhere around. The good thing is she paid attention to her mama's snort and ran back to safety. If she had been a much more mature doe, the snort most definitely would have saved her life. Her mama didn't know it, but her baby was safe with me on this day anyway.

FENCES & FREEDOM

In our day, we need more parents who snort. We need parents who are on task, doing their job, watching out for their children, expecting obedience to their wisdom and snorting like crazy when the children are headed for danger. I have heard that some of the most angry kids are teens whose lives have been messed up by bad decisions. They are angry because deep down they wanted parents who laid down some boundaries. They had no one to snort. Snorting says, "I love you. I don't want anything to happen to you. I want to give you the good life."

It has been proven that little children play happier and more securely on playgrounds that have fences. And I've seen plenty of stray dogs running around free, getting into trash cans, and looking like they were having all kinds of fun. But when I look more closely, I see their hair is matted, they scratch constantly, and they are "skin and bones." They have no one to care.

Even whitetail deer, that have been raised on farms with fences, prefer them. Terry Kennedy, of Southern Yankees Whitetail Farm, once told me of an occasion when all his deer got out through an unclosed gate. Would you believe they all came back? They were worn, frazzled, and bummed up from being chased by dogs. They wanted back in the fence. There was security there. They once again wanted Terry's care and attention (Isaiah 1:2-3), rather than what they got when they tried to run away.

Ironically, one of the bucks that escaped was named T-R-O-U-B-L-E. He was bottle-fed when he was little. He came back from his escapade with no antlers which, from a distance, made him appear to be a doe. As he got closer to home, Terry finally recognized him. With great joy, Terry shouted, "Trouble!" The runaway heard his voice and immediately ran to him. What a story!

I'm reminded of the parable Jesus told of the prodigal son. Oh, how that young man wanted out of what he thought were stifling fences. And off he ran. He wasted his life on prodigal living and ended up wanting to eat with the pigs. But what a change the circumstances produced in his rebellious heart. When he left home, he was saying, "Give me..." When he returned, he said, "Make me..." (Luke 15:12,19). Since he came home wiser, it may well have been the best money he ever spent.

Our heavenly Father has commanded us to teach our children His ways. He lays that responsibility on parents, especially us dads (Ephesians 6:4). We need it. Too many times fathers go AWOL. The book of Proverbs is a manual for rearing kids. It is written in the tone of a dad speaking to his son trying to give him wisdom to live life and know where the dead-end roads are. I've enjoyed reading it with my son at the breakfast table before he heads off to school. Cereal helps the body, but only God's word helps the soul. Refuse to eat either one and you will die. I beg us all to use it during the teen years.

When we see our kids making choices that will not be good—SNORT! When they disobey—SNORT! When they are disrespectful— SNORT! I didn't say SNORE. Don't go to sleep at the wheel. We might doze off in a tree stand and lose a buck. But if we go to sleep on this parenting thing, we could lose the most valuable thing in the world...an eternal soul.

LIVING BETWEEN HEAVEN AND EARTH

The Bible shows us some godly people who never snorted. It is said of King David's rearing of Absalom, who tried to take over his daddy's kingdom, *"And his father had not rebuked him at any time by saying, "Why have you done so?"* (1 Kings 1:6). Absalom ends up dead largely because he never had a dad who snorted. This young man attempted to take his father's throne and forced his dad to run for his life. But in the end, this long-haired, handsome young man's mule "went under the thick boughs of a great terebinth tree, and his head caught in the terebinth, so he was left hanging between heaven and earth. And the mule which was under him went on" (2 Samuel 18:9). Even though he had been told not to harm him, David's commander took three spears and thrust them through Absalom's heart while he was still alive in the midst of the terebinth tree (18:14).

The passage about David's grief when he hears the news is hard to read. It says...

"Then the king was deeply moved, and went up

to the chamber over the gate, and wept.
And as he went, he said thus:
'O my son Absalom—my son, my son Absalom—
if only I had died in your place!
O Absalom my son, my son!' "
2 Samuel 18:33

Some SNORTS all through life could have made the difference in Absalom. The book of Hebrews teaches us that God disciplines his children and so must we. Take time to read Hebrews 12:3-11. When children have a loving home where they are taught well, expected to listen and obey, praised when they do, and disciplined when they do not, it blesses them so much. They become great young men and women.

"Now, no chastening seems to be joyful
for the present, but grievous;
nevertheless, afterward it yields the peaceable
fruit of righteousness
to those who have been trained by it."
(Hebrews 12:11)

If you were blessed with this kind of parent, you probably didn't like it much when they snorted or spanked (oops, did I say that nasty word?), but now I'm pretty sure you are so thankful they did. You probably think you deserved it even more. God, thank you for dads and moms who snort!!

Am I a parent who "snorts" warnings to my children? Do I trust God when He says I need to warn, correct, and discipline my children? Have I witnessed the rudeness and rebellion of a child left to himself with no one to discipline him? How might I help a child whose parents did little or nothing to teach him about God?

Eyes

I'm always excited to hear hunting stories my friends share with me. Some of them are funny; others are scary; and sometimes they are both. One of the funniest ever shared with me was when a friend of mine got scared right out of his pants! He had entered the woods early one morning, before daylight. He stopped for a moment in a spot and then turned slightly to his right only to meet two big glassy eyes that were face-to-face with him—only a foot away! He jumped and let out a slight "yikes" before realizing it was a cow! But he says it was lots better than the morning a friend of his was run out of a pasture by a BULL! I'm sure he was making some really fast "moo"ves!

There are lots of eyes in the woods. God has equipped each animal with precisely the kind of eye it needs. There are eyes for the *predators* and eyes for the *prey*; eyes for the *hunters* and eyes for the *hunted*.

PREDATOR OR PREY? WHICH ARE WE?

Now, here's an amazing observation. Animals that are *hunted* generally have eyes that are located on the side of their head, and the pupils are elongated horizontally. This gives them fabulous peripheral vision and a great advantage. They have a wide field of view and can detect a wide range of movement. Even if their head is down while grazing, they still can see around them. They may not be able to tell how far away a predator is, but they don't care. Most of the time they are out of there and quick!

Animals that are *hunters* by nature have eyes very close together and to the front of the head. The pupils are round. Bobcats, owls, coyotes, foxes, and other hunters have them. These eyes give them the ability to determine distance and zero in on the prey.

Guess what kind of eyes we have? We have the eyes of a hunter...eyes that were designed for hunting by the One who made everything "very good" (Genesis 1:31). Esau had them (Genesis 25:27). Every person has them. Even non-hunters will be glad they have those kinds of eyes if food ever becomes scarce.

One of my favorite "go to" persons regarding deer hunting is Grant Woods of GrowingDeer.tv. Grant is a wildlife biologist and knows so very much about the whitetail. Recently, he replied to a question of mine giving me a great quote about the way God made hunters. He says, *"That's why I hunt— because I'm fully alive while I'm hunting! The sights, sounds, smells— my senses are triggering constantly! I'm not just watching Creation— I'm part of Creation— a predator as God built me to be. I have canine teeth and a gut designed to eat meat and forage—not just forage. That's why I hunt."*

Those predator eyes along with a God-given intelligence are the only things that keep us from becoming prey ourselves. And we better use that intelligence tool when it comes to lions, bears, and wolves! It reminds me of the guide who was cautioning hikers in a wilderness area. Before they set out, he informed them about two kinds of bears in the area. He also gave them some useful things in the case of an attack. He gave the hikers pepper spray to shoot into a snarling bear's eyes and bells to wear on their shoes. The bells would help them to be heard by others if they were running from a bear. He then said, "To help you know if you are in Black Bear or Grizzly territory, you can analyze their droppings. A Black bear's droppings will be about this big, have berries in it, and smell like honey. When asked, "What about Grizzly bear's droppings?" he said, *"A grizzly bear's droppings will be MUCH larger, will have little BELLS in it, and smell like PEPPER!"* Too funny!

THE EYES OF THE LORD

The greatest eyes in the universe are the eyes of the Lord. He was the first to have night vision. *"The eyes of the Lord are in every place, keeping watch on the evil and the good"* (Proverbs 15:3). Everything is out in the wide open before Him. *"And there is no creature hidden from His sight, but all things are naked and open to the eyes of Him to whom we must give account"* (Hebrews 4:13).

I am thankful I serve the God who sees **everything**. He can see my good deeds and one day reward me for them. He can also see my bad ones. And He can see my plight and come to my aid (Genesis 16:13).

I am so thankful there's an all-seeing eye watching me. God is omnipotent (all powerful), omnipresent (present everywhere), and omniscient (all-knowing). It keeps me safe. No matter where I am on the earth, I am always within view. King David says it best. Be sure you read these next verses slowly and with great meditation.

"O LORD, You have searched me and known me.
You know my sitting down and my rising up;
You understand my thought afar off.
You comprehend my path and my lying down,
And are acquainted with all my ways.
For there is not a word on my tongue,
But behold, O LORD, You know it altogether.
You have hedged me behind and before,
And laid Your hand upon me.
Such knowledge is too wonderful for me;
It is high, I cannot attain it.
Where can I go from Your Spirit?
Or where can I flee from Your presence?
If I ascend into heaven, You are there;
If I make my bed in hell, behold, You are there.
If I take the wings of the morning,
And dwell in the uttermost parts of the sea,
Even there Your hand shall lead me,
And Your right hand shall hold me.
If I say, 'Surely the darkness shall fall on me,'
Even the night shall be light about me;
Indeed, the darkness shall not hide from You,
But the night shines as the day;
The darkness and the light are both alike to You."
Psalm 139:1-12

THE EYES OF A MOTHER

My mother had eyes like a hawk. Very little got past her. It always amazed me. It reminds me of a song years ago by Shenandoah entitled ,"Mama Knows." Here's a little of it.

> *Me and Jimmy Crowder and a single cigarette*
> *Crouched down in a stall out in the barn*
> *Three puffs later we were sick as we could get*
> *Prayin' we'd get better before we got home*
> *She saw me comin' through the back door screen*
> *I knew the minute that she looked at me*

> *Mama knows, Mama knows*
> *Sometimes I think she's got a window to my soul*
> *Mama knows, Mama knows*
> *Even when I think it doesn't show*
> *Mama knows*
> (Writers: Tony Hazelden, Tim Mensy)

Recently, I was studying with a young man who told me of his confession to his mother that he had been drinking again. He said, "I told her because, first of all, I'm a grown man. Secondly, because she's my mother. And lastly, because she would find out anyway!"

I remember once, when I was young, I had done something wrong. Instead of "givin' me a whippin'," Mama knelt down in front of me, looked into my eyes, and simply said, "I'm disappointed in you." That hurt so much. I couldn't stand seeing the look of disappointment in mama's eyes. The whippin' would have felt much better!

Later, when I was old enough to drive, Mama said, "Jeff, I can't be with you everywhere you go. But God is able to see everywhere, and God sees everything." She's right.

When I was preaching in Tennessee, there was a service station where I often did business. At the gas pumps, the owner had an airbrushed sign with a big eyeball on it. It simply said, *"The eye is on you!"* It was there to keep people from driving off without paying for their gasoline. I appreciated the sign but he didn't need it for me. Mama had taught me that a long time ago. Thanks Mama!

THE LORD TURNED AND LOOKED

I still do not want to hurt my mama or my daddy. I want them to be proud of me. I want them to pillow their head every night never having to worry about where I am, what I am doing, or what trouble I have gotten into again (Proverbs 10:1).

But more than that, I do not want to disappoint my Lord in any way. I think so often about Peter's denial of Jesus as recorded in Luke 22:54-62. He swore that final time that he did not know Jesus and was never with Him. The rooster crowed just as Jesus said it would. It must have sounded like an alarm in Peter's ears. Jesus, a short distance away, heard it too, and the text simply says, ***"The Lord turned and looked at Peter."***

I've always wondered what was in that look. The text continues, *"And Peter remembered the word of the Lord, how He had said to him, 'Before the rooster crows you will deny Me three times.' Then Peter went out and wept bitterly"* (22:61-62). I would have too.

It doesn't happen often, but every once in a while I hunt within earshot of a farm. And occasionally at daybreak, I will hear a rooster crow in the distance. Oh, the meditation in that! I'm persuaded Peter never forgot the Lord's eyes and probably never wanted to see that look again.

One day, I will look in the eyes of Jesus. I want to see a gleam of happiness proceeding from them. I want to hear Him say, *"Well done, good and faithful servant; you were faithful over a few things, I will make you ruler over many things. Enter into the joy of your Lord"* (Matthew 25:21). What a day, glorious day that will be! God, help me keep my eyes zeroed in on it.

THE ARROW STRIKES Do I live with an awareness that God sees everything I do? Is He mostly pleased with what He sees? If not, does the thought of disappointing Him bother me? How will thinking of His eyes help me every day?

Clues: What Was I Meant to Do?

God loves variety. He could have made just one kind of tree, one kind of bird, one kind of flower, one kind of deer, and one kind of person. But He didn't. He let His mind run wild with creativity. Think of all the color God painted with when He created the world. Artist Bob Ross on PBS used to hold me spellbound as he'd say something like, "Let's throw in a little Prussian blue here and some Van Dyke brown and a touch of burnt umber. Oh, this space needs this. This will add a nice touch. Maybe a soft, quiet, little tree lives right here. Just drop it in. Use your imagination. Let it go. Let it happen. Have fun." And then with such ease he'd scratch his knife or slide his brush across the canvas, and a thing of beauty came to life!

It's easy to imagine Jesus, through whom all things were made (John 1:1-3), doing the same thing. All God had to do was speak and it happened. God said, "Let there be"...and it was. Wow!!

And don't think for a minute that God is some "stiff." In creation, we see His intelligence, power and artistry, but we also see that He obviously is playful and has a sense of humor. Don't you think monkeys are funny animals? I wonder who thought of that? And who hasn't laughed at the crazy things animals do on America's Funniest Home Videos? I once saw a dog, sit by a crying baby, and every time the baby would cry, the dog would sing a lullaby of sorts. The baby would stop crying! And who made my grandmother's Mina bird? He would whistle at good-looking people and cry out her name in a long drawl—"Vonceille!" When Granddaddy came in, the bird would say, "Hello Granddaddy." Who made my little

Yorkie bark at me this morning at the breakfast table, wag his tail and shake his toy for me to throw it across the room? God created him to press me, as if to say, "Let's play!" See why I love Him? I wonder how beautiful heaven must be if earth is only the footstool. Isn't He amazing!!

God's love for variety also explains why every deer has its own unique features. This past season, a good friend of mine harvested a piebald deer. It looked like a paint pony. I can see God having all kinds of fun when He made him! Talk about unique!

Whitetails vary in other ways too. Bucks each have their own scent which serves to mark their territory. Some are wiser than others. This is why some bucks live to a ripe old age and some mature does become expert leaders of the pack. Some are prone to be a little more nervous and suspicious. Some have outstanding genetics. Others are less endowed. Forget a cookie-cutter God. He may use a basic mold but He loves throwing in a little bit of *this* or *that* here and there.

YOU TOO ARE UNIQUE

We are all different. DNA proves that. And when it comes to life, all of us have unique features and roles to play. First, there are male and female differences. Remember the childhood nursery rhyme...

> *What are little girls made of?*
> *Sugar and spice and everything nice.*
> *And what are little boys made of?*
> *Slugs and snails and puppy dog tails.*

And I think when He made me, there were some
*rifles, racks and big deer track*s!!

Secondly, there are individual differences. When God stitched you in your mother's womb, He used a pattern especially designed for YOU. Your fingerprints prove it. No one else has yours. You were "fearfully and wonderfully made" (Psalm 139:13-14). Each of us has interests, passions, talents, and abilities that to a large degree shape who we are. The same is true with our children. As they grow, they leave us clues on how the God of heaven shaped them. Many Bible students believe this is the meaning of Proverbs 22:6.

> *"Train up a child in the way he should go,*
> *And when he is old he will not depart from it."*

Some believe the passage is teaching that every child comes with a bend in a certain direction. Children have strengths and abilities and certain things come easy for them. Effortless. These become clues on where they will perform best in life. Parents should take time to discover these clues and then tailor the training of their children to fit each one.

I wonder, was Jeremiah meant to be a prophet from the womb? Isn't that the very point of Jeremiah 1:5? *"Before I formed you in the womb I knew you. Before you were born I sanctified you; And I ordained you a prophet to the nations."* And what about Paul? Did God always plan for him to become an apostle? It sounds like it. Paul says, *"...it pleased God who separated me from my mother's womb and called me through His grace that I might preach Him..."* Paul had choices, yes. But God had plans (Proverbs 19:21; 16:9).

Even in the church, God loves a variety of talents and roles. God wants us and our gifts placed in just the right spot in the body of Christ. We passionately do what He wants and what we do best. And we rejoice in those who can do what we cannot. We are many, but one!!

> *"If the whole body were an eye,*
> *where would be the hearing?*
> *If the whole were hearing,*
> *where would be the smelling?*
> *But God now has set the members,*
> *each one of them, in the body,*
> *just as He pleased."*
> 1 Corinthians 12:17-18

PONDERING MY PASSIONS

In my life, I have had a passion for preaching, teaching, writing, and broadcasting. I've been running my mouth and pushing my pen for a long time. In recent years I have had an explosion of interest in the outdoors and the whitetail. I guess that seed just laid dormant for a while.

As I track backwards, I can see the progression. My parents first taught me to love God. Then my daddy tapped into my love for music and lyrics. The first notes of a song would barely start, and Daddy would stop, turn up the volume, and say, "Jeff, listen to this." I came to love songs that had melody and meaning. I hate rap! It's a bunch of noise to me. I was attracted to the storytellers like Red Sovine, Jimmy Dean, bits of Tom T. Hall, the Statler Bro's, and more recently Brad Paisley. Ever heard, "When I Get Where I'm Going"? (I miss you, Granddaddy. I look forward to walking with you again. Just had to say that.) It has been said of me, *"Jeff May doesn't just listen to songs; he devours them."*

Then at the age of twelve, a radio station came to our town. I was mesmerized by the disk jockey and all the buttons and knobs on the control board. I stopped in to visit every day. Another clue? In a short time, I became a pilot of the airwaves.

I remember as a young kid sitting in the library at study hall, and over and over again I was drawn to a section of wildlife books. I would look at all the pictures of the animals, marveling at how each was made. And then, when I had seen them all, I'd do it all over again. I also loved watching Mutual of Omaha's *Wild Kingdom.* Were these clues? Hmm. And why did the student council vote for me to be the chaplain?

In college I continued disk-jockey work, but I also learned to do television news and special interview shows. Even today, I tell people, *"I'm still a news reporter. It's just GOOD NEWS"*—that's what the Gospel is. And I offer a great fire insurance policy (Rev. 21:8). Also, in school, all the speech classes were easy for me. Math was very hard. Did I even need to be concerned about it? And all the while, I knew serving Jesus faithfully was the highest priority.

Aren't all of these passions flowing throughout this book? Here I am writing about the great outdoors: connecting the *woods* to the *Word* with my pen. Are you picking up what I'm putting down? Hmm, again.

WHAT ABOUT ME, DADDY?

I see the same thing happening in my children. When Bethany was ready to go to college, she said, *"Dad, I've decided I* *want to go into nursing.*" I said, *"Okay,"* but inwardly I was thinking, *"That's not Bethany."* This is the same girl who just two days ago was with me outside when I was dressing a deer. Accidentally, blood spurted onto my face and began to roll down toward my lips. She saw it just as I was about to wipe it off, and she began convulsing with the **"Raaallllppphh, EEEaaarrrllll, Buuuiiiiccckkk** routine!*" Now come on! How would she ever be able to handle a dear, sweet old lady's bedpan?

Well, we arrived at the admissions office a few weeks later and it was time for her to declare her field of study. She said, *"Daddy, I've decided I want to go into cosmetology."* I smiled and thought, *"Now, that fits the young lady I know."* That's the little girl who set up "Nail City" in our house. It was her childhood nail salon. And it's the same girl who was always into makeup and dress up. Like Dad, she stunk at math too. She hated reading and had a terrible attention span UNLESS she was working with her hands. Ah, clue! That's why I didn't get too upset at some classes she didn't excel in. It probably didn't matter much anyway. I didn't see calculus in her future.

Then there's Henderson. He has always loved tractors, four-wheelers, and monster trucks. He has a good attention span and pays attention to details. He surely is an outdoor person. He has voiced his love for beautiful nature scenes—*"Look at that daddy!"* What will he do? Well, I can see something in the outdoors and perhaps an agricultural setting. Will he preach full-time? That would thrill me but I will not push him to do it unless he really wants it.

DO YOU WANNA PREACH?

When Henderson was two years old he was looking at a big crane doing construction work. We asked him what he wanted to do when he grew up. He said, "Drive a crane. Drive a dump truck." His mom said, "Don't you want to preach like daddy?" He said, "No. I wanna work." Too funny! Hey, don't knock it.

I love the joke where the little boy thinks his preacher dad makes more than anyone else because on Sunday, it takes six men to take up all the money! Truth be known, good preachers say, "If you can't pay me. I'll pay you." Churches should take care of them well, but it's not about money. Maybe Henderson will blend his worlds.

He is a good speaker, so maybe he will be a public relations person of some sort. We shall see. The clues are still rolling in.

Let me mention one more. My brother-in-law John, since childhood, has loved the outdoors and any kind of machinery. "Brrrmm, Brrmmm" was in his vocabulary before "ma-ma" and "da-da." If it has a steering wheel, he can drive it. Was he meant to sit behind a desk and push a pencil in some high-rise building in New York City? Never! He'd suffocate in no time at all! It's just not *his* bent and I'm pretty sure it is not the way *he* should go. Am I surprised he now walks the woods and cruises timber for a living? Am I surprised that he delights in the noise of massive machinery cutting trees and stacking up logs like they were toothpicks? Am I shocked that the inside of a tractor is his sanctuary? Is it an accident that one of his greatest joys is the family farm? No, not at all.

THE WAY YOU SHOULD GO

Now, having said all of this, I don't think we are supposed to drive ourselves crazy thinking, "What is my life's calling?" All I am saying is that we should take all this into consideration when deciding what to do with our lives. And it may be that we feel that we must go in a certain direction. I like what Dee Bowman says about his own preaching, *"I think a person can go to heaven without being a preacher. I just don't think that I can."* Maybe he is saying what Paul said, *"Woe is me if I preach not the gospel"* (1 Corinthians 9:16). He felt necessity!

What about you? What are the clues concerning the kind of person you are? What are your interests, passions, and abilities? Take time to notice them. If you have kids, take time to help them see who they are. They love it when you do that. I'm reminded of a dad who began telling one of his children the special traits he saw in him, and then one by one the others chimed in, "What about me dad?" They want to know who they are. Once discovered, the next phase is to channel these talents in a God-honoring direction.

Let me throw in one disclaimer. Not all inclinations should be lived out. There are some things I might like to do that I must not do. But if your desires are clean and pure, you can use them in manifold (multi-colored) ways.

Any God-approved job a man works hard at and uses to provide for his family is a great job. But wouldn't it be great if you could find your niche and get to do it all your life? Paul Harvey once said, *"Take your hobby, and make it your job, and you'll never work a day in your life."* It's true. Yes, I am supported financially to preach but Bible study is also much like a hobby to me. It's never really work for me to do it! It's a great joy. I hope and pray you can do what you really like to do. Money isn't everything!

I'm persuaded you can choose any number of things to do with your life that will please God. You and I are created differently. But **one thing** was intended for all of us and if we don't get on board with it, all of life is a waste. We need eyes that are "single" in purpose (Matthew 6:22 KJV). Paul ultimately stayed fixed on "one thing" (Philippians 3:12-16). We were made *by* the Lord, *for* the Lord. *"All things were created through Him and for Him"* (Colossians 1:16). That means YOU. You were made to serve Jesus and be with Jesus forever. Don't reject the only thing that satisfies.

A good friend of mine once told his wife, "We are all the same." When she said otherwise, he said, **"God gave just one book for all of us. We must be the same. We all need the same thing."** In that sense, he is right. We will never find ultimate happiness and fulfillment until we realize that. Let's enjoy our work but put aside any agenda that clearly is not God's. Get in His word today, and be what you were meant to be!

"Lord, thank You for the unique way You stitched me in my mother's womb. I like it. I am comfortable in my own shoes. Thank you for giving me passions, interests, and jobs that make me smile and that mostly feel effortless to me. I may not do them that well, but my heart leaps when I get to try. May my feeble efforts bring great glory to You, the Maker and Designer of us all. Amen."

THE ARROW STRIKES Can I see the unique and special way God made *me*? Can I make any changes so that I might do more of what I love to do? Am I picking up the clues on how my children are made? Am I helping them see how special they are? In what ways can I adapt their training to their passions and abilities?

Rattlers

Yesterday, I strapped on my "Rattlers" for some scouting along a snake-infested wildlife refuge. The previous week, eight were seen swimming in the creek, and, yes, some of them were water moccasins. I'm not really terrified of snakes, but I surely don't mind a little insurance by wearing the snake-proof chaps. After gearing up, I got to thinking about one of my favorite snake stories.

It is a legend about a girl walking through the woods who almost stepped on a snake. Instinctively, she pulled back in horror, but to her amazement, the snake called out, "I'm so glad you came along. I'm cold and need a friend. Please pick me up and put me under your coat so that I can get warm. And will you be my friend?"

In fear, the girl replied, "I cannot possibly do that. You're a rattlesnake and you will bite me. I *can't* pick you up."

"No, I promise I won't bite you. I really want to be your friend, and after all, am I not also a creature of God, just like you? I'm so cold; please pick me up."

She began to feel sorry for the snake and sat down to think it over. As she looked at this creature of God, it began to look beautiful. Previously she had not noticed its many colors. She admired its graceful lines and movement, and gradually it began to look harmless.

She thought, *"Well, he's right. He is a creature of God. And just because most rattlesnakes bite doesn't mean this one will. It seems like a nice snake, and shouldn't I be willing to be a friend when someone asks me? Someone who needs me?*

"Yes, I'll be your friend," she said, and picked up the snake and put it under her warm coat. Immediately, the snake bit her, and the pain and poison shot through her body. She cried out, "Why did you bite me...You promised you would be my friend!" The rattlesnake slithered away, turned with a smirk, and said, *"You knew what I was when you picked me up!"*

VENEMOUS VIPERS

Spiritual vipers are all around us. They look alluring. They hold out a promise that they will not bite. But they will. Don't pick them up!

How many lives have been devastated by **alcohol and drugs**? Liquor companies love to show the chilled froth rolling down the side of the mug, but they never show you the car wrapped around a tree. God Himself calls strong drink a snake and warns us not to pick it up.

"Who has woe? Who has sorrow? Who has contentions?
Who has complaints? Who has redness of eyes?
Those who linger long at the wine, those who go in
search of mixed wine. Do not look on the wine when it is red,
when it sparkles in the cup, when it swirls around smoothly;
At the last it bites like a serpent,
and stings like a viper."
Proverbs 23:29-32

There is often a sad and deadly progression in drinking. A man takes a drink. The drink takes a drink. At the last, the drink takes the man.

Then there are those who "pick up" adultery dressed up in a pretty little word called *"affair."* It sounds less harmful doesn't it? Or maybe it's fornication called *"friends with benefits."* What could possibly be wrong with a *benefit*? Here too, we are dealing with a rattler.

*"With her **enticing speech***
*she **caused him to yield**.*
*With her flattering speech she **seduced him**.*

> *Immediately he went after her,*
> *as an ox goes to the slaughter,*
> *Or as a fool to the correction of the stocks,*
> *Till **an arrow struck his liver**.*
> *As a bird hastens to the snare,*
> ***He did not know it would take his life.* "**
> Proverbs 7:21-23

I know several men and women too, who wish they had never picked up pornography. This snake has poisoned and destroyed many marriages and lives. The devil has found a way to slither into our homes with it. Who will ever know? So…click, click. A snake loves a mouse, especially the tasty one with the long tail connected to your computer and to the world of darkness.

Yesterday, I saw an episode on TV where a person feared he might have to lose his hand after being bitten by a snake. Losing a hand is terrible, but it beats losing a life. This is why you may have to radically amputate pornography from your life. I've known of men who confessed their addiction to a friend (James 5:19-20), asking him to hold them accountable, check on them often, ask hard questions, and assume access to their computers. That's what it takes. The devil loves working undercover. Bring it out of the darkness: out of the secrecy. You might have gotten into it by being a *male;* you will get out of it by being a *man.* Listen to Jesus…

> *"But I say to you that whoever looks*
> *at a woman to lust for her*
> *has already committed adultery with her in his heart.*
> *If your right eye causes you to sin,*
> *pluck it out and cast it from you;*
> *for it is more profitable for you*
> *that one of your members perish,*
> *than for your whole body to be cast into hell. "*
> Matthew 5:28-29

PARDON ON A POLE

There are other snakes we could mention. Whatever the species, the action needed is the same.

And if you have already been bitten by the serpent of old (Revelation 12:9), you need to look to Jesus for the cure. There is an interesting event in the Old Testament about a bronze serpent. The children of Israel murmured against God. *"So the Lord sent fiery serpents among the people, and they bit the people and many of the people of Israel died"* (Numbers 21:6). They repented and prayed to the Lord for help. Moses was told to make a bronze serpent and put it on a pole. If a serpent had bitten someone, when he looked at the bronze serpent, he lived! All indications are that God did not take away the snakes, but He did give the cure. Likewise, God has not taken away the evil snakes around us. They will be there until the end. But He has warned us not to pick them up. That ought to be common sense, but then again we do some really stupid things sometimes, don't we? And when we sin and are bitten, we must look to the cross of Calvary for our forgiveness. Jesus said, **"As Moses lifted up the serpent in the wilderness, even so must the Son of Man be lifted up"** (John 3:14). If you are not a Christian, cleansed by the blood of Jesus, Calvary has the cure (Mark 16:15-16). If you are a Christian and have been bitten again, there is still a cure (1 John 1:9-10).

Watch out for the rattlers of life and stay focused on the cross!

THE ARROW STRIKES Am I wise to know the vipers around me that can easily destroy my life? Have I picked up one recently thinking it will not bite me? Am I simply deceiving myself?

Association Without Contamination

I read an unusual story recently in a hunting magazine. The headline read, "Hunter Exposed to Rabies While Field-Dressing Deer". It was about a man who after field-dressing a deer, became even more concerned because of the behavior he had seen in the deer before harvesting it. The hunter said, "I saw the deer standing in a creek, straining, and growling." He thought there was a coyote nearby from the sounds the deer was making. After hearing the hunter's account and testing the deer, authorities determined that the deer was rabid. Because the hunter had scratches and cuts on his hands from field-dressing the deer without wearing gloves, he was urged to have post-exposure rabies shots. I hear those shots are very painful.

Ironically, I told this story to a few people, and a year or so later one of my friends called me and said, *"Jeff, do you remember that story you told me about the rabid deer?"* "Yes," I replied. *"Well,"* he said, *"I have a cousin who just got attacked by a six-point buck. He got cut some by his antlers. Do you think the buck was rabid?"*

His cousin was not even hunting. He was setting fence posts, when all of a sudden this buck came from the woods charging at him. For a little while the man was in the fight of his life until a helper saw what was happening, ran to help and killed the buck with his hammer. One of them had to have some relief! My initial answer to him was that it probably wouldn't hurt to get checked out since he had an open wound. But since it was during the heat of the rut, the deer was likely just amped up, and attacked. Such attacks on humans are rare, but it does happen sometime. They get a little crazy.

I have since been told that the greater probability is that the buck that attacked him was someone's bottle-fed buck. They have no fear of humans because of the close interaction they had when they were little. Their instinct to flee is lessened and during the rut they choose to fight anything even close to their does.

I'm not done yet. Recently, a landowner told me that his son didn't hunt anymore. "Why not," I asked. "He's allergic to them," he said. "You are kidding me!" I exclaimed. At that moment, my hunting buddy laughed and said, "Jeff, that would be terrible, wouldn't it?" Allergic to deer! I'd be okay with being allergic to cats, but a whitetail? May it never be!

Every time the landowner's son would process a deer, he would break out with spots all over his body. It was confirmed. He was allergic to deer hair much like my son is allergic to pet dander. He once had an allergic reaction while we were in an arena where horses were on show. But a whitetail? This stuff is getting more dangerous by the minute. Honey, if the phone rings, don't answer it. I've had enough.

So, what will I do with all this news coming at me? Should I quit deer hunting because of the danger of contamination? Not for a moment! I am not about to miss the joy and rewards of deer hunting just because there are risks of contamination. I'm just gonna get me a claw-foot hammer and a bodyguard! Ha!

I already take some protective measures. Last year, I passed on a deer that had a huge left foot, was limping, and had fallen off in weight especially in his hips. Since I was unsure about it, I did not harvest it for food. Even with the ones that appear healthy, I always try to field-dress and process them with gloves. What am I doing? I'm seeking to have association without contamination.

THE DOCTOR WHO NEVER LOST A CASE

Isn't this what our Lord did while seeking to save the lost? He was "a friend of sinners" (Matthew 11:19). He associated with them in order to help them. Actually, He was hoping that He would rub off on them, rather than allowing them to infect Him. Jesus had great compassion as the Great Physician (Luke 5:31).

To be sure, Jesus came under fire for His associations. Would you believe the religious leaders, of all people, criticized Him? The most disgusting moment to me is when Jesus was taking time to help a woman, and Simon the Pharisee "blew a gasket" and said, *"This man if he were a prophet, would know who and what manner of woman this is who is touching Him, for she is a sinner"* (Luke 7:39). Do you hear it? "She is a sinner!" Haven't we all been? Haven't we all come from the wrong side of the tracks (Titus 3:3-7)?

This arrogant attitude is precisely why the Pharisees had a hard time reaching those who had made terrible mistakes in their life. Jesus said to Simon, *"Do you see this woman?"* I think that was the problem. Pharisees didn't see people needing help. They saw people to condemn and dismiss. Jesus was different, and those who could see their sin were drawn to Him like a magnet! And you guessed it; when they saw the crowds going to Him, they were jealous: jealous enough to later kill Him (Matthew 27:18).

Old time preacher Marshall Keeble, once preached a sermon calling Jesus "The Doctor Who Never Lost A Case." He's right. Jesus never lost a case with anyone who came to Him and "followed doctor's orders." He warned about the dangers of associating with bad people, but He sought approved situations to be with them, love them, and teach them. Yet, He never did the bad things they did nor aided them in it.

In a real sense, God has sin allergies. A holy God cannot fellowship sin. Therefore, Jesus was very careful. His closest friends were those who were seeking God. He would take chances with ordinary diseases, but He never took chances with sin. He even once touched a leper who hungered to be touched by someone... anyone (Mark 1:40-42). I have a preacher friend who once touched a leprous young child in a foreign country, who pleaded with him not to do it. When he took his chances and hugged the child, the child burst into tears. My friend couldn't heal the boy's body, but he did touch his heart. And that often becomes the door for the gospel: the healing everyone needs. Simply put, Jesus sought association without contamination. He died not by carelessness but at the hands of deliberate men who couldn't stand His love for all people. And He died with no traces of the sin virus (1 Peter 2:21-22; Hebrews 7:26)!

The Pharisees were a different story. I think they did care in their own way about God. And I think they wanted to be pure in their own twisted way of thinking. But they were diseased with pride as they compared themselves to "sinners." They also rebuked and ridiculed Jesus for eating with "sinners." But it occurs to me that any person we eat with is a sinner or has been. We all have sinned.

DO NOT BE DECEIVED

Of course, we must not run with people who are going to hurt us spiritually. We must not be deceived. Several verses and one-liners teach us so.

My favorite Bible verse along these lines is 1 Cor. 15:33. It says, *"Do not be deceived: 'Evil company corrupts good habits.'"* Said another way... *"He who lies down with a dirty dog picks up fleas."* And... *"We are in the world, not of the world."* *"It's okay for a ship to be in the water. But we must not let the water in the ship."* All of this is in 1 Corinthians 5:9-10. Things can rub off on us without us realizing it. A person who walks into a coal mine with a white shirt, even with great carefulness, still has high risk of getting a smudge on him. Great carefulness is needed. More than once I have seen someone decide he is going to bring someone up by "buddying" with that person. Oh, he does bring the guy up a little, but the guy brings him down some too. They meet in the middle, and now neither are pleasing to the Lord. Are we getting this principle balanced?

Jesus balanced it well. Sinners knew that He did not condone their sin but they also felt loved by Him enough to want to come to Him. People without Christ need to be exposed to genuine Christians. We must not keep our salt in the shaker (Matthew 5:13). They need to see Christ in us as we seek to be a good example to them. But we cannot do the sinful things they do or go to the sinful places they go. We do what we can, when we can. And there is no greater joy than the moment someone we have cared for obeys His gospel and gives their life to Him.

THE CURSE AND THE CURE

Oh, there will be moments when you become contaminated. Even as Christians, we sometimes, in a moment of weakness, sin. That doesn't excuse it, but it does happen. The good news for the Christian is we don't have to take a painful shot. Jesus took the shots at Calvary, the strokes that were due to us (Isaiah 53:8), and can take our crimson sores and make them white as snow (Isaiah 1:18). While I would never minimize the pain someone goes through to take rabies shots, it pales in comparison to the six long hours of pain Jesus suffered on the "torture" stake. I praise Him and love Him for taking the curse while I take the cure. As the hymn says, *"Love so amazing, so divine, demands my soul, my life, my all."*

Will I go hunting again after hearing such scary contamination stories? If God wills, I will. Of course, I will be careful, but go I must. Will I reach out to people who could contaminate me? Yes. The rewards are worth the risk. True love is always risky. You can get hurt. Just ask Jesus. But then again, some people who hurt you in this life may thank you in the next life. I can picture Saul of Tarsus thanking Stephen, a man he watched die while he held the garments of those who stoned him (Acts 7:54-60; 22:19-20). Some of Jesus' penitent murderers will thank Jesus in eternity (Acts 2:36-47). His mother probably joined and fellowshipped them in the Jerusalem church (Acts 1:14). Now, that's forgiveness!

THE ARROW STRIKES Would I ever quit hunting because of the danger of contamination? Should I completely stay away from those living in sin because they might rub off on me? Am I thankful that Jesus, although perfect, mingled with the lost in order to teach them and save them? Do I have any friends in my life who have contaminated me by their bad influence? Have I had a bad influence on anyone? What changes, if any, do I need to make in my relationships?

"My Thung is Thuck"

Hunters can get themselves into some unbelievable predicaments. Some of the stories are simply hilarious.

James, a friend of mine, makes for one of these stories. A few years ago he went hunting on a tremendously cold winter morning, in the teens to be exact. Brrrr! He awoke with great excitement as he thought about the potential opportunities the day might bring.

James tossed his climbing stand in the back of the truck. While James and his huntin' buddies were enjoying the warm cab of the truck as they traveled, his metal tree stand was being subjected to freezing winds blowing across it. Once they were at the hunting property, he took his stand out of the truck. It would be interesting to know just how cold the steel had now become. It numbed his fingers quickly just by picking it up.

Now James is probably a lot like me. Once I have selected a tree to climb, for some reason I feel like I need to hurry and get on up the tree. But on a cold day like the one with which James was dealing, it is easy to have fumblefingers. They just don't work very well, and often gloves get in the way. James worked to loosen the wing nuts on the stand, and then he had another problem. With all that had to be done, he really needed a third hand. A place was needed to put the wing nut while he adjusted the stand. Can you guess where this story is headed?

You guessed it. James put the sub-zero wing nut in his mouth and immediately felt the sting! Quicker than you can say Jack Frost, the nut froze to my friend, who now felt like a nut himself. Instantly the wing nut seized his top and bottom lip fastening them together, and his tongue got in the action too. His "thung was thuck." He then did the only thing he knew to do. He ripped the nut loose. Now, he was left with a constant reminder of his mistake. A wing impression was left seared on his lips. This isn't the way to earn your wings! He thought, *"How thould I be tho thupid?"*

TOOTHPASTE AND TAILBEARERS

Our tongues can get us in a world of trouble. God spends a lot of time warning us about the danger of the tongue. Some of the best words about it are in the book of James.

"For every kind of beast and bird, of reptile and creature of the sea,
is tamed and has been tamed by mankind.
But no man can tame the tongue.
It is an unruly evil, full of deadly poison."
James 3:7-8

Have you ever said something you wished you hadn't said? I remember Andy Griffith, in one of the episodes of his show, spoke without thinking and said to his girlfriend, "It was just one of those greasy words that slipped out." Wouldn't it be great if some words would just freeze to our lips so that they were never spoken? How many people has the serpent of old hurt by falsehoods, unkind words, and gossip. There's a hiss in "gossssssip!"

When my daughter was little, I was going to teach her about gossip during one of our family nights where we did a little devotion with an activity to reinforce the lesson. I gave her a tube of toothpaste and told her to squeeze it out on a paper plate. I then told her I would give her five dollars if she could put it all back in the tube. Bless her heart, she tried but it wouldn't go. She began to cry. I didn't count on that, so I gave her the five dollars just to console her. But she got the point. Once some things are out, we can't get them back. Our words are like that. You can't retrieve them very well once they slide out. And they can hurt reputations and kill friendships (Proverbs 16:28).

A preacher-friend of mine once wrote, "I have learned that to control myself, I must talk to myself. Most people would say that you are crazy for talking to yourself, but they are the same people who have slippery tongues."

Slowing down to think a little would have helped James an awful lot. It will help us, too. Think before you speak. Freeze the words to your lips. Don't say them. Brand this lesson on your brain. Sometimes it's better if our "thung gets thuck." It will save a lot of hurt and a few scars, too.

THE ARROW STRIKES Am I known for being a person of pure speech? How much better would my relationships be if I froze more words to my tongue and didn't say them? Can people trust me not to gossip about them? Do I stand up for those who are being run down by gossip?

Go Back to Where You Went Wrong & Start Over

Hunters sometimes go wrong leaving the path they need to be on. It often happens when following a blood trail in search of a deer. An anxious hunter scours the ground looking for that first speck of blood. It goes something like this. *"Where is some blood? I don't see any at all. I know he ran this way. Wait! There's a drop. And...there, I see another. Yes!"* He's on the right path.

But sometimes, there can be a big distance before you find the next drop on the ground or a smear on a sapling. Which way from here? It's right here where the hunter can so easily go wrong, walking a long way in the wrong direction. The slightest veer off the path can lead you far, far away from where you should be. Once he realizes he is off track, there is only one reasonable option. *Go back to the spot where you went wrong and start over.* It works. Some hunters use toilet paper for back-tracking, marking each spot where blood was found. It's biodegradable, and rain will clean it up. Just go back to your last marker. And from there, if the wound hasn't dried up, there will be more signs to follow. You just have to go in a different direction.

Doesn't the same thing happen in life? *The wrong road will never turn into the right road.* If you discover you are on the wrong road, you must turn around. Go back to where you made the wrong turn and move forward from there.

THANK GOD FOR U-TURNS!

I've seen it happen in marriages. A couple begins their life together and love is aflame! Their quest is for each other. But if they are not careful, they can slip off the trail of love. They get caught up in the demands and stresses of making a living, rearing kids and handling finances. I've heard it said that, "A honeymoon is that time between bells and bills." I've always thought that saying was sort of funny except when I see it erode a marriage. Couples grow further and further apart from one another and at last lose the intimacy they once shared. What should a couple do when they realize they have lost their way? *Go back to the spot where they went wrong and start over.* Rekindle the fire. Take a weekend retreat. Pursue each other again. Find that once familiar ground and go forward.

I've seen it happen among family and friends. Sometimes even family and friends hurt one another. How do you restore the relationship? Go back to where you went wrong and start over. The Bible shows the offender backtracking (Matthew 5:23-24). It also shows the offended one backtracking (Matthew 18:15). It has been pointed out that if each are headed back to each other, they will meet each other on the way. Often, a relationship that has been strained for years, with a good meeting and good hearts, can be mended in a matter of minutes. Really.

I've seen it happen to some in their relationship with the Lord. What do you do when you realize that your walk with the Lord is not as strong as it once was? What if you lose your way? Jesus gives the answer to those who leave their first love. *"Remember therefore from where you have fallen; repent and do the first works"* (Revelation 2:5). Jesus is calling for us to remember how it was in the beginning. *Go back to the spot where you went wrong and start over.* Light the fire. Fan the flame. If you once were on a trail where you were giving Him your time, devotion and talents, now is the time to go back and *"stir up the gift"* (2 Timothy 1:3-6).

I remember a time in my life like that. I got off track. I slowed up on studying my Bible daily, got wrapped up in my broadcasting work, and was not choosing spiritual people to spend time with after hours. I started losing my way. One day my cousin, who roomed with me, made a simple statement to me, but it rattled my cage. He simply said, *"I wish you were like you once were, studying the Bible every day."* He missed the better Jeff. You know, you don't have to deny Jesus with your mouth to be guilty. You can live and act like you don't know the Man (Titus 1:16).

DOC, GET IT ALL

For some reason, my cousin's words sounded in my ears like a rooster crowing. Then and there, I made the turn around. I started studying once again, let go of some bad influences in my life, and eventually I could no longer be satisfied delivering the evening news with all its dirty laundry. I knew I had "good news" (the gospel) to share. What did I do? I went to the spot where I went wrong and started over. It was that simple. I cannot say it was without pain. Cutting some things out of our lives sometimes hurts.

And get this, when it comes to sinful things in our lives, we can't cut out only a little bit. If you had cancer and the doctor was going to do surgery, would you ask him to only take a little out, or would you want him to get all of it, if possible? Recently I was preaching in a place where I was told of a guy who was trying to overcome an addiction in his life. He let it go but kept his old friends. They pulled him back to it. He repeated the cycle a time or two more. At last, he let go of the troublesome friends. His words of victory are priceless. He said, *"I found that if I didn't let go of everything, I couldn't let go of anything."* Amen!

I'm sure there are other applications we could make. Make your own. Fill in your own blank with the turnaround you may need to make. The Lord will bless the turn. It is what He most desires for us, for **there is only one path that leads to heaven**. It may be narrow, but it can be walked if we are willing to be diligent (Matthew 7:13-14).

The devil will place many detours before us, and foolishly we may take them. But there is always a time and place where we can backtrack. If that is what you need to do, my prayer today is that you will! You will not be sorry you did.

THE ARROW STRIKES If I have lost my way, can I see where I went wrong? Can I go back there now and start over? What course should I take for the rest of my life?

Mama Said There'd Be Days Like This

Preparing to go hunting can really be a hassle. Hunters have so much stuff to remember and to pack. But that is compounded when you are trying to get two people ready to go, and the second one is a young boy. You have to think for two.

But hey, that's no problem. I pride myself on organization. I'll just start early and think ahead. Friday night arrived, and the family enjoyed an early supper. This allowed plenty of time to stop by the sporting supply store. A little doe estrus urine would help us to flirt with a big buck. The night was really running smoothly. I started my cell phone charging, got the boy in bed early, and Susan and I "hit the sack" too. Plenty of time remained for a good night's rest, even though I planned to get up at 4:00 a.m.—two whole hours before we had to be settled into the deer stand. Perfect! Or so I thought.

The next morning, the alarm sounded, and I had no reason to hurry due to my precise planning. This allowed time for me to go to the bathroom. There's nothing worse than nature hitting you while you are strapped twenty feet up a tree. I took my no-scent bath and then went to catch Henderson's bath water. He got ready in good time, and everything was right. I even remembered to get the shooting stick so Henderson would have a good rest for his young arms. It felt so good not to be in a "tizzy" (that's what Granny used to call it) as we left the house.

We were off. I was relishing in all the time I still had left when ten minutes down the road, "it hit me." Oh no, I left my fanny pack at the house. My brain kicked into the alert mode. "Can I do without it?" "No." My flashlights, gloves, hood, grunt calls, windicator, and rattling horns were all in that bag. I told you hunters had a lot of stuff. No problem. We've got plenty of time thanks to my planning. I swung the truck around and headed back, being careful to watch my speed. Meeting Barney Fife and getting a ticket was the last thing I needed. I made it to the house, ran inside, got the bag, and eased back out. I was still trying to have that relaxed feeling, but I felt it fading a little.

About ten minutes down the road I had another problem. I couldn't believe it. I actually had to go to the bathroom. No problem. I allowed plenty of time today. So, once at the hunting place, I left Henderson in the truck and stepped aside to "attend to my needs." I was happy to get this behind me, until I looked and saw that in the dark I had "attended to my needs" on my coveralls. They were soaking wet. So much for my scent-killer bath!! No problem. I'll just strip these things off, leave them at the truck, and spray a double dose of no-scent cologne. I felt a chill hit my legs because now I was down to much thinner clothes. I had just ruined my insulation. No problem. "Just be tough," I said to myself.

Day was just beginning to break. No problem. I actually think it is better to ease in with just barely enough light to see without using a flashlight. Henderson and I made it to the stand, and I made four trips up and down the ladder trying to get all our stuff in the two-seater. Hen said, "Dad, did you bring the estrus stuff?" "Of course son, I remembered everything. It's right here in my...oops, coveralls." I had left the scent wick in that newly-scented front flap back at the truck. No problem son, I'll just squirt some doe urine on "this 'ere tree." I don't know how well that works, but at least he thought it was pretty cool.

I finally got seated and wiped all my nervous sweat from me. "Granny, now I know what you meant by 'tizzy'." I found a place for all our stuff and rested the shooting stick beside my leg and was so happy I remembered it. A moment later, we heard a big thud at the bottom of the tree. "What was that?" I said. Henderson mumbled, "I think you dropped the shooting stick." No problem. "Henderson, just prop on your leg. You did bring it, didn't you?"

I sat there thinking, "My wife will never believe all of this. I'll text her later and let her know we are okay. I've got my phone right here in my..." That panicky feeling stabbed my heart again. I could see my phone still nestled in its cozy cradle next to my side of the bed, and I wondered if in bed was where I should have stayed.

CHARACTER IN A CAVE

Maybe this day was meant to be so that I could now write about something very serious. God does not insulate us from trials and tribulations in life. Rather than saving us *from* them, He saves us *through* them. He's not wanting us to become *bitter*. He wants us to become *better*.

I refuse to call this day a bad one. As a preacher, I have sat too many times beside grieving and mourning people to dare call this day a bad day. It feels irreverent toward them. They can tell me about bad. There will be evil days in our lives. Just ask Jesus, or Joseph, or Job. That's why we brace for them with God's armor (Ephesians 6:13). Have you known such a day?

As I sat in the stand, my mind roamed back to the days when David was being stalked for some ten years (as some count it) by an envious King Saul. There were no trail cameras waiting to flash on David but there were plenty of eyes in the wilderness helping Saul to look for him. At last a day came when David and his men were hidden in a cave and Saul went in to attend to his needs (1 Samuel 24:3). That was still fresh on my mind and on my coveralls too.

While Saul was attending to his needs, David's mighty men saw their chance. Get him now!! They said, "This is the day" (1 Samuel 24:4). For a moment David's vengeance spoke to him. He ever so carefully eased up behind Saul. I've seen bobcats move just as stealthily. David reached out, gently grabbed Saul's robe, and cut off a corner. And would you believe, even this bothered David afterward? He felt bad for even snipping off a piece of the king's robe. What profound respect David had for the Lord's annointed, even if this king had roamed about like a sniper! After Saul was done "attending to his needs," he exited the cave. David also went out, and called to Saul. He showed Saul the corner of his robe. Basically, he was saying, "I was within an inch of you. I could have easily killed you." Saul melted and wept, but his remorse was short-lived.

Now these were bad days! My day was loaded with nothing more than small inconveniences. Yet, some guys might have fussed and cussed with every one of those petty mishaps. It can be easy to do. But don't ever forget, there might be a little boy watching. Greater yet, your Father is watching. It reminds me of the country music song which talks about a son picking up his dad's "cussin' " (southern for nasty talk) and blurting out a four-letter word. The dad responds...

"Son, now where'd you learn to talk like that. He said, 'I've been watching you dad, ain't that cool. I'm your buckaroo. I want to be like you. And eat all my food and grow as tall as you are. We got cowboy boots and camo pants. Yeah, we're just alike, hey ain't we dad? I wanna do everything you do. So, I've been watching you.' "
(Rodney Atkins)

The tough days test our mettle (1 Peter 2:6-7). We find out what kind of strength we really have. And those days often are good for us spiritually. Some key verses teach us that we can even rejoice in trials because we know we can grow spiritually through them. I always emphasize the phrase, *"knowing that,"* in each of the verses (James 1:2-4; Romans 5:3-4). King David faired better in the *cave* than he did in the *palace*. Some of his greatest psalms showing dependence on God came from his cave days. It was at the palace where he saw and committed adultery with Bathsheba.

Character is not always made on the bad days, but it is most always revealed. So, learn to grow from the days that don't go just the way you hoped. Mama said there'd be day likes this.

How well do I behave under pressure on the difficult days? What does this say about me? In what ways could I do better? Who do I remember is watching, listening, and learning?

I had never felt a major adrenaline rush before I began deer hunting. Oh, I heard people talk about it, but I had no idea what it felt like. I played sports, went to amusement parks, and other such things but never felt the rush.

But the first time I ever heard the unmistakable crunching of leaves made by deer hooves, it hit me like a lightning bolt. So sudden and unexpected. Then to see such a serene and majestic creature right in front of me. And this time, he has no idea I have entered his world. Among earthly things, it gets no better to me.

Yet, I know a moment is coming that will blow my mind. The rush will be magnified a million times over because a sweet anticipation has been building for years. I can only imagine the jolt to my whole body and soul when I see Jesus with my own eyes.

Thank God, I'll have a body that will be powerful and can withstand the blast and take it all in. Oh, that will be glory to me!

FALL

In the world: Cool air graces the mornings. High school stadium lights illuminate their little piece of the autumn sky. The "Boys of Fall" are back in their helmets, cleats, and shoulder pads. Alabama and Auburn are muscling through their schedules. Hummingbirds will soon depart. Leaves are changing color and beginning to fall. Goldenrod blooms. Cornstalks are turning brown. Soybeans are yellowing. Combines and grain trailers will soon enter the often dusty fields. Kids will enjoy Fall Festivals, trick-or-treating, pumpkins, and candy corn. Teens will go looking for haunted houses and corn mazes. Bowhunting shops are buzzing with activity. Sweaters are being unpacked. There's Thanksgiving, turkey and dressing and cranberry sauce. Food plots are planted, and I start playing my fall theme song: "The First Winds Of Autumn."

In the woods: White oak acorns are ready. Whitetails are eating as much as possible to put on weight for the coming winter. They seek a good fall and winter habitat: food, water and cover.

Velvet has been rubbed away from the buck's antlers. Scrapes will be made on the ground as the bucks do their "courting." The heat of the rut will come. The bucks will be looking to score, but so are the hunters who pursue them. There lies our greatest opportunity. They throw a lot of wisdom to the wind. Do they know we are coming?

Leaves may lose chlorophyll and die, but it's the season hunters feel most alive! This is the season of great outdoor adventures and opportunity for a trophy whitetail.

In the Word: If the days of your life are eighty years (Psalm 90:10), the fall season is when you are forty to sixty years old. Your hair may be turning grey or turning loose but wisdom has come with the years (Proverbs 16:31). Your salvation is nearer with each passing day (Romans 13:11). You love God and life more deeply and are now more emotional about spiritual things.

Your children are possibly Christians by now. You may see your first grandchild born. Don't blink. They grow fast. Hug all you can. You have prayed for them even before conception (Deuteronomy 29:14-15). In a sense, you see the grandchild as *your child* (Psalm 78:2-4). You dream of a dynasty of faith in your family: *you, your son, your grandson* (Deuteronomy 6:1-9). Your aged parents may need your help soon (1 Timothy 5:4).

A lot of life is behind you, and if God is willing you have about as much in front you. You are more humble. You have a strong sense of how much you have needed God's grace. You drop your stones more quickly (John 8:9).

Spiritually, you feel you can offer more now. You should be wiser and able to help others with their problems. You may even be an elder in the church. You are working on what matters and avoiding time wasters. And since you know the last years, God willing, are around the corner, you are getting away more with the love of your life before the difficult days come. You slow down more to soak in the special moments. It's a great time in life. Make sure you live it fully, but live it cleanly.

> *"...Solid food is for full grown men,*
> *even those who by reason of use*
> *have their senses exercised*
> *to discern good and evil."*
> Hebrews 5:14 - ASV

Weatherman

It's fall! A lot of things change. I change. From September 24 (give or take a day or two) to January 31, I transform into an amateur meteorologist reading the weather signs in two states, Alabama and Tennessee. I guess you might say I am trying to see "weather" or not I should hunt. You can rest assured the deer make their decisions based on the weather. And if they do, we should too. It's time to use our brain. It is our greatest asset in hunting whitetails.

God graced the whitetail with the keen ability to detect oncoming weather conditions. They will prepare and protect themselves when they know bad weather is coming their way. That's why hunters like to hunt just ahead of a front coming through. Deer are more likely to be moving. I'm told that barometric pressure plays a role in deer movement, and they can sense its changes naturally. They feel it. They don't watch the 10:00 p.m. news trying to catch the forecast. But I tell you, I do think they can read a calendar! I once found a hunting guide in their bedding area, and it was opened to the pages that had the season dates! Just kidding— but it sure seems like they read the book.

Hunters on the other hand have to rely on a look at the sky for weather signs. Cloud formations can foretell conditions for several hours or a couple of days. We also surf the internet and watch the local weatherman. We use all these tools to help us make our decisions. How cold will it be? What direction is the wind coming from today? Will my scent likely rise to higher elevations today, or will it linger low?

More than once I have wanted to kick myself for not checking the weather more closely. I got punished for a while in conditions I never prepared for. I had no one to blame but myself.

Why is it that we hunters can get so serious about reading the signs when it comes to deer hunting, but we often neglect the most important signs of all? Why don't we study the signs that tell us we should prepare ourselves for eternity? Life can end as suddenly as a flash of lightning. It can catch you as unready as you have been in pop up thunderstorms. How can we be expert prognosticators about tomorrow's hunting conditions and often so unwise about what matters most?

ADJUSTING TO THE FORECAST

Jesus saw the same problem when He came to earth to be our Savior. He was trying to get people to see who He was. It was so clear to see, but many of them *would not* see it. Notice I didn't say they *could not*.

In spite of the bucket-load of signs He had already given them, they wanted a great sign from heaven. He answered and said to them, *"When it is evening, you say, 'It will be fair weather, for the sky is red'; and in the morning, 'It will be foul weather today, for the sky is red and threatening.' Hypocrites! You know how to discern the face of the sky, but you cannot discern the signs of the times"* (Matthew 16:3). They could read the sky better than they could the Old Testament prophecies, His miracles, or His unprecedented ability to teach. His teaching was so astounding it once even stopped some men from arresting Him. When they returned to the so-called authorities, they were asked why they had not brought Him. They answered, *"Never a man spake like this man!"* (John 7:46). Not only did His preaching stop them from arresting Him, it arrested them. He didn't just teach with authority. He sounded as though He was the AUTHORITY. And He was!

The reasoning should have gone as follows: "If He can perform miracles, He is from God (John 9:31-33)—the very Son of God. If He is the Son of God, His words are true. If His words are true, I should obey them. I should become His disciple."

Jesus went on to say that He would not give them a sign from heaven. But He would give one more major sign before He left earth. He called it "the sign of the prophet Jonah" (Matthew 12:38-

40). He meant that just like Jonah was in the belly of the great fish for three days and three nights, so He would be in the grave, and then come forth! The resurrection was the greatest proof that Jesus was indeed the Son of God (Romans 1:3-4). And yet, some of them knew the tomb was empty and still would not come to Him. None are so blind as those who will not see.

Fellow hunters and outdoorsy people, let's not be guilty of the same. Evidence for God is everywhere (Acts 14:17; Romans 1:20). Surely, you can't spend all those hours in the woods and then fail to see Him. And there is more documented evidence for Jesus than any other historical character in all of history, even George Washington. He lived. He walked among us. And the Bible which recorded His life is reliable (1 Thessalonians 2:13). It proves itself to be the word of God. Read it. Someone once said, *"I believe the Bible is the word of God because I've been reading it."* It will prove itself.

If you can read the signs of the weather, and **adjust your day's hunt** according to it, then you can know Jesus is the Lord and **adjust your life** to Him. Listen. I doubt anyone loves this hunting stuff more than I do, but I know it will come to an end one day. God is not going to ask me on judgment day what my biggest trophy scored.

BEWARE OF IDOLATRY

To deer hunt, I have had to make adjustments. Before I started deer hunting in the fall and winter, people would sometimes ask me, "What's your hobby?" My answer always was "I love reading the Bible." Even when I wasn't studying to teach, I still loved sitting and reading the Bible. I still do. I am blessed to do what I love to do. But I am probably somewhat of a workaholic. I tend to overload myself.

When Eddie and I met, he sensed this tendency in me. He said to me one day, *"Jeff, we all need to smell the roses sometimes. Go catch a big bass. Go to the woods. Watch the animals. Harvest a deer. We need that. It's okay."* I knew all of that with my head; I just had to accept it in my heart.

Even Jesus didn't work all the time. He rested, recreated, restored His soul, and recharged His batteries. He had to deal with the limitations of the flesh too. He is the one who made us with limitations. It was His idea. He left margin for going to private places to simply "be." He was teaching us that our time in private will make us better when we return to the public discussions and the crowds. There are times when we don't need to have a job to do but to just "be." Best of all, "be" with God in solitude. We don't need to let our bodies outrun our souls.

This adjustment was hard for me. There were times I felt guilty deer hunting because I had never done much recreational stuff...mostly studying. I felt like I was cheating God in some way although I knew I still had things in balance. Being alone with God and "sharpening my saw" through relaxation was my main reason for going to the woods anyway. But being with Eddie was loosening me up and bringing my world alive as I started seeing a world I didn't take much time to see before.

Having said all of this, the words "beware of idolatry" ring in my ears. I have seen too many deer hunters turn hunting into antler worship. An idol is anything that takes more of your thoughts, time, energy, and devotion than God. For example, covetousness is called idolatry in the Bible (Colossians 3:5). We might not make a gold image, carve out a block of wood or stone, but we can do our kneeling and bowing in our own ways. Hunters can think so much about hunting that God is squeezed out. Deer hunting is a great gift from God, but it becomes wrong when we love the gift more than the Giver.

Think about it. Compare the time you spend thinking, reading, researching, talking, and pursuing the deer to the amount of time spent pursuing God through reading your Bible, praying, meditating, and worshipping him with other Christians. I love trophy rooms. You know I do. I have one. But with the wrong focus and zeal they can become shrines...little temples to what we love the most. It's all about keeping God first (Matthew 22:37). It has been compared to a shirt that has been buttoned up wrong. If you don't get the top button right, everything else will not line up. Our lives turn terribly wrong when God is not King, holding the top spot with no rivals.

God is a jealous God. His name is even called "Jealous." The Bible says, *"...for you shall worship no other god, for the Lord, whose name is Jealous, is a jealous God"* (Exodus 34:14). God loves us. He pursues us in His love. He has invested all He has (even Jesus) so that He might one day freely give us all things! And He is jealous for our love. He will tolerate no rivals.

Can we understand this? Would you be okay with your spouse having a lover on the side? Would you tolerate a rival?

Let me borrow some good words here from Kyle Idleman and his helpful book called *gods at War.* "Imagine going to a local restaurant and seeing me having a romantic candlelight dinner with a woman who is not my wife. Imagine walking up and asking me who I was with and what it was all about.

Picture me smiling nonchalantly and saying, 'Oh, I'm on a date!'

'But what about your wife?'

'What about her? I love her too. I've taken her out plenty of times.'

I'm pretty sure you'd walk away angry and disgusted and you'd have good justification.

Can you imagine my wife, afterward, meeting me at the door with a big smile? She would say, 'Hi, honey. Did you have a good time on your date?'

News flash: this would not happen.

Her hurt, her anger and her pain would be enormous. And in fact, I would be offended if she *didn't* feel that way. If she was anything other than jealous, it would show me she really didn't care" (pg. 46,47).

Are you following me? We need to adjust our lives to God. We must be God-centered. I cannot tell you *exactly* where the line is crossed. But I do know I have seen hunters who love the creature more than the Creator. I don't want to be one of them.

THINGS LOOK GOOD FOR SUNDAY

Let's prioritize what matters. Sunday, for that matter, need not be just another day to hunt no matter how good the weather conditions may be. Jesus arose on that day, appeared to the disciples on that day, and one week later appeared to them on that day (John 20:1,19,26). John is stressing the first day of the week for a reason. The early Christians observed the Lord's Supper on that same day (Acts 20:7). My studies indicate Pentecost always fell on Sunday. If so, that means the Lord's church began on the first day of the week. It's a most fitting day for His church to begin.

It's a day to treat with utmost reverence. It's His day, not mine. It's a day of public worship and encouragement to other Christians. I have heard people say, "I can get closer to God out in the woods or on a lake than you church people can in a pew." Granted, God is in the woods, and we can love that time with Him, but God has commanded us to gather with other Christians to worship on the Lord's Day. We cannot please Him by being off somewhere other than where He has told us to be. It's disobedient and dishonoring.

We must let our sport lead us to spend more time with God and not more time away from God. It should draw us to God, not become our God. Never put creation in the place of the Creator (Romans 1:25). See Him on your hunts and then come home to spend time in His word, reaching out as He did to help others and lead people you love to Him.

So, the next time you look in the heavens and ask, "What should I do today—stay or go?", realize that question is not just for hunting; it is for getting right with the Creator. The future has been forecasted for every person (Matthew 25:46)—one way or the other. Let's all make our plans based on the forecast.

THE ARROW STRIKES Have I often made decisions based on the weather forecast? Am I convinced the signs prove Jesus was here and is the Son of God? Should I make any changes? Has my deer hunting been a wonderful way to enjoy quiet time with God? Or do I see evidence that the gift has taken the place of my devotion to the Giver? What plans do I have for Sunday? Does the forecast for my future look good?

Rejected

Deer hunters love hunting the rut. It's that time in the deer woods where "love is in the air." Bucks spend a lot of time with their snoot to the ground or lifted high in the air seeking a doe in estrus. Simply put, they are looking for a girlfriend. Yet, love always has its risk. Rejection hurts!

It reminds me of our little love ritual in elementary school. I still remember the day I fell in love with a cute little girl across the room. I nervously wrote, *"I love you. Do you love me? Yes or no?"* I sent it across the desks and waited for her to circle one or the other, all the while yearning for a "yes." She smiled and sent the note back. I slowly opened the paper, and she had circled "or"! What do you do with an "or"? It may have been her way to keep from hurting my feelings but it wasn't a "yes" and it felt just like a "no." Rejected!

Deer have their love rituals too. A buck will make a scrape on the ground, digging away all the debris on the ground until only fresh dirt remains. He will then pee on the tarsal glands of his back legs mixing the scents to trickle into the dirt. It is his way of saying, "I love you. Do you love me?" A doe is supposed to come by and hopefully leave a "yes" answer by leaving her scent in the spot as well. Once he has his "yes" he goes looking for his newfound girlfriend. It may also be his way of telling others bucks, "Back off; this is my turf." Researchers differ in their conclusions on scrapes but they all agree that scrapes are for communication, like my note to the cute little girl.

Recently, a hunting friend of mine called me, and as I answered the phone, he was already laughing. He said, "I know you can tell I am ecstatic but I just saw something in the woods I have never seen before. I've got to tell you about it."

He explained that he was watching a small field, and some does entered. One of them stopped in the field and proceeded to perfume herself. I suppose she had a certain fellow in mind. Well, after a moment or two a small buck strutted onto the field. He had a little rack but must have thought he was really something. He trotted up to this doe and expressed his intentions to court her. She read his intentions, looked him in the eyes, and...HEADBUTTED HIM!! Ouch, that hurts! More than that, it hurt Buckey's feelings. I know it did. I remember first grade.

Well, ole Buckey thought she was playing the "hard to get" routine. He circled around, still working his snoot in the air, and approached her again. She headbutted him again. She kicked at him several times, too. Finally, as my friend watched and laughed, the little buck turned and walked away all by himself with his head low to the ground. Rejected!! It happens in the woods too.

TO REJECT OR NOT TO REJECT

We all know that one of the greatest gifts God ever gave to a husband and wife is the gift of sexual relations. It was God's idea. He was the One who dreamed of it when He created us. And it is not just for procreation. God intended it for the pleasure of a man and his wife. But, God regulated it. It is not for anyone, anywhere, anytime.

Sexual relations *outside* of lawful marriage are to be rejected. The Bible calls it "fornication," and to live in it will keep us out of the kingdom of heaven (Galatians 5:19-21). The Bible says, *"Marriage is honorable and the bed undefiled; but fornicators and adulterers God will judge"* (Hebrews 13:4). That's pretty plain, isn't it?

To illustrate, I once heard of a family that was working together on putting sod down at their new home. As the children were putting sod down on the ground, the mother said, "Oh, that's beautiful sod." Seeing how excited she was, the youngest child wanted to make mom extra happy. Later, when she was inside the house, he came in with some sod and dropped it on the living room carpet. She wasn't happy at all! She shouted, "Get that nasty dirt out of here!" The little boy was confused. At one moment she called it *"beautiful sod,"* and now she calls it *"nasty dirt."* Why the difference? Well, it all depends on where you put it. Sod belongs outside the house, not inside the house. And so it is with God. Sex inside of lawful marriage is beautiful to Him. He looks upon it, smiles, and in essence says, "That's exactly what I had in mind." But outside of marriage it is nasty dirt to Him. What we need is some big-time headbutting!

If you are yet to marry, and someone is pressuring you for sexual relations... headbutt them! If you live your life as you should, they probably already know exactly how you feel about it and will not even make advances. Your virginity is a wonderful gift worth waiting to give. You are a gift wrapped up tight. One day it will be okay to unwrap the gift for the love of your life, but not until then. Premarital sex will not make a relationship stronger, and a part of you will be taken you can never get back. Consider these two poems.

I met him; I liked him.
I liked him; I loved him.
I loved him; I let him.
I let him; I lost him.

I saw her.
I liked her.
I loved her.
I wanted her.
I asked her.
She said, "No."
I married her.
After sixty years,
I still have her.

If you are married, and someone other than your spouse makes advances toward you, headbutt them! If you are at work, send strong signals to coworkers that you are happily married. Talk about your family. Place pictures of a happy family all around your office. This tells the wild folks to back off. You don't belong on this food plot! And make sure you keep sending that signal. Too many homes have been destroyed at the office. And there is no greater hurt in all the world than the rejection of an unfaithful, cheating spouse. These "back-off" signals are much like a posted sign which reads:

POSTED
PRIVATE PROPERTY
**Hunting, Trapping, Chasing,
Hitting On, Or Asking Out,
For Any Purpose Is
Strictly Prohibited
Under Penalty of Law**

Sexual relations *inside* of marriage should be celebrated. In my preaching, I actually call it "the celebration." It is here that a godly man and woman celebrate all they share together. They are one spiritually. They are one emotionally. And they celebrate their relationship by becoming "one flesh." God designed it for devoted Christians to experience this on a level like no other. The "outside-of-marriage" stuff is counterfeit...not the real thing. And God says it is okay to be "intoxicated" with married love (Proverbs 5:15-19). He gave you a cistern from which to drink. Drink from it. He designed it for you. And don't drink from another well.

And while we tell the unmarried in regard to sex, "You sin if you do", God says in marriage that you sin if you don't. Don't headbutt your spouse. God teaches that your body belongs to them and their body belongs to you. You are to freely share with one another. Look carefully at the words of 1 Corinthians 7:3-5.

*"Let the husband render to his wife the affection due her,
and likewise also the wife to her husband.
The wife does not have authority over
her own body, but the husband does.
And likewise the husband does not have
authority over his own body, but the wife does.*
Do not deprive one another except with consent for a time,
*that you may give yourselves to fasting and prayer;
and come together again so that Satan does
not tempt you because of your lack of self-control."*

In the simplest language God is telling the married couple to have sexual relations and not stop except with consent for a little while and then get back to it. If you headbutt your spouse, it hurts. It hurts down deep. And if it continues, you may wake up to a nightmare. If there's no food in the kitchen, your spouse may go out to eat. Satan has a "heyday" with unfed spouses! In the words of an old country song: *"It's so easy not to care about what's right and what's wrong. It's too hot to fish. It's too hot for golf. And it's too cold at home"* (Bobby Harden). Beware! Nurture your love life!

A POWERFUL PARALLEL

God uses the most powerful bond on earth (marriage) and the sexual privileges that go with it to describe His relationship with His bride (His people). It expresses the longing and the excitement God feels for us and we for Him. Take for example His Old Testament bride: Israel.

- God found her in Egypt as an abused baby, thrown out to die. But God loved her, and cleaned her up. She grew and became beautiful in body and soul. God married her. He uses fairly graphic language to describe how beautiful she was to Him (Ezekiel 16:7-8)

- But she was unfaithful to Him. Using the ways of the wild, God says she *"sniffed at the wind"* (just like a deer does) in her desire (Jeremiah 2:24). He says Israel was like *"well fed lusty stallions; every one neighed after his neighbors wife"* (Jeremiah 5:8). And in the strongest language possible you can hear God as an angry husband say, *"You built your high places at the head of every road and made your beauty to be abhorred. **You offered yourself to everyone who passed by**,* and multiplied your acts of harlotry" (Ezekiel 16:25).

- Because she cheated on God, God divorced her for her adultery with stones and trees (Jeremiah 3:6-10). It is the one hurt that He truly understands and the only cause He gives for divorce and remarriage today (Matthew 19:9).

In the New Testament, Christians are the bride of Christ. We are married to Him. In First Corinthians 6, sexual immorality with a harlot is put in contrast to our being *"joined to the Lord* (vs. 17).*"* As His bride, we are joined to Him in the deepest intimacy one can ever experience.

Often in scripture, when a man had sexual intimacy with his wife, God would say "he *knew* her." It is a word describing the depth of that union—body, mind, and soul joined together. They totally open themselves up to one another. It is a trusted-revealing.

In a similar fashion, what God most wants is for us to know Him. No, we don't have sexual intimacy with God, but we do have deep spiritual intimacy. It would be natural for a Christian couple after "knowing one another" to think of their union with the Lord and enter into a prayer of thanksgiving for all He is to them. They can then drift off to sleep in the sweet peace of their relationship with Him and one another. And the greatest marriage supper of all is ahead when we join Him face-to-face in heaven (Revelation 19:7-9; 21:9).

"Thus says the Lord;
'Let not the wise man glory in his wisdom,
Let not the mighty man glory in his might,
Nor let the rich man glory in his riches;
But let him who glories glory in this,
That he understands and knows Me,
That I am the Lord,
exercising lovingkindness, judgment,
and righteousness in the earth,
For in these I delight,' says the Lord."
Jeremiah 9:23-24

THE ULTIMATE REJECTION

Rejection can be serious business with God. He is a jealous lover. He wants our love and will tolerate no rivals. He wants and deserves the top spot in our hearts.

In the Bible, Samuel felt the sting of rejection. After all the years of serving Israel faithfully, he was rejected as a leader in Israel. They didn't want Samuel. They wanted a king. Their hurtful words were, *"Look, you are old, and your sons do not walk in your ways. Now make for us a king to judge us like all the nations"* (1 Samuel 8:5). God told Samuel not to take it too personally. God was the one hurting. He added, ***"They have not rejected you but they have rejected Me"*** (1 Samuel 8:7). God was their KING. How could they want a little k-i-n-g? Our rejection hurts God.

Likewise, Jesus told the apostles not to take rejection personally as they tried to teach people about Him. He said, *"He who hears you hears Me, he who rejects you rejects Me, and he who rejects Me rejects Him who sent Me"* (Luke 10:16). Do we see it? When we say "no" to the gospel message preached by the apostles, we are rejecting Jesus and thereby rejecting God. Our rejection stabs His holy heart.

But the most serious thing we need to see is that if we reject the Lord, He will be forced to reject us on the day of judgment.

"Therefore whoever confesses Me before men,
him will I confess before My Father who is in heaven.
But whoever denies Me before men,
him will I deny before My Father in heaven."
Matthew 10:32-33

So, the next time you see a little love ritual going on in the woods, think about a Lord who loves you more than anyone could—and has proved it. Think of how He so desires for you to come to Him. Jesus wept over Jerusalem's rejection of Him (Matthew 23:37). It hurts. And at last, ask yourself, do I really want to hurt Him by my continued rejection? Do I want to be hurt by His rejection in the last day?

We ought to do like Saul of Tarsus who later became the apostle Paul. He kicked against Jesus for so long (Acts 9:5). The day finally came when he could kick no longer. Jesus' love for him was too hard to resist, and he became a Christian (Acts 22:12-16; 26:19-23). Shouldn't we also do a little soul-searching?

Not long after writing the opening to this devotional, I found out what might have been going on when little "Buckey" was headbutted. A veterinarian and deer enthusiast told me it was probably the doe's **son** that was approaching her. And her headbutting was designed to run him off. And she will. She will force him to leave her neck of the woods. It's God's way of helping them against inbreeding.

Would you believe a man in the Bible did something like that, going after his father's wife? And the church at Corinth drew a line in the sand and gave him the strongest disciplinary headbutt! They withdrew from him in an effort to save him (1 Corinthians 5:1-13). He could not continue in willful sin and have fellowship with the church. It's okay for whitetails to do what whitetails do. But we must not. We are not animals, and we must not live like them! We are made in the image of God, and God calls us to abstain from sexual immorality (1 Thessalonians 4:1-8). He demands sexual purity. It's the difference in swimming in a mudhole or swimming in the ocean. He's trying to give us the best. He always does.

THE ARROW STRIKES Have I ever felt the hurt of rejection? Am I understanding how God feels when we reject Him? Do I nurture my relationship with my spouse? Do I put up clear, no trespassing signs toward those who would tempt me to be unfaithful to my mate?

Bobcat!!

The sun was slowly setting when I saw him. Something was crouching down and moving stealthily across the field. I quickly glassed him and discovered it was a bobcat—a.k.a. Mr. Predator.

I had never taken a bobcat, so this was a first. I slowly lifted my rifle to the shooting-house ledge, settled the cross hairs, and fired. He fell on the spot. Then I thought, "Uhh, what do I do now?" It was getting a little darker, and I knew I had to go get him. I thought, "What if I just wounded him? What if the shock just knocked him out? What if I walk up to one angry kitty?"

I eased down the stand, bolted my rifle again, and walked out to my trophy. Fortunately for me, the deal was done, and I could put my fears to rest. Others have not been so fortunate with predators.

Not long after taking this bobcat, I happened to see a story in a local newspaper. It had a picture of man sitting up in his hospital bed, and he was sliced and diced worse than a tomato in a food processor. A bobcat had worked him over.

The wounded hunter said that he had gone on a morning hunt and ascended his tree with a climbing stand. After settling in a little, he heard noise above him. He looked up and stared eyeball-to-eyeball with a face full of bobcat! And then it was on! Talk about waking up on the wrong side of the bed! The bobcat pounced on him and began to wreak havoc. There was no "pause" in the action, mostly just "paws!" As Jerry Clower would say, "Knock him out, Johhhnnnn." Meanwhile, John hollers out, "Whawwww!! Shoot up here amongst us. One of us has got to have some relief!"

According to the hunter, he was able to get his hands on the cat and—as best he could— slam him against the tree. It worked. Infused with adrenaline, he killed the cat but not before being left in a world of hurt. I remember this incident often when I am headed up a tree. More times than not I take the time to look at my stand and even above it to make sure nothing has rested there for the night.

YOUR ADVERSARY THE DEVIL

Certainly a deer has its predators in the woods. I am one of them. It has to watch carefully for the enemy. This is one reason they do not like windy days. Too much is moving around, and they can't detect predators as well. Likewise, the Bible wastes no time showing us our enemy: the serpent of old, the devil, Satan (Genesis 3; Revelation 12:9).

Read no further than the third chapter in the Bible, and there he is seeking to destroy Adam and Eve (John 8:44). Start reading Job and before you even finish chapter 1, there he is planning to wreak havoc in Job's life. Read about Jesus' life in the gospel of Matthew; immediately Satan was working to devour Him. In chapter 4, Jesus is tempted three times in the wilderness yet defeated the devil by knowing the scriptures. Three times Jesus fired the words, *"It is written!"* And the predator ran away. The devil cannot beat scriptures we are determined to stand upon. But know this— he'll be back. The devil left Jesus, but when a good opportunity presents itself, he'll return (Luke 4:13).

Did you know the name, Satan, means "adversary"? He is a prowler, a predator seeking the greatest game on earth - you and me. He goes to and fro on the earth, walking back and forth on it (Job 1:7). Peter, who himself once became a victim of Satan, warned us saying:

> *"Be sober, be vigilant;*
> *because your adversary the devil*
> *walks about like a roaring lion,*
> *seeking whom he may devour."*
> 1 Peter 5:8

Satan is no small bobcat (not that I am minimizing his potential). He is a roaring lion! He is fierce. He studies his prey. He patterns you. He learns your weak spots and he will attack them

(2 Corinthians 2:11). We need to watch out for him as warily as we watch for other physical predators. What he is trying to do to us is far more costly. We must watch and pray. This is what Jesus told Peter (Matthew 26:41).

Are you on alert daily watching out for the devil's efforts to destroy you? Are you aware that he knows what bait to dangle before you and when to dangle it? And he's in no hurry. He loves the slow kill (James 1:13-16). Be sober! Be vigilant!

The good news for the Christian is that if the devil does manage to get in a painful swipe on us, we can conquer him through the forgiveness of the Lord. Our enemy is fierce, but He who is in us is stronger than he who is in the world (1 John 4:4). In essence, Jesus slammed the cat to the tree when He died on the cross for our sins (Colossians 2:11-15). Victory is ours if we will resist the devil. He will flee (James 4:7-8). Yet, if we do sin, His blood is available for cleansing all His children (1 John 1:7-10). We must confess our sins and turn from them. Watch out for the cat!

THE ARROW STRIKES Can I see any areas where the devil is influencing me? Am I aware of my weak spots? What bait could he dangle before me that I might take? What can I do to better resist him? Have I recognized how Jesus can help me overcome the devil?

The Day the Hunter Became the Hunted

It was Friday, the 13th. No kidding. It really was. It might have been an unlucky day for my prey, but it was a great day for me. I had wanted a bobcat for several years. As you read earlier, I had taken one when my son was about three-years-old but never had it mounted, because I didn't think my wife would want such critters around the house. I was wrong. She is pretty "easy" about it. So, I have long wanted another, and this day was the day.

I got myself all settled in the tree and was hoping for a mega-buck. After about an hour, something caught my attention trotting in from the left. Because it startled me, I reacted quickly and jerked my head and eyes to the left. It was a bobcat! My movement must have startled him because he checked up and stopped dead in his tracks, out in the wide open, and peered at me. We engaged in a stare down for a good while. There was nothing I could do. My gun was on my lap, and any movement would cause him to bolt. All I could do was hope for him to settle down and attempt to ease away. I'll never forget the look in his eyes. It was a look that said, *"I have messed up. How do I get out of this situation?"* If he would have just kept his eyes on me, he would have had a way of escape. But he didn't. He cowered back two or three steps, turned his head from me and at last was turned broadside. It happened so fast, in a moment, on one day in time. The hunter had become the hunted. The stalker was defeated by a man attached to a tree. And the spiritual applications here are so joyful to write about.

HE STIRS UP THE PEOPLE

Jesus was a hunted man while He walked on earth. Satan was the hunter. Jesus was stalked by the devil and his followers (Mark 3:6). It started at His birth and continued until the day He died. The book of Revelation says, *"The dragon stood before the woman who was ready to give birth, to devour her Child as soon as it was born"* (Revelation 12:4). They wanted Him gone!

Jesus was a threat to their lifestyle, their traditions, and their hypocrisy. And to add even more heat to their fire, everybody liked His preaching better than theirs. The religious leaders were envious. Their twist was, "He stirs up the people" (Luke 23:5). They wanted to take Him out of this world (John 11:47-53).

Over and over the Bible shows there is enough power in envy to kill. It killed Abel. It sought to kill David. In due time, it did kill Jesus (Matthew 27:18). So, Jesus had to watch His steps and move about carefully until He was ready to lay His life down for our salvation. They would not take His life. He would give it (John 10:18).

Satan must have been so thrilled as the pace picked up during the Passover. Judas had betrayed Jesus, and the wheels of death were moving toward Him. Soon, Jesus would be murdered upon a Roman cross and His impact upon men ended. The hunter was closing in.

But Satan never knew he was actually walking the corridor to his own defeat. He was influencing his boys to kill Jesus (John 8:44) but actually assisting God in His plan of salvation (Acts 2:22-24). **If Jesus dies on the cross, it will be the means of saving those held by Satan and will strip Satan of his power and his claim on us.**

> *"...that through death He might destroy him who had the power of death, that is the devil, and release those who through fear of death were all their lifetime subject to bondage."*
> Hebrews 2:14-15

"COME INTO MY WEB," SAID THE SPIDER

This was all a trap for Satan. He never knew what was really happening. Jesus would triumph over Satan at the cross (Colossians 2:14-15). And guess what God was doing as Satan moved in? He was laughing! Yes, He was. He was laughing because all of this was working out just as He had planned from the beginning. *"Come into my web"* said the spider to the fly. On the greatest day in all of history, **the hunter became the hunted** and was **defeated by a man** *nailed* **to a tree** (1 Peter 2:24). Listen to what Psalm 2 says about that gathering of authorities around Jesus. Be sure to later read the whole psalm.

"He who sits in the heavens shall laugh;
The Lord shall hold them in derision."
(Psalm 2:4)

Oh, the old devil had been told what was going to happen to him, but it didn't register with him. He may be old, but he's not omniscient. All the way back in Genesis, right after Adam and Eve sinned, God told Satan the day would come when One would come from woman (that's Jesus) and would bruise the head of the serpent (that's the devil). But in the process Jesus would be bruised.

It's a picture of someone using his foot to bash the head of a snake but gets bruised doing so. Well, the bruise hurts, but just look at the snake. This is what Jesus did at the cross. He delivered a crushing blow to the devil while only temporarily hurting Himself. Read it for yourself in Genesis 3:14-15. The devil didn't get it. He really wasn't supposed to. God kept it veiled in dark, shadowy words. It really was meant for us to see and rejoice in after it was too late for the devil.

We look back in hindsight with the cross shining upon the words, and we go, "Ah ha! I see it." There would never have been a Bible if the sins of Genesis 3 had never occurred. The rest of the Bible is about "fixing" (one of my favorite southern words) the problem of sin: in the lives of Adam, Eve and all who would follow them, including me.

My cat tried to back up and reverse course. In contrast, the "roaring lion" (1 Peter 5:8) did not. He pressed on to his own undoing.

Oh, he can still work to tempt us, but he cannot claim us as his unless we give ourselves to him. Jesus has ripped the power of death away from him. Satan cannot say of all of us, *"They are mine,"* because some of us have come to the Savior. And when Satan does tempt us there is always a way of escape. God will provide it (1 Corinthians 10:13).

A big key to overcoming temptation and snares is to keep our eyes on the Man who was on the tree. If the bobcat had never taken his eyes off of me, there would have been a way of escape for it. If you are already a Christian, keep your eyes on Jesus and His will for your life. You will escape death and obtain life eternal, while the devil who has hunted you will be shut away in a terrible place of death (Revelation 20:10).

Thank God there was a day the hunter became the hunted!

THE ARROW STRIKES Have I thought as deeply as I should about the sacrifice of Jesus to destroy the works of the devil in my life? Have I thanked God lately for drawing Satan (my predator) into His trap? Am I, as a Christian, fighting Satan daily with power, knowing the victory is mine as long as I stay faithful and claim the forgiveness provided by the cross?

Inner Voices

Confidence is essential in deer hunting, especially bow-hunting. In the "moment of truth," when that buck sporting his nice rack appears, believing in yourself is paramount. However, it is easy for inner voices to trouble you: silently saying something like, *"You can't make that shot. You are going to miss."* The words are devastating to performing well.

This is why practice is so important. Practice allows another voice to enter that says, *"You've got this. You've practiced this shot hundreds of times. Chip shot!"* This is the voice you need to build you up. It says, *"You can do it. Pick a spot. Maintain form. Execute the shot. You've got him."*

You better believe this same scenario plays out in the spiritual world. It's like the old Looney Tunes cartoon from my childhood where a cat had a little demon sitting on one shoulder whispering negative things. On the other shoulder sat an angel whispering encouragement. Whose voice will you listen to? It's up to you.

It happens with Christians who formerly lived a regretful past. Isn't that all of us? Peter talks about *"our past lifetime"* and teaches us to let the past be the past and live life anew (1 Peter 4:1-3).

ONE VOTE FOR YOU, ONE VOTE AGAINST YOU

Both the devil and God want to use your past. The devil loves to use it to drag you down and keep you from performing well in your walk with the Lord. God wants you to build on it, using even your failures. Think of what great things He did with the murderous Saul of Tarsus who became the apostle Paul (1 Timothy 1:12-17). He "failed forward" and used his past to help others see that they could rise to better things.

The enemy is masterful in planting defeating thoughts in our heads (John 13:2). It may be something hateful someone says to you. It may be your own thoughts you allow to float around. Regardless of how these detrimental things get in your head, the devil loves it. He loves it when you hear things about your past: *"You're a piece of filth. You ought to be so ashamed of what you did. What makes you think you can be a good Christian? God doesn't want somebody like you. God doesn't love you. Nobody loves you."* It's all a lie from the father of lies (John 8:44).

The truth is altogether different. When you become a Christian, God removes all of your sins, no matter how bad they are and buries them. Listen to what He says about you. All of this is found in scripture although I am grouping it. *"You are loved. You are accepted. You are My child. You are Jesus' friend. You are redeemed and forgiven. In My Son, you are free from condemnation. I am promising you great and precious things ahead."* This is the voice of victory. This is the voice to listen to. It comes from the Father of truth!

HELPFUL HINTS

Let go of all of your hurtful thoughts about your past. Tell Satan to get behind you (Matthew 4:10)! Let go. I am reminded of the story of how some natives of the jungle kill monkeys. They get a coconut, cut a hole in it, hollow it out, place peanuts on the inside, and then tie it to a tree. A monkey comes along and sticks his hand in the coconut, but with a clenched fist around the peanuts he cannot remove his hand from the hole. The tighter he grips, the greater the bondage. What's the key to being free? Let go. But he will not do it. Is letting go what you need to do with your past?

Listen to the voice of truth. I'm told that one of the reasons some pilots crash at night over the ocean is because they stay out too long and everything gets dark. They lose all sense of what is up or down. Now, if they have had instrument training, all they have to do is believe and follow the instruments. They never lie. However, many pilots just can't let go of what they *think* is right and *feel* is right, and they fly the plane right into the ocean. An airplane mechanic once told me, *"Your mind will scream at you but you must follow the instruments. They are true."* The point? Keep listening to God. Only His voice is true!

Maybe there's a great challenge out there. Maybe it's the need to step out of the comfort zone and do something you haven't done before. Listen to the voice of truth. I love the words to a song so titled. It takes us to two scenes: Peter walking on the water and David killing Goliath.

Oh what I would do to have
The kind of faith it takes to climb out of this boat I'm in
Onto the crashing waves

To step out of my comfort zone
To the realm of the unknown where Jesus is
And He's holding out His hand

But the waves are calling out my name and they laugh at me
Reminding me of all the times I've tried before and failed
The waves they keep on telling me
Time and time again. 'Boy, you'll never win!'
"You'll never win"

But the voice of truth tells me a different story
And the voice of truth says "Do not be afraid!"
And the voice of truth says "This is for My glory"
Out of all the voices calling out to me
I will choose to listen and believe the voice of truth.

Oh what I would do to have
The kind of strength it takes to stand before a giant
With just a sling and a stone
Surrounded by the sound of a thousand warriors
Shaking in their armor
Wishing they'd have had the strength to stand

But the giant's calling out my name and he laughs at me
Reminding me of all the times I've tried before and failed
The giant keeps on telling me
Time and time again "Boy, you'll never win!
"You'll never win."

But the voice of truth tells me a different story
And the voice of truth says "Do not be afraid!"
And the voice of truth says "This is for My glory"
Out of all the voices calling out to me
I will choose to listen and believe the voice of truth.

But the stone was just the right size
To put the giant on the ground
And the waves they don't seem so high
From on top of them looking down
I will soar with the wings of eagles
When I stop and listen to the sound of Jesus
Singing over me.

I will choose to listen and believe the voice of truth.
(Mark Hall & Stephen Curtis Chapman)

Loosen up, please! Just admit that we all have done stupid things. Call it what it was. It was a stupid moment. And when you have been forgiven by the Lord, get on with business (Hebrews 9:13-14).

Just recently, a neighbor was talking to me about some changes she had made in her life. One Sunday, her preacher said that when you are tempted, say to yourself, *"Don't be stupid."* Still being weak, as her habit was, she pulled into a bar that very same week. She turned the car off, and then the thought hit her. She brought her hand down on the dashboard and said, *"Don't be stupid."* And with that, she cranked the car and left. That's it. Just call your past what it was. It was stupid. I was stupid. And move on.

I love the Andy Griffith episode where Gomer Pile entered the army and for a prank, his comrades convinced him to put on the sergeant's uniform. Well, the sergeant was livid when he saw him in it and made him sit in the hut with a bucket on his head and think about what he had done. Andy finds Gomer and asks why he is wearing the bucket. Gomer explained, and Andy said, "Gomer that was stupid." Gomer candidly replied, "Whuttin it though?" That's it. Quit riding yourself with defeating thoughts. Loosen up. If you are a Christian, you are forgiven. And it hurts the Lord, who died for you, to see you keep killing yourself with it. He died to set you free. Now, live in that freedom.

Remind the devil of his future. Someone once said, "The next time the devil reminds you of your past, remind him of his future." He sure has one. Hell is prepared for him and his kind (Matthew 25:41).

Remember, it hurts the Lord who died for you. Imagine how hurt Jesus is when He has suffered so much to give you freedom from your sins and you keep acting like you are not forgiven. It's a trust issue. Do you trust Him when He says your sins are gone? Our refusal to accept Him at His word is an insult to His truthfulness and hurts Him just as much as the nails.

Okay, back to the woods now. That Goliath-size buck is in front of you. Rest the pin on the spot. You've got this. Take him!

THE ARROW STRIKES — When I think of my past, do I have defeating thoughts, or do I use my past to see God's grace, and then use it to help others? Are there any "peanuts" (forgiven sins) I need to let go of? Do I need to forgive myself? Do I realize how very special I am to God?

God & the Taxidermist: Two Artists at Work

It matters WHO does your taxidermy work. Not everyone can take something dead and bring it alive...making it lifelike.

It's a little hard to explain, but when the long pursuit of a great trophy buck turns from dream to reality, it matters who does the artistry on him, because a strange kind of bond is developed with this magnificent animal.

I recently read such a story called *"Quest for Hurley: A Long Special Relationship Between A Buck and a Bowhunter Comes To A Bittersweet Conclusion"* by Barry Wensel.

Hurley was a 14-point that field dressed at 248 lbs. and measured at 190 1/8 inches. Wensel got his first opportunity at Hurley in 2009. He shot over his back. He says, *"I named him Hurley because I felt like hurling every time I relived the thought of the arrow flying high."* Two more years of hard pursuit, and daydreams became reality in 2011.

In the afternoon sun, Wensel finally got to see Hurley on the ground. His next words are touching. I emphasize the words that grab me. *"I instantly **had very mixed emotions**. I had attained my goal, my dream, yet it suddenly **seemed too final**. I kept thinking I was going to wake up and find it actually was all a dream. **I was honestly choked up**."* Speaking of the bond that develops, he says, *"This personal closeness is something I feel a lot of hunters cheat themselves out of. Because of the intimate relationship that develops, **one senses a loss** similar to the death of a loved one. We* *must accept these emotions, just like we do other personal losses"* (Bowhunter, November 2012, pg. 20-24). I understand. The pursuit is over, but there's a part of you that wishes it wasn't. The journey itself was so rewarding. But what do you do now? Of course, a buck like Hurley must be mounted, but whom will you choose?

I personally am very picky when it comes to choosing who will get his hands on my deer. This trophy will be preserved for a lifetime and will always be a reminder of all the hard work, patience, and the time on the stand it took to finally be rewarded at the end. It will be looked at and talked about with friends. In a great article, Daniel Gooden says of his work, *"I am driven by the happiness and joy our work brings to the clients.* **Knowing that each time they view their mount, it takes them away from where they are and puts them in the time and place where they were when they harvested the animal is important to me"** (The Art of Taxidermy, Whitetail Times, Winter 2012, pg. 45). This is the kind of whitetail trophy artist I want!

Where am I going with this? I want someone who really cares to work on my trophies, and I certainly want THE BEST to work on *me.* Did you know that God sees you like a piece of His art, and He wants to perform His wonderful work on you? I like the parallels I see in a taxidermist and God.

BOTH ARE WORKING WITH SOMETHING DEAD

The best taxidermist is one who can make the mount look exactly like the living animal. In contrast, God doesn't make us *look* alive. He actually makes us alive. The same God who raised Jesus from the dead *physically,* raises us from the dead *spiritually.*

Resurrection power worked for Jesus and me. Ephesians 2:1 says, *"And you He made alive, who were dead in trespasses and sins."* It is the same power that continues to work in our lives, keeping us pressing on with no fear of the grave (1 Corinthians 15:54-57).

BOTH START WITH A VISION

A taxidermist will first ask what pose you want. Here's where you get to envision things. You get a chance to "see the end from the beginning." He knows exactly what he wants to do. With the greatest work of all, God had a vision for the beautiful piece of work He wants you and me to be. Would you believe He is striving to make us look like Him: to have His traits, His character and His nature? Wow, what a dream! But it's a dream He can make reality. It's all over the Bible.

- To be holy as He is holy (1 Peter 1:13-15).
- To partake of the divine nature—be like Him and Jesus and the Holy Spirit (2 Peter 1:4).
- Be transformed into the likeness of Jesus (2 Corinthians 3:18).

God has made it very simple for us. He sent His Son Jesus and in essence was saying, "Watch Him and do what He does," for He is "God with us" (Matthew 1:23). And step by step, little by little, the transformation occurs. The taxidermist starts with an ugly raw mannequin or form that looks little like my buck, but oh what he does from there! Likewise, I come to God "just as I am"—nothing pretty at all. I yield to His hands at my conversion, and the wonderful transformation begins (Colossians 2:12). It gets more glorious at each phase of my growth...ever and ever more like Him.

"But we all with unveiled face,
beholding as in a mirror **the glory of the Lord,**
are **being transformed into the same image**
from **glory to glory**, *just as by the Spirit of the Lord."*
2 Corinthians 3:18

BOTH MUST HAVE A LOT OF PATIENCE

The process is laborious for the taxidermist—skinning, salting, drying, tanning, preparing the form, and placing the hide on the form. He then must work carefully with the eyes, ears, nose and mouth, and then to think that he has to do it over and over and over again. But the best ones don't lose their passion for it.

There is one thing that reduces his frustration greatly. The deer doesn't argue with him and stays still. Well, of course he does! God's job takes more patience because we choose whether we will let Him work on us. If you don't want to be a MASTERpiece, you don't have to be. Yet sometimes, even those who say they want to be like Him still offer too much resistance. Of all of His creation, we are the only ones who resist. Do you remember the story of Jonah? Everything did what God wanted (wind, waves, sea, the repenting people of Nineveh, a plant, and even a worm). Everything and everyone but Jonah!

God works long with us, and how frustrating it must be at times when we are so slow to come along. I know Jesus got frustrated with the apostles but He loved them and stayed with it. ***Jesus didn't focus so much on what they were but rather what they were becoming!***

We have to be patient too. God's not in a hurry. He never is. Someone once said, *"If you want to be a mushroom, God can do that overnight. But if you want to be a giant sequoia, you better give that some time."* I know a masterful taxidermist who has had a man's deer for three-and-a-half years! Is that too long? Well, to me that's unanswerable. If it is the buck of a lifetime and this guy is GOOD at what he does, it just might be worth the wait. And with God, I know it's worth the wait. The word "wait" is all over the Bible, and we surely need "wait training."

So, be patient. God is doing the greatest work of all, making you like His Son. You are a work in progress. I have a kid's class I enjoy so much, and we regularly sing.

"There really ought to be a sign upon my heart.
Don't judge me yet, there's an unfinished part.
But I'll be perfect, just according to His plan.
Fashioned by the Master's loving hand.

He's still working on me.
To make me what I ought to be.
It took Him just a week to make the moon and the stars,
the sun, the earth and Jupiter and Mars.
How loving and patient He must be.
He's still working on me."

And yes, you play a part in this. How does it happen? Read your Bible; watch Jesus; imitate Him; obey what He says (and don't forget the words of the apostles and prophets in the Bible are His words too). He speaks through them. Little by little it's happening. You start to look like Him in all you say and do. Live life thinking of Jesus living inside of you, and let Him work from the inside out (Galatians 2:20).

BOTH DO "FINISH WORK"

I have a taxidermist currently working on a bobcat for me. His turnaround time has been normal, but his "finish work" seems to be the longest part. Finish work is stuff like the base with materials like a field would have. It also includes a fence post with barbed wire. I'm even adding a "No Hunting" sign from our family farm written by our beloved Uncle Dick. I guess you could say the animal is being fitted to its environment.

God also has "finish work" to do. The idea is that we are to strive to be as much like Jesus as we can be in this life. When we make mistakes as Christians, we confess our sins, and God makes us perfect in the blood of His Son. After we have given our all to be like Jesus, God caps it off at the last. And it seems that He does it instantly. His finish work is fast!

> *"Beloved, now we are the children of God;*
> *and it has not yet been revealed what we shall be,*
> *but we know that when He is revealed,*
> ***we shall be like Him,***
> *for we **shall see Him as He is**.*
> *And everyone who has this hope in Him,*
> ***purifies himself, just as He is pure."***
> 1 John 3:2-3

BOTH SEE IT AS THEIR "WORKMANSHIP"

The best taxidermist takes pride in his work understanding that it says something about him, the artist. When I see a mount that is done poorly, it tells me a lot about the man who did it, and I have no interest in him doing any work for me. Simply put, I'm turned off.

Then there's the flipside. I sat down recently with a taxidermist that in my opinion is one of the best. He'd rather not do it, if it's not going to be done right. For example, he spends a great amount of time on just the eyes. As he says, "*The life is in the eyes. And a woman who sees it, whether a female hunter or the hunter's*

wife, will first look at the eyes. Eyes matter greatly to a woman."
He's right. The eyes have to be right to bring it alive! He has a great
backlog of clients. Why? They love his mounts: his workmanship.

Here's where I get so excited. A true Christian is the
workmanship of God! You can see wonderful things about God just
by looking at what He has done with this person. Many times I have
marveled at the great difference God has made in the lives of so
many people.

> *"For we are His workmanship,*
> *created in Christ Jesus for good works,*
> *which God prepared beforehand*
> *that we should walk in them."*
> (Ephesians 2:10)

When we yield our lives to Him, it creates a new man that
others can see. In a real sense, you are on display so that others will
see God through you. Hopefully they will want the same Artist to
work on them (Matthew 5:16).

BOTH HAVE A SPECIAL PLACE TO DISPLAY THEIR WORK

Every taxidermist I have ever visited has a room where his
work is proudly displayed. With God, that trophy room is heaven.
If you are a true Christian, Jesus is now preparing a beautiful place
for you (John 14:2). Some other very special people will be there
too. Just read Hebrews 11. Some beautiful works of God you have
known in your lifetime will also be there. Oh, the Lord is the
centerpiece but all around Him are His "trophies." He is so pleased
with His beloved sons and daughters: His family. He wants to show
for all eternity what He has done with us (Revelation 21:9).

Let this sink in. Have you ever thought, "What does God get
out of all of this He has done"? We get Him. We get heaven. But
what does He get? What makes Him so happy He never aborted the
project? I think the answer is: *His people...His workmanship.* They
are His inheritance, His possession (Ephesians 1:14,18). They shine
as the sun (Matthew 13:43). I don't know why He wanted me, but I
am so humbled He did.

GOD SPARED NO COST!!

When you choose your taxidermist, don't go cheap. Trust me, you will get what you pay for. I once saw a sign in the lobby of an excellent taxidermist that read, ***"The bitterness of poor quality remains long after the sweetness of the low price is forgotten."***

Listen. God is never about poor quality and He didn't buy His trophies with money. It wouldn't do. He bought us with the precious blood of His Son (1 Peter 1:18-19)! It was a ransom. Those are never cheap! He envisioned it before the foundation of the world. He then invested into it 1393 pages of scriptures (at least that's how many pages my Bible has), and a few thousand years of time. He watched as many of His prophets and people were mocked and killed. At last, He gave His Son, which really means He gave totally of Himself!

You matter to Him. Yield to Him. Let Him get His skillful hands on you. Heaven will surely be worth it all.

THE ARROW STRIKES Have I thought much on how God wants to make me like His Son? Do I realize how much it cost God to save me? What things in my life need to be made new? Do I have any part of my life I have marked as "off limits" to God, refusing to yield to Him? Am I someone God would love to display to the world? Will I be added to heaven's beauty one day?

Give Him the Best

I was perched along a hillside in middle Tennessee looking down a lane and I saw him coming. But something wasn't right. His head was bobbing up and down in an awkward kind of way. Then I realized he was limping. He stopped at the property line on the other side of the fence. I knew he was about to jump. I hated it for him because I knew it might not be easy and the landing would likely be painful. He bounded up in the air, cleared the fence, and came down allowing only his good, right front hoof to put on the brakes.

He continued his limp toward me and stopped less than ten yards away and munched on some little Beautyberries. I now could see his hoof clearly. It was all puffed up the size of a softball. I don't know how he hurt it, but he must have gotten into something. I also noticed his hips were lean. Obviously, he was falling off in size. I probably should have taken him before a four-legged predator with sharp teeth got hold of him. It may have been the best thing to do, but I was on a mission to get a good buck, and I didn't want my shot to disturb things and ruin my hunt. And since I didn't know what was going on with "Limpy," I was a little concerned about eating the meat. I was hoping he might get well. So, I let him walk.

"HEY, I KNOW!! LET'S GIVE IT TO GOD!"

You are probably aware that in the Old Testament, animal sacrifices were offered in worship to God. When they offered such sacrifices, God called for the best saying things like, *"Your lamb shall be without blemish"* (Exodus 12:5).

Over time some of the worshippers lost their reverence for God. They began to live immorally but would still "go through the motions" of worship. Guess what kind of animals they picked to offer to God? You got it. Ole Limpy! Anything that was coughing or broken up, they gave. You know, anything that wouldn't be a real SACRIFICE on their part. Now, if the governor or somebody *really important* came along, they would be sure to present themselves in the very best way...but this was *only God* you see! The whole thing made God furious, and He basically told them to shut the doors and go home.

> *"And when you offer the blind*
> *as a sacrifice, is it not evil?*
> *And when you offer the lame and sick, is it not evil?*
> *Offer it then to your governor!*
> *Would he be pleased with you?*
> *Would he accept you favorably?"*
> *says the Lord of Hosts."*
> Malachi 1:8

The same thing happens too many times today. I'm reminded of the family who went to worship. After the services were over and they were heading home, the dad commented about how terrible the song leader was. The mother said something about the preacher's sermon being too long. On and on it went, until finally their child chimed in and said, *"Well, I thought it was a pretty good show since we all got in for a dollar."* Hey, that's a pretty funny story to tell, but I doubt God is laughing. The best was lacking.

When people begin to lose their reverence for God, they tend to become slackers in everything that has to do with Him.

YET, GOD GAVE HIS BEST

What a contrast to what God does! When the fullness of time came and it was time for God to give what was needed for our salvation, He gave the best heaven had to give. He gave His Son:

the same Son who never did anything wrong. We are not surprised to read passages about Jesus which talk about how perfect He was.

"Knowing that you were not redeemed
with corruptible things like silver or gold,
from your aimless conduct received by
tradition from your fathers,
but with the precious blood of Christ,
as of a lamb without blemish
and without spot."
1 Peter 1:18-19

No spots, no blemishes, no sin...that's Jesus, God's gift to us (1 Peter 2:22). He's *"holy, harmless, undefiled, separate from sinners, and has become higher than the heavens"* (Hebrews 7:26). Now, that's a sacrifice.

LET'S DO BETTER

God deserves the best...ALWAYS. He is excellent and should receive excellence from us. And when you really think about what He has done for us, how can we give him the "Limpies" of our life?

I know we expect excellence in less important places. In my home state of Alabama, football is a god to many. We are the home of one of the greatest rivalries in the nation—Alabama versus Auburn—the "Iron Bowl." And it matters little which team you pull for; the fans on each side want coaches who demand excellence from the players. They will accept nothing else. Subpar will not do! Listen to such a quote from coach Nick Saban.

"Somebody tells you to do something.
*Somebody **sets a standard** of how you are gonna do it.*
You understand it. It's defined.
*And then you show that you have the **ability***
*and the **accountability** to do it that way."*

But isn't something really out of whack if we take football so seriously and then give shabby service to God? Why does the vast majority of the 110,000 fans who sat in a stadium on Saturday fail to sit in a pew on Sunday?

Everything we do in service to God ought to be done with our might (Ecclesiastes 9:10). And there ought to be some sacrifice, some cost. I love the words of David when a man named Nashon offered to give him all he needed to sacrifice to God, FREE OF CHARGE! David's response was, *"No, but I will surely buy it from you for a price; nor will I offer burnt offerings to the Lord my God with that which costs me nothing"* (2 Samuel 24:24).

If we are on the job, our work ought to be of the finest quality. We are not slackers, only working hard when the boss is looking. The Bible calls that "eyeservice." We work with excellence at every moment because we are always aware that our work is for the Lord (Colossians 3:22-24). And a great payday is coming.

In our homes each evening we strive to be excellent parents. It would do us well upon driving into our driveways at the end of the day, to turn the ignition off and pray to God. The greatest work we have done all day will be done between the sheetrock walls of our house. It's worth our best (2 Corinthians 12:14-15).

In our worship on the Lord's day or any other worship period, let's enter into it with reverence. Let's come to worship unblemished, having already cleared anything between us and God. Let's focus when the Bible is read. Let's pray fervently when the prayers are offered. Let's sing with strength. Let's listen attentively when the word of God is preached. When we see our flaws and defects, let's make needed corrections.

Once while preaching in Virginia, I was told a joke about three men who went hunting: a preacher, a lawyer and a doctor. After an unsuccessful hunt, they were standing together, and a big buck ran across the field in front of them. All three pulled their guns up and shot at the same time. The buck collapsed. They began arguing about whose bullet killed the deer. About that time, a game warden came up and asked, "Who shot the deer?" They replied, "We don't know. We all shot at the same time." He said, "I'll go look and come back and let you know." After a brief moment, he returned and said, "The preacher shot him." They asked, "How do you know the preacher shot him?" He said, "It went in one ear and out the other." Maybe that's why Jesus often said, "Listen."

I fear that in America too many people treat worship like another entertainment venue. Os Guinness has said, "The modern world has scrambled things so badly that today we worship our work, we work at our play, and we play at our worship." Folks want everything that is done to be entertaining. They come as though they are an audience. Folks, we are not the audience. We are the participants. **GOD IS THE AUDIENCE.**

I know of a preacher who was asked if he thought clapping was proper in a worship setting. I liked his answer: *"I want to focus on doing the worshipping and hope that God is clapping."* It seems to me he understood WHO was the object of worship! I'm reminded of an opera singer who left the stage crying because one man didn't clap. Someone said, "Why are you concerned about one man? Listen to the crowd. They loved you." She said, "That one man...is my teacher." If He doesn't clap, it doesn't matter if the whole world is standing in ovation!

Don't offer "Limpy." Offer the best!

THE ARROW STRIKES Have I thought much about God giving His best for me? Have I been a slacker at work because I failed to see I should offer my best? When I arrive at home after work, do I ask God to help me do my best for my family? When I go to worship, do I find myself wanting to be entertained, or do I strive to truly worship God with all my heart?

Shame

In the whitetail woods, I have done some things I didn't want to tell my hunting buddies for fear they would laugh at me. Or maybe they would think I wasn't a very good woodsman or hunter.

- I have gotten lost going to a stand, and yet I knew where it was. It should have been easy to find.

- I once shot at a big buck, with a muzzleloader, at a mere twenty yards and missed! Talk about embarrassing.

- I have shot and walked to retrieve does that turned out to be...bucks. I've done it even after studying them very carefully, trying not to make a mistake. It makes me so mad when I do that! The first time I did it, one of my hunting buddies held three fingers above his head every time he saw me and would say, "Three-point doe!"

These moments are really just small stuff. Other things I have done bother me even more. Like the time I unbolted my rifle and a round popped out I didn't know was in it.

Another day, I was walking from my stand and looked down, and my rifle was in the "fire" position. Evidently, I had clicked the safety off when a deer was approaching, never got the shot opportunity, and then failed to put the safety back on. This makes me very ashamed and mad at myself because I am a Hunter Safety

Instructor! How could I do that! It just proves that even the best intentioned person can mess up!

My most memorable moment of shame totally blindsided me. I had always said that if I was bowhunting I might take a mama doe if her little one was unspotted and eating on its own. On opening day of the season, that scenario presented itself. I awoke with excitement because one of my goals that year was to improve my bowhunting skills. Not long after settling in, I saw two deer, and both were browsing and eating berries. From a distance I saw no spots on the smaller one, and when the bigger doe came to forty yards, I released an arrow and took her. It was then that I saw spots on the smaller one. I don't believe it's wrong to harvest a doe like that and wouldn't fault anyone who did. The little one can still eat, and I can too. But I felt sorrow on that day unlike any day before, and I decided that I probably would not do the same again. For some reason, my feelings led me to think of what my sins did to Jesus on the cross. When I field-dressed that doe and blood cascaded over the rocks in the creek, I told Eddie, "Look at that Eddie. That's what Jesus did for you and me." Innocence died for me. And it may sound crazy to you, but when I later packaged my venison, I wrote "Salvation" on the package as a reminder of the hunt.

THE HEART OF SHAME

I think it is right here that I need to make one thing clear. Hunters have hearts. I know I do, and the men closest to me do. It's just that if you hunt long enough, you are going to have some tough, difficult moments in the woods. Isn't life the same way?

At the dawning of the Lord's day, I was still thinking about yesterday's hunt. I also was preparing to think about the Lord's Supper which I would soon eat. It's a weekly memorial to bring Jesus' sacrifice very near to my heart (Acts 20:7), as He said, *"Do this in remembrance of Me"* (Matthew 26:26-30).

Strangely, two deaths were still merging in my mind, yesterday's and today's...*hers* and *His*. I wondered if any other hunter had ever written about the emotions I was feeling. I checked Steve Chapman's excellent book, *A Look At Life From A Deer Stand*, and there I found words that helped me.

"I have told my son, Nathan, that if he experiences no remorse after taking a deer, he's simply a killer of animals. If there is remorse, however, he's a hunter" (pg. 109).

"A good hunter is committed to the deer after the shot, especially if the arrow or bullet was off the mark and not in the vitals" (pg. 109).

"It's hard to explain to a non-hunter how the sight of blood affects those of us who stalk into the woods every season to fill a game tag. Each time I'm confronted with two powerful emotions. One comes quickly and the other settles in later. When I down a deer, the quiet screams of success go off in my mind. I can't classify it as victory because this is not a battle. The deer doesn't shoot back. It's a success because this man has outwitted one of the smartest animals alive...
The second emotion I invariably deal with came that night when I lay down to sleep...When I closed my eyes that night, all I could see was red. That night the thought of it hurt. That morning the color of success was red. That night a necessary shame clouded the same color. Though it had done nothing to harm me, I took the life of that innocent creature. Once again the pendulum swung from joy to sorrow" (pg. 111-113).

"I have often wondered if other hunters go through this same mixture of emotions. (May I interrupt to say, "Yes, we do Steve."). *I have a feeling they do, but I suppose few ever talk about it. Yet, I believe it is part of the bond that exists between us" (pg. 113).*

Christians have a blood bond too. We are all connected to the shed blood of Calvary. As we sing, *"There is a fountain filled with blood drawn from Immanuel's vein and sinners plunged beneath that flood lose all their guilty stains."*

I can't help but think, if hunters really share a bond and all have experienced moments of shame and remorse in the woods, why don't we talk about it? Can you sense where I am headed? When I finally told a hunter or two about some of those embarrassing things and the shame I felt, they each said, *"I have done the same thing and*

I have had those same emotions." Recently a hunter and preacher-friend of mine said he once shot a button buck accidentally when his little boy was with him. He said, *"I felt as if I had taken a young boy before his time."*

I guess some things are better just left in the woods, yet it felt good to know that I wasn't the only one. And it may be okay for hunters not to talk about their mistakes, but I am convinced that Christians must always talk to God and sometimes talk to others in order to overcome sin. It simply helps to know others struggle too.

SHAME IS A GOOD THING

Who do you think created shame? God did. I suppose He created it the same day He created the conscience. A conscience can become seared to the point where it will not work (1 Timothy 4:2); but when it has been taught correctly by God's word, it will sound an alarm. That's a good thing. God designed it to bring us back to Him when we have sinned.

It's all over the Bible. David's conscience ate him alive after committing adultery with Bathsheba (Psalm 51 & 38). Peter wept bitterly after betraying Jesus (Luke 22:54-62). Those who crucified Jesus were pricked in their hearts, repented, and were baptized for the remission of their sins (Acts 2:36-41). Shame is a wonderful thing. It can bring us back to God.

I personally believe that some of the depression many people are dealing with is because of sin. Now, don't get me wrong. Righteous people can have times of depression, but I'm just saying there are lots of people who feel very bad about what they have done, and they find a good psychiatrist who will help them *silence their conscience*. And that's not good.

We need to take our sin and shame to God and let Him purge the conscience (Hebrews 9:14). That's what David did, and he felt so much better (Romans 4:6-8). Even our baptism at the beginning of our journey with God is an appeal to God for a good conscience (1 Peter 3:21). I know it was for me. I remember the relief of knowing my sins were washed away in the blood of Christ.

I believe the same thing that happens in the *woods* also happens to people of the *Word*. We sometimes do embarrassing things, and we don't tell anyone because we don't want them to think differently of us. I believe there are many sincere Christians who struggle with some particular sin in their life, and yet they feel they have nowhere to go and no one to talk to heart-to-heart. So, what do they do? They cover it up and continue in shame. Spiritual masquerades are not fun. Just ask King David. His greatest relief was when his sin was brought out in the open and he confessed, *"I have sinned against the Lord"* (2 Samuel 12:13).

A NEED FOR OPENNESS

Not only does God want us to bring our sins to Him for Him to cover. He also encourages us to confess our faults *one to another*, help each other, and pray for one another.

> *"Confess your trespasses to one another,*
> *and pray for one another,*
> *that you may be healed.*
> *The effective fervent prayer*
> *of a righteous man avails much."*
> James 5:16

> *"The sacrifices of God are a broken spirit,*
> *A broken and contrite heart -*
> *These, O God, You will not despise."*
> Psalm 51:17

For example, in the last several years there has been an increase in the number of men (and I might add women too) who struggle with pornography in their lives. Greater access to it and privacy has probably led to the increase. They feel intense shame but they don't feel they have anyone who will truly understand, help them, and not feel differently toward them. What do they do? They keep trying to *appear* as squeaky clean Christians while *feeling very nasty*.

We need to do better in helping each other with sin, and I think we are beginning to. All Christians need to quit pretending that we never struggle with temptation. Let's talk in such a way when we are together that those who are struggling begin to think, *"You know, I can tell he cares and has a heart of compassion. I really think I could share with him my struggles."*

Recently, I went way out "in the boonies" with a group of about thirty men and stayed in a cabin. For an evening and a day we listened to great lessons and had refreshing discussions on issues men deal with. It was great.

One brother spoke on purity. He spoke about his struggle with pornography with great openness. Everyone listened, and I could see that he was appreciated for sharing it. He taught about some measures he had taken: some keys to overcoming. He encouraged finding someone to hold you accountable (not controlling you but holding you to the task), bouncing the eyes away from anything immodest, kicking out bad thoughts, and knowing what triggers *you* to sin. Don't excuse it. It is sin you know: a sin where men especially are vulnerable (Job 31:1; Matthew 5:27-30). This brother got into porn by being a *male*. He got out by being a *man*!

Some sins are best left with God alone, but in those cases where breaking free is helped greatly by confessing to another...do it. By all means, be careful with whom you choose to share it, but do it.

TIPS FOR THE LISTENER

If we are to help those who come to us seeking our help and our prayers we have to learn to be great listeners. Let me share four very important things.

1. **Listen with great compassion.** We all sin. What has happened to my brother could happen to me (Galatians 6:1-2). As they confess, don't have that "How could you ever do that" look on your face. They are already feeling plenty of shame. That's why they came to you.

2. **Hold everything they say in utmost confidence**. It may later need to be confessed to others but for the moment hold it tight. NEVER BREAK PROMISES OF CONFIDENTIALITY. I repeat...NEVER. If you do, they will never come to you again. And I wouldn't blame them. Talebearers destroy friendships (Proverbs 16:28).

3. **Help them with a plan for victory.** Agree to hold them accountable. Did you know they even make computer

software that will send an e-mail to someone if you look at a porn website? Ask them tough questions in the days ahead. *"Are you still clean?"*

4. **Be prepared for relapses.** Sometimes after committing to overcoming, a person will yet sin again in a moment of weakness. They may be even more ashamed to tell you this time, because they had been doing so well until then. Tell them you believe in them. Identify what led to the fall. Help them grow wiser from it and above all, pray with them for God's help in breaking free from the bondage.

Father, help me to be a humble Christian. Help me to freely confess my sins to You. And help me to have a heart of compassion and helpful words toward brothers or sisters who share their sin struggle with me. Help me be a person they know they can trust to pray with them and help them be victorious in Christ. Provide me also with those who will help me in my moments of weakness. Thank you for the gift of your Son and the cleansing He gives. May He live within us helping us live in the Spirit and not in the flesh. It's in His saving name I pray. Amen.

THE ARROW STRIKES Have I ever done anything while hunting that I didn't share with others? Are there things in my life that cause me to feel shame? Have I freely talked to God about it? Do I need to find a trusted friend with whom to share my struggles? Am I understanding that shame is a good thing to bring me back to God?

Uptight Hunter

When it comes to deer hunting, there are no hard and fast rules. That's the beauty of it. You can hunt any way you like. The important thing is to make sure you are enjoying it and coming away blessed by what the whitetail and the woods have to offer. Let's look at two hunters and their vastly different approaches.

HUNTER #1

This hunter's approach will settle for nothing less than a trophy buck. Those who use this approach are not having fun unless they know a nice buck is in their future. They wash their clothes in scent-free detergent, perhaps even using a washing machine that is used for nothing but hunting clothes. They may decide to let them air dry outside and then put them in a Rubbermaid container to keep out all household scents, food odors, etc. If cedar is natural to the area they hunt in, they may put some cedar branches in the plastic tub to fill the clothes with the aroma.

They take a bath with no-scent soap, brush their teeth with a special toothpaste, and wait until they get to the hunting property to change into their clothes and rubber hunting boots. More than likely these clothes are camouflaged with the perfect pattern and are made with no-scent carbon technology to effectively absorb organic odors. Doesn't that sound cool?

Those who use this approach refuse to hunt a stand if the wind is not right and they consider the wind direction even as they make their way to the stand. The route they take to the stand is the one less likely to bump deer. They have a detailed plan for every hunt and love the strategy involved to outsmart the experienced buck. More than likely, they don't have snacks in their fanny pack either. They may boldly go where "no man has gone before" in search of the creature. They may even use waders or a boat to cross swampy areas in order to get where deer are hiding and feel safe. Sooner or later, this approach will result in the trophy buck they have longed for.

HUNTER #2

This hunter's approach is the exact opposite of the first hunter's approach. The guy using this approach gets up and searches for his clothes. Most of them are still in the cab of the truck where they have been riding with him all week. They have not been washed in a while. He doesn't take a bath. He took one the night before with whatever soap he had. He makes himself a pot of coffee and fries some sausage for a biscuit. If he doesn't have time to do that, he'll stop by Mama Sue's Quick Stop, talk to the regular crowd, and perhaps smoke a cigarette. Later, he might smoke in the tree stand. He'll pump some more gas in the truck for his journey and eat his food on the way to the hunting place. He has a pretty spot he always likes to hunt. The wind might not be right today, but he loves this stand. If he walks by a cow patty, he might conveniently and deliberately step in it for a little cover scent. He eats some snacks about midmorning and falls asleep often, but he's having a great time. And sooner or later, he'll probably get his trophy buck, too, when the wind is right or during the crazy time of the rut.

MY APPROACH

How does Jeff May go about this thing? Well, I have to say this. One year I did all of the things guy #2 did (except for the cigarette), and I had my best year ever. I put my first two trophies on the wall. I had lots and lots of fun!

Having said that, I do believe the wind direction worked in my favor on both occasions. It also was during the rut, and they were harvested on spots I seldom hunt. Not much human scent was there in the first place. So, there you go.

What do I really believe is the best approach? Well, it all depends on what *you* want to do. Have fun. That's the main thing. But I think what's fun varies from person to person. At this point in my life as a hunter, **I am more like the first man**. I do a good bit of scent control except I am still too cheap to buy the no-scent clothing. And I know someone is already reading this and thinking, "That's a mistake."

I do try to consider approaches to the stands whenever possible, watch for wind directions, and strive not to overhunt a particular stand. But I know you can be wound too tight and take much of the fun out of deer hunting. If you have the highest of goals every time out, you are bound to be disappointed. I mostly believe you should take a few important measures and then "do the time." Be willing to sit longer, enjoy the time in God's creation and let whatever happens, happen.

There are so many variables in deer hunting. No matter how many scent control measures you take, I believe you still smell a little when you get to the stand. You just do. To a mature whitetail, the human smell is as offensive as a skunk is to us. **Bottom line: you stink!** And God put the fear of man in the beast every time he smells you. They run for a reason. They may second guess their eyes or ears. But they never second guess their noses. If they smell you, they run first and think later.

> *"The fear of you and the dread of you*
> *shall be on every beast of the earth..."*
> Genesis 9:2

Sometimes your goals will vary based on your weapon. If I am bowhunting, I am happy even to take a doe. If I am using a primitive weapon like a flintlock, a 125-yard harvest on anything might be very special. Plus, I love to eat!

Goals may also vary on where you are hunting. Alabama has intense hunting pressure, and our whitetails walk around looking up in trees! What might not be a trophy somewhere else is a trophy here. You may hunt small farms which are hunted on the perimeter by other hunters. You can't control and manage as many things, so don't get uptight about it.

Do you see what I mean? There's no way to tell every person how to hunt, and deer hunters often disagree. There are simply too many things factoring in.

A PREMISE HARD TO ARGUE AGAINST

I cannot argue with one basic premise. *A mature whitetail buck is hands-down the smartest big-game animal on earth. He is so experienced he basically does not mess up. The margin for error is very small. Play careless and without attention to detail and most likely you will not see him, much less kill him.*

God might be very forgiving, but mature whitetails are very unforgiving of your mistakes. The only times when you might get a little forgiveness is when the wind happens to be right, or during the heat of the rut. Truth is, the big one in your territory probably knows you are there and he may even know from the moment you get out of the truck. You thought you were hunting him but he's also hunting you. Sometimes deer choose to stay near your truck or lodge because you will be *going away* from there. Really! They aren't dumb.

On the day you were careless you probably thought, *"Wow! I didn't see a thing! The deer just weren't moving today."* The truth is, they probably smelled you a long way off and dared not come near where you were. The whitetail lives and dies by his nose. You have to respect it. Man #1 is probably going to kill more trophies. I believe that. But if being man #1 makes you tense and destroys the joy of hunting, why not relax a little like man #2. Just do what you want to do. That's the way it is in the *woods*. But let me be abundantly clear, it is <u>not</u> that way in the *word of God*!

PURSUING CHRIST: YOU <u>CAN'T</u> JUST DO ANYTHING

I believe there is only ONE approach to Christianity that is Biblical and leads to great joy and happiness. In a nutshell:

> *Your heart must be moved and captivated*
> *by a Lord who died on a cruel cross for you.*
> *Your aim is now to be as much*
> *like Him as you can possibly be.*

It's shooting for PERFECTION.

Every piece I have written in this book has made some exact parallels from deer hunting to our walk with the Lord. **But it is here that parallels stop!!** You can do whatever you want, within the law, while deer hunting. But in your relationship with Jesus, you cannot!

Just as a deer will not tolerate your smell, God absolutely, positively, will not tolerate sin. It stinks in His nostrils. Download this into your hard drive and never erase it: God is a holy God who cannot live eternally with sinners. We have to be cleansed. Heaven is the purest place because it is the home of this holy God. Sin will not enter that place, period (Revelation 21:27). Why do we seem to think it will? Why does most every person get preached into heaven regardless of their lifestyle choices?

Most of us are aware of work places that have sterile rooms in which to work. Whatever they are working on must not be contaminated. People who work in those rooms have to take baths first and then put on special sterilized suits. *Even these measures cannot touch the sterile holiness of heaven.* And I've even heard of places that demanded that such workers not eat French fries and the like because they make their fingers oily. If a person got fired for eating French fries, we would understand and even agree. But when it comes to sin, we cut ourselves all kinds of slack and treat it as if it doesn't matter. How crazy is that? We must be holy as He is holy (1 Peter 1:13-16).

God wants us to be like His original Son, Jesus. Jesus committed no sin. This is the standard that God sets before us, and He will never lower it (1 John 2:1-2; 1 Peter 2:21-22). There is a dividing line between those who live life however they want as compared to those who truly want to be like Christ. Ephesians 4 speaks of how some people live, but then says of Christians, "***You did not come to know Christ this way***" (Ephesians 4:17-24 - NIV).

RELAXED INTENSITY

Putting on the new man. Putting on Christ. This is what true Christians strive to do every day, and they love doing it. It gives them great joy. The commandments (the do's and the don'ts) are not just do's and don'ts. They are the means of becoming like the One they love. They **do** as He would do. And they **don't do** what He wouldn't do.

It's commandment-keeping that has a thrilling purpose: being like Jesus. The commandments are not a burden to us any more than practicing at the archery range (1 John 5:3). Just as we love practicing in the off-season, Christians love practicing righteousness in every season of life. **Practice makes perfect** and makes us a home where Jesus wants to live (John 14:15,21,23-24).

And get this: God knew we wouldn't smell good at times. If we do sin in a moment of weakness, we humbly bring it to God, and He cleanses us. *What are we then? Clean. Pure. Holy.* **Perfect.** And little by little there is a magnificent change taking place. We are gradually transforming into His likeness (2 Corinthians 3:18). Christ is living in us and through us. These are the people who go to heaven (Colossians 1:27). And they are *"happy on the way."*

God will use even our mistakes to grow us. I'm convinced whitetails learn from their mistakes. They say to themselves, "I will not do that again!" Will we be as smart? We don't excuse our mistakes, but we learn from them and build upon them to become more like Him. I call it RELAXED INTENSITY. We are *intensely serious* about performing well, but we are *relaxed enough* to play well. It's much like a good football coach who calls for perfection from his players on every play. If they fail on any given play, they simply *play the next play with the same intensity.* But he doesn't want His team so uptight they don't play well at all and fail to enjoy the game!

Likewise, some Christians get way too uptight. I used to be one of them. They lose sight of God's desire to work with them and help them grow. It seems they have a *"works mentality"* to being saved. They see salvation hinging totally on whether they do everything perfectly and never mess up. They live a tense life and are never quiet able to enjoy the journey of being a Christian. They inwardly even wonder if they will make it to heaven. It's just not a lot of fun to them because the journey has been reduced to merely a bunch of rules and regulations. They have *a ledger concept.* They have good deeds in one column on the page and bad deeds in another column on the page. They hope the good deeds tally up to be more than the bad. But they will never give up, because they are hoping to do well enough that God will give them a home in heaven. A loving, active, trusting relationship with the Christ who died for them is missing (Galatians 5:6).

Friends, Jesus came that we might **have life <u>now</u> and have it more abundantly** (John 10:10; 1 Timothy 4:8). He wants us to **enjoy this eternal life even now** (1 John 5:13). I so enjoy the pursuit of Jesus. It is my *greatest adventure*. It's fun. It really is. Studying the Bible is enjoyable. Worshipping with brothers and sisters is enjoyable. Serving others and seeing their smile is enjoyable. Seeing God in the wild is exhilarating! *Christians have more fun…especially later!*

CRIMSON "WHITE-OUT"

Now, in those moments when we are overtaken by sin, we hate it because we *"missed the mark"* (an archery term and the Bible definition of sin). We want to be straight shooters, and we resolve not to commit that sin again. Grace energizes us to get up and go at it again. Grace gives incentive. Without it, why try again?

Let's use this illustration. Jesus' blood works like liquid paper or as some call it "whiteout." In the days of typewriters, bosses provided the "whiteout" to their secretaries. They weren't giving them permission to type carelessly but rather providing a solution when a mistake was made. The secretary could apply the "whiteout" and then retype. At last, she has a perfect paper! Likewise, this holy God never gives us permission to sin but provides a "whiteout" to cover our sins – ironically it is the crimson blood of Christ. How blessed we are (Romans 4:7-8)!

The Bible basically calls it "whiteout." Isaiah 1:18 says, *"Though your sins be as scarlet, they shall be white as snow."* His blood covers all my mistakes, and at the end **I can have a perfect paper, not because I have been perfect, but His blood makes me perfect.** God knew there would be some mistakes along the way. He doesn't give a license to sin (Romans 6:1-2) but He knows we can grow even when we have regrettably made mistakes.

Simply put, God is looking for **progress,** and that is what we seek day by day He wants to see us abounding— **increasing in His characteristics** (2 Peter 1:5-11). We will not be *sinless,* but God ever wants us to *sin less.* And let me add, *less and less and less.* It is not progress when our sin does not grieve us. It is not progress when we do not repent. It is not progress when we do not carry it to the cross. It is not progress when we keep doing it. I love this quote: *"You can never make the same mistake twice. Because the second time you make it, it's not a mistake, it's a choice."*

Just as I can become a better deer hunter by staying in the game and putting in the time needed, I can also become a better Christian by doing the same. Accomplished Christians have no secret. They just do the same thing every day, week after week, month after month, and year after year. It's called discipline. And it's that simple.

If this is not your approach to the Christian life, you will never be truly happy. It's all about Him and our desire to be a little replica of Him. Hunt the way you want to, but do Christianity HIS WAY! Anything else stinks to Him.

THE ARROW STRIKES As I think about this devotional, am I Hunter #1, Hunter #2, or somewhere in between? Do I strive for perfection in the woods and in my relationship with God? Are most Christians I know serious and uptight, or are they serious yet joyful? Does it thrill me to know that I can be a perfect paper when this life is over because all my sins have been blotted out in the blood of Jesus?

Night Light

I love the way Genesis, chapter one, describes the creation of the world. I especially enjoy reading of the two lights God created on day four. The Bible says:

> *"Then God made two great lights:*
> *the greater light to rule the day,*
> *and the lesser light to rule the night.*
> *He made the stars also."*
> Genesis 1:16

The woods provide many opportunities to experience the presence of God, but to me none bring greater peace and tranquility than moonlit paths. I remember one particular morning I had a long way to walk in fairly unfamiliar territory. I couldn't have been more delighted to see that God had provided me a "nite lite" to help me navigate along. I could see perfectly without a flashlight. My body shadowed on the ground beside me as I walked. The "lesser light" was ruling the night well. It was soft, yet powerful. It may have been that every deer around could see me walking but I didn't much care. I was enjoying the Lord more. What serenity! My heart was stirred by God's gentle light.

When it comes to having a godly influence on others, God needs soft lights. Some people are abrasive in the way they approach others about the Lord. They shine their lights in people's faces so bluntly that they turn away. Have you ever covered your eyes when someone suddenly turned the light on when you weren't ready for it? If so, you have the idea. Isn't there a big difference in "shining your light" rather than "letting your light shine"? God said the latter.

> *"Let your light so shine before men,*
> *that they may see your good works,*
> *and glorify your Father in heaven."*
> Matthew 5:16

Even Jesus was not a noisy character (Matthew 12:19-21). Jesus moved slowly among the people, paying attention to people's hurts and needs. Most of the good He did was done as He passed by (John 9:1). The person who gently shines from within doesn't need a spotlight.

Please realize that you can have a great impact on others simply by letting your light shine. Don't underestimate the power of simply living the life. It happens when you work hard each day on the job, when you patiently deal with an overbearing boss, when you do a kind deed to help another, when you show faith in the midst of a great trial, etc. It is seen by others in the way you treat your spouse and your children. I have known of many instances where someone expressed an interest in Jesus and eventually became a Christian because a friend simply let their light shine. I once heard of a man who formerly had mocked his Christian coworker, but when his wife threatened divorce, he ran to his friend begging him to pray for his family. His very words were, *"I didn't know anyone else to come to but you."* How about that?

Have you ever heard the hymn, *"Let The Lower Lights Be Burning?"* I was a grown man before I ever understood the song. It's a song about a seaman desperately trying to make his way to shore. He can see the greater light of the lighthouse but he also needs the lesser lights along the shore lest he dash against the shoreline and suffer ruin. We are those lesser lights. Listen...

> *"Brightly beams our Father's mercy*
> *from His lighthouse evermore,*
> *But to us He gives the keeping*
> *of the lights along the shore.*
> *Let the lower lights be burning!*

Send a gleam across the wave!
Some poor fainting, struggling seaman,
you may rescue, you may save. "
(Philip P. Bliss)

Someone may be out there in the dark waves struggling and looking for light. Will you be that light? The Master will never fail to be the Great Lighthouse He is, but let's keep the lower lights burning.

THE ARROW STRIKES Is my light shining so that others can see God in me? Have I ever shone my light rather than simply letting my light shine? Am I seeing that I can have a great influence on people as I quietly do things like working hard on the job, being a good family man, helping others, and showing faith in times of adversity?

Wrapped in Bacon

Eating venison is a bit of an adjustment for some families… especially *my* family. My wife is the kind who doesn't like her fish to be fishy (How can a fish not be fishy?). She cuts her hot dog wiener in half because it's too "meaty." And I remember her saying of some pork once, "It tasted like a boar hog!" See the difficulty of this?

Since I believe in someone eating what is taken in the woods, somehow we have got to find a way to get this food down.

> *"The slothful man does not roast what he took in hunting.*
> *But diligence is man's precious possession."*
> Proverbs 12:27

Since venison can have a wild game taste, you have to either acquire a taste for it or discover the secret to preparing it. I want it to be all savory like Esau's wild game was to Isaac. He loved sending Esau to the field. He even requested it for the special day he would bless Esau.

> *"Now please take your weapons, your quiver and your bow,*
> *and go out to the field and hunt game for me.*
> *And make me savory food such as I love,*
> *and bring it to me that I may eat,*
> *that my soul may bless you before I die."*
> Genesis 27:4

For my family, the best way to consume most of it is by making jerky. We love it! Curing salt and special seasonings probably have a lot to do with it. When my buddy Eddie shares deer jerky with people, he jokingly says, *"Now listen. Deer jerky is the one thing in life where it is okay to be totally selfish. If you don't want to give it to anyone, you don't have to. It's okay. You can just eat the whole bag all by yourself!"* We also like to "butterfly" the backstrap, pound it out like cube steak, and batter fry it. Mmmm good! We all like it.

Then I found a recipe for grilled back strap I thought was "out of this world!" I am sharing it with you at the end of this devotional. It has a special marinade but is also wrapped in bacon. I mean, how can something not taste great when wrapped in bacon? Give it a try.

Well, of course, all of this great food wrapped in bacon got me to thinking about some spiritual things. Jesus often used food and water to speak of Himself. He is the *"bread of life"* and *"living water"* (John 6:35; 4:13-14).

Jesus teaches us that when we are trying to teach others, we often need to wrap our words in bacon. Actually, His ambassador, Paul, called it "salt," but the idea is the same. We try to be tactful with our words so that they are received more easily.

"Let your speech always be with grace,
seasoned with salt, that you may know
how you ought to answer each one."
Colossians 4:6

There have been so many times when I have wished certain Christians lived by that verse. They don't have any tact. They don't even know how to wrap their words in bacon. Forget the salt, they just give it to you harsh and straight...always! Open your mouth; you are gonna take the medicine whether you like it or not! They drive people away rather than drawing them closer by the graciousness of their words.

Jesus used a lot of "bacon" in John 4. He talked to a woman at a well who was in false religion and had five husbands. It's a good thing she didn't run into some people I have known along the way. Jesus tenderly addressed both issues and had the woman intrigued by His love and care. He knew He needed to season His words with salt.

But hold on a minute. Let's balance this picture because Jesus also gave it straight and strong to some people. He tried for a long time to tenderly reach the Pharisees but at the last He blasted away at their hearts with words of dynamite. Some people simply should know better. They have been privileged with access to God's word for years and they can be approached more strongly. We just need wisdom to use the right approach with each person. Jesus knew all men. His approach was always right. But we may have to study people to know how to answer.

> *"On some have compassion, making a distinction;*
> *but others save with fear,*
> *pulling them out of the fire,*
> *hating even the garment defiled by the flesh."*
> (Jude 22-23).

Jesus said to the hard-hearted Pharisees, *"Woe to you, scribes and Pharisees, hypocrites! For you travel land and sea to win one proselyte and when he is won, **you make him twice as much a son of hell as yourselves**"* (Matthew 23:15). Whew! I don't smell any bacon on those words. They had to eat it wild! But there is just as much love in these words of Jesus as all the rest. He loved these people and this was a last ditch effort to break into their rock hard hearts. This is the same Jesus who cried over Jerusalem (Matthew 23:37; Luke 19:41). Don't ever make the mistake of thinking Jesus was soft.

I feel that I have probably made mistakes both ways. I have used bacon when I should have served it straight. And I have served it straight when I needed to wrap it, hold it securely with a toothpick, and let the person savor the goodness of the words. I'm not Jesus. I just need to study my prospects better and do a better job teaching. I need to pray about it, seek God's wisdom, and try to get it right.

Can I share two examples from my life? I remember talking to one young woman about the way of the Lord, and it was very emotional for her. Her parents were in false religion, and it was very hard for her to accept what she was clearly reading in her Bible. When I talked with her, I had to make sure she understood the truth but also had to wrap my words in bacon. She was eventually converted to Christ. When I later moved from that city, she sent me a goodbye card. I'll never forget her final words. She said, *"Thank you for being **bold** enough, yet **tender** enough to lead me to the truth."* I smiled because it told me that "wrapping in bacon" was what she needed.

On the flip side, I once had another friend to call me one night filled with frustration. He was tired of living the Christian life. Perhaps because we were close friends, he spoke plainly, telling me of his plans to move away, pursue a woman he had no right to, and "party away." I said to him, *"You better have all the fun you can because you are not going to have any fun when this life is over."* No bacon in those words!! And that's not judging either; it's just stating what the Lord said about adultery and works of the flesh (Galatians 5:19-21). That same man called me several months down the road all broken and in tears. He had lost all and wanted to come home to his family, his friends and most of all the Lord. Sound familiar (Luke 15:11-32)? We are still the best of friends, and every once in a while he will furrow his brows, look at me, laugh and say, *"You better have all the fun you can!"* He never forgot the words. He knew they came from a friend who loved him. He knew that friend would always be there.

So, the next time you grill, wrap it in bacon. You'll be glad you did. You'll probably want seconds or thirds. I did! But also take the time to meditate on the power of your words. Is there someone you need to gently lead to the Lord? Is there someone who needs some gentle rebuke? Don't forget the bacon. Is there someone to whom you need to give it straight? Remove the toothpicks, unwrap the salty slab and speak. You are not really a friend if you don't (Proverbs 27:6; Psalm 141:5).

> *Lord God, thank you for teaching me that life*
> *and death is in the power of the tongue.*
> *Help me to carefully consider my words*
> *when speaking to people I love.*
> *Help me to know when to apply salt*
> *and when to give it straight.*
> *I need your wisdom.*
> *Above all, help me to be motivated by Your love*
> *in all I say. Help me dare to care.*
> *Make me like your Son in whose name I pray. Amen.*

Spicy Bacon Backstraps

- Venison Backstrap chops
- 1 package bacon
- 2 cups Italian dressing
- ½ cup Frank's Red Hot
- ¼ cup soy sauce
- 1 Tbsp garlic powder
- 1 Tbsp meat tenderizer (optional)
- 1 tsp black pepper
- 1 tsp Creole seasoning

Marinate the chops in Italian dressing, Red Hot, soy sauce, garlic powder, meat tenderizer, black pepper, and Creole seasoning. Wrap each chop in bacon and secure with a toothpick to hold together during cooking. Grill on foil until done so that the bacon fries while cooking. You may need to spoon off some of the juices while cooking. Enjoy!

THE ARROW STRIKES Have I ever corrected or rebuked or tried to teach someone in a manner I now believe was the wrong way to go about it? Do I see the need with some people to salt my words? Is there anyone I need to talk to today? Should I give it to them straight or season my words? Have I received it well when others, with genuine concern, had to correct me?

Revival—Do You Need One?

It was a cold, rainy morning, so I decided to go deer hunting. I chose a place we call "Shack Attack" to get out of the rain a little. "Shack Attack" is an old feed crib obviously used years ago on someone's homeplace. It's a bit dilapidated with several holes at the bottom of its remaining walls, but a little burlap added to it makes it a great shooting house the deer are very used to seeing.

On this particular morning my mind was distracted as I sat there in the dark waiting for a little daylight. I looked at the old, gravity-fed feeder and imagined some days gone by. I pictured an old man in overalls coming in, lifting the lid off a barrel, adding more feed, and maybe bellowing out over the hills... *"here, here, here!"* In fact, I had used the barrel lid to cover a big hole in the corner.

Well, I was paying little attention to hunting when suddenly something stormed the shack from outside. It ran through the hole, banged the barrel lid and RAN ACROSS MY FEET!! Let me tell you, I had my own version of Ray Stevens' "Mississippi Squirrel Revival," except this was an Alabama boy's rendition! I jumped up from my seat and wanted to shout, *"Something's got a hold on me!!"* It was *"a fight for survival, that broke out in revival."* I never did see exactly what it was, but the fact that *"something was among us was plain to see."* Needless to say, I paid much better attention after that. It was a revival for sure!

NO ONE SITS STILL

When it comes to our lives before God, nothing is more important than revival and we surely need a good reviving from time to time.

A mature Christian understands that when it comes to spiritual growth we are never at the same level, never standing on the same rung. It's interesting to note that the book of Hebrews speaks of **going forward** and of **drawing back,** but the one thing it never speaks of is sitting still. We just do not do it. Honestly, can't we all say we have had both highs and lows spiritually?

God's desire is for each of us to keep a constant watch over our spiritual zeal and keep our fervor meter topping out. But the sad truth is that too many times we don't. We don't ask God to help us be "on fire" for Him. Our hearts grow a little cold to the cross. Our enthusiasm wanes in the greatest cause of all. Our drive to lay hold of heaven becomes lethargic.

We must take time to talk to our souls. Deeply spiritual people always have (Psalm 42:5,6,11). We must keep the cross fresh in our minds. We must stay in the word daily to feed our passion. We must stay alert to the devil's desire to work us toward the downhill slope.

SOUL SHAKERS

When our spiritual lives become dilapidated, God is not beyond allowing things to come our way that are intended to revive us. Amos 4:6-12 is a classic example. Israel had long been unfaithful to God, so God brought famine, blight and mildew, plagues, death in battle, and so on. None of it worked. After every effort God says, *"Yet you have not returned to Me."* We never know what these soul-shaking things might be. I have witnessed several along the journey and it is sad that it took some of these things to bring people to obedience or revival.

It might be an untimely death. Consider Acts 5 where Ananias and Sapphira lie to God and are struck dead. You would think such a thing happening in the church would stifle its growth...but no! It brought great fear to all who heard of it (vs. 11), and believers were increasingly added to the Lord (vs. 14).

I once heard of a young man who continued to put off his obedience to the gospel. He knew God's plan of salvation but would not surrender in spite of his wife's prayers for him and continual encouragement. Tragically, a day came when his wife was killed in a terrible car accident. It moved him to obey the gospel. He literally trembled entering the baptistry and it surely was not because the water was cold (Acts 24:25).

Would it take someone close to you dying to awaken your need for God?

It might be a close call for you personally. Acts 16:25-34 recounts the conversion of the Philippian jailer. Seeing the prison bars open after an earthquake, he was about to kill himself. Had Paul not cried out, "Do yourself no harm," he likely would have died at his own hands. What a close call! But praise God, the circumstances rattled the bars around his heart and he became a Christian, obeying the gospel after midnight.

Those close calls can come at any time. Once when I was returning home late at night from a gospel meeting, I was heavily engrossed in listening to a sermon. It didn't register with me that because of construction work my four-lane road had become a two-lane. I topped a hill, saw nothing but headlights in front of me, and almost "met my Maker." It can happen suddenly and without warning (James 4:13-17).

It might be sin bringing you "to the end of your rope." That's what brought the prodigal home (Luke 15:11-24). A pig pen and memories of his father's house did the trick. Too many times, I have seen even Christians take a path that leads nowhere. I've even prayed for them to hit bottom in hopes of revival. Is this what it will take for some?

It might be a sermon that "storms the will" much like Peter's did on the day of Pentecost when about three thousand repented and were baptized (Acts 2:22-41). Sometimes a sermon is preached, and there are multiple responses. At other times, the same sermon can be preached with no responses. You never know what words, at what moment, will finally break through.

It may be seeing a bad example in another Christian and then realizing you haven't been such a good example yourself. Are you leading your friends toward God? Or is your double life blaspheming God and hurting Him (Romans 2:21-24)?

It could be **experiencing God's grace after a fall** that ignites you like it did King David (Psalm 51:10-13).

What if you **envisioned the Lord's disappointing look** that Peter saw (Luke 22:54-62)? He was a blazing fire for the Lord after that (John 21:15-19). The point is, it sometimes takes such things to stir some of us.

ONE BURNING QUESTION

Does it have to take a tragic death, a close call, cancer, a 9/11, a hard road, or such like to revive us? Do we not have enough before our faces every day to stir us to a life of devotion to God? How about the following?

Without Jesus, I am lost (John 3:36; 8:21-24). If I'm not a Christian, I am lost. If I depart from the faith, I am lost. Hell has not gone away. Is there a need for God to put something else, some greater soul-shaker in front of us? Is there a greater one?

Jesus of Nazareth was crucified to save me. Does it take more than this sacrifice to break into our hearts? Do we understand what He did? He became poor that we might be rich (2 Corinthians 8:9). He died the death of "even the cross" (Philippians 2:9). Isn't it interesting that the word excruciating, which we use to describe intense pain, references the cross? "Ex" means "out of"; "cruci" relates to "crucifixion." Put it all together; it is pain like that which came out of the cross.

Back when the movie, "The Passion of the Christ" was popular, I decided to go see it in case it provoked some good conversation with a seeker. The scourging and crucifixion were so hard to watch. When we all walked out, there was no laughing, no chatter and no stops for popcorn. I just got in the car, drove away, and headed toward home. Those who saw the real thing had a similar reaction (Luke 23:48).

I drove to the church building, walked to the front pew and talked to God for a long while about what He had done for me.

Someone later asked me, "What did you think about the movie?" I said, *"I don't want to watch it again. Only if I needed a dynamite blast to my cold heart, would I ever watch it again."* To this day, I haven't. Is a crucified Lord, written about on the pages of your Bible, enough to revive your heart?

A resurrected Lord lifted my burden off my back. I get so upset at the lies of nonbelievers who want to suggest that Mary Magdalene was immoral and had a sexual relationship with Jesus. Some have asserted, without any evidence, that she was even married to Him.

Let me tell you...yes, she loved Him, but there was no physical relationship with Jesus. She loved Him for reasons mockers in their cold blasphemy will never understand! She loved Him because He took a mega-burden off her back (Mark 16:9). Has He taken your burden away? Go to the tomb and weep with Mary and then feel her revival when she knew He was alive (John 20:11-18). I love these words penned by Ken Young in the song, "Rabboni."

> *So I come once again bringing all I have to offer,*
> *Just to find a dark and empty tomb,*
> *Your holy frame somehow exhumed.*
> *Then I hear someone say,*
> *"Why are tears so freely falling?*
> *Can't you hear the voice that's calling?*
> *A voice that knows your name."*
>
> *Rabboni! My Teacher and my God!*
> *You're alive and my burdens melt away.*
> *Rabboni! Sweet Son of God Most High!*
> *I know death has lost its power*
> *And Your glory's here to stay.*

Is your sin, a crucified Lord, and resurrected Saviour enough to revive you and give you fuel to finish the race? Are you thankful for everything God has done and still does to revive your soul? Do you need a revival? Do I? If we do, I pray it happens today.

THE ARROW STRIKES Do I believe God can and does bring things into our lives to wake us up spiritually? Can I think of times in my life when God may have been trying to get my attention? Is it possible that God is reaching out to me even now? Is my sin and the death of Jesus enough to bring me to conversion or revival?

Stroke!!

There was no warning before it happened: nothing at all. It was a beautiful day in the middle Tennessee hills, and we were doing what deer hunters do in the spring to get a woods fix. We were trying to find us some "live action" with some thunder chickens! Turkeys!

If we had been horse hunting, I could have bagged a big one because most of my morning was spent watching a horse sniff my decoys. A mile or so away, by the way the crow flies, Eddie's outlook was more optimistic. At 8:45 he sent a text message that simply said, *"Got one gobbling."* After a few minutes, I wondered how things were going, and I sent a text asking for some MRI (Most Recent Information). There was nothing. No response. I wasn't alarmed. I thought, "The game is on for him. He's after one hot and heavy." I went back to watching my horse.

Then came the call I will never forget. It was Eddie. I prepared to hear an excited voice saying, "I got him!" Instead the voice on the other end was tired and winded. He said, *"Hey man, I've had a bad accident."* Terrible images flashed across my mind. I could see Eddie with a shotgun blast to his chest and was wondering if I would ever find him. Nervously I said, *"Aw man, Eddie! What happened? Where are you?"* He said, *"I fell back in the creek bed and broke my arm."*

True to the man I knew, he was already back in his Jeep, fighting through the pain and driving back to me. During this same time, our friend Chester's day could not have been better. I called him to tell him we had to get Eddie to the ER, and I found out he had turkey feet in his hands and a great bird draped over his back. I hurt for Eddie but I was relieved it was only a broken arm. Things could be so much worse. Little did I know, they were about to be.

One day later Eddie had a successful surgery on his wrist but they told us they fought his blood pressure. At home he sent me what I thought was a groggy text that said, "Im hzme" (I'm home). I laughed when I saw it and jokingly wrote back "Oa kae" (Okay). But soon, I would no longer be laughing. Somewhere between the time he went into surgery and the next morning, Eddie was blasted with what one doctor called "a fatal stroke"—the widow-maker kind. By the grace of God he survived it. His having built his body up through the years also helped. The neurologists later said, "Your physical strength probably saved your life." His strong body had absorbed the blast, but things still did not look good. Only time would tell.

I watched my friend being carried by ambulance to a larger hospital, and I felt so alone. Superman was hurt, and there was nothing I could do to help him. But I knew God could. I watched until I could no longer see the ambulance. After visiting him later that night, leaving him in intensive care was so hard for me. If you have a regular hunting partner you probably understand the incredible bond that builds between two men who share the predawn moments together. I realized that in my mind Eddie had become a hero to me. I admired him. I respected him. I looked up to him. Our ages were far enough apart to allow for that. When he graduated from high school, I would have been in kindergarten. Over several years, Eddie had fed a side of me I didn't even realize I had, and I was loving it. He pulled every ounce of manhood out of me: a wild side. I have a hard time explaining it, but my outdoor adventures with him and God always made me feel so alive! It was surely "life at full draw."

I needed Eddie. The outdoor world as I knew it with him had just been blown to pieces...like a lightning bolt exploding a giant oak. I realize that hunting is not the most important thing here, but still it was what we were. Every day, on the phone, Eddie and I conversed easily moving from the woods to the Word and back again. He was like a Jonathan to me (2 Samuel 1:26-27).

"YOU MUST NOT QUIT"

The Lord's day came and worship was so meaningful to me. I was preaching a series on *God's Providence in the Life of Joseph.* It seemed providential to me that I was preaching the series at "such a time as this" (Esther 4:14). I was looking for purpose in everything that was going on and resolving to trust God.

As I went to bed that night with the greatest wife any man could ever have, I was emotionally shot. I was holding so much inside. We lay in bed and talked about Eddie and then the dam broke. I began to cry. I cried for Eddie. Selfishly, I cried for *me*. I wondered if the Eddie I knew would ever pursue the whitetail with me again. My voice quivered as I said, "Honey, I don't think I can do it without him." I couldn't see myself even wanting to climb those hills without him.

I think Susan sensed that it was possible I would give it up. It was then that this woman who has lifted me so many times spoke gently and firmly. *"No matter what, you can't quit hunting. It has become a part of you. It's who you are."* Only a true hunter's wife could speak those words. Only she comes close to understanding. At that moment, I could not have loved her more. Her man had three addictions in his life: the Word, his wife & children, and the whitetail. The last addiction was created by a dealer named Eddie Simmons. Step by step, he had made *me...him.* I wiped my tears and prepared to get up the next morning and take my burdens and my prayer to the one place in the world that made sense. All my tears were dripping into God's bottle (Psalm 56:8). He had seen them, and collected them, and early the next morning I would feel His great love for me and my friend.

OPEN LETTER TO EDDIE

For this part of the story, I will let you read a portion of a letter I wrote to Eddie during his ordeal for him to read at a later time.

"On Sunday night, I told Susan I had to go to the Ponderosa in the morning. No other place on earth would do. I had to go to the perfect place to pray. In a strange way, I wanted to feel connected with you again...and if I was there...I knew I would.

I got up at 5:00 a.m. as if it were a deer hunting morning. A cool 46-degree morning graced me. As the morning went on, I would see God script the morning as if He knew everything I needed to receive a measure of comfort. I drank coffee, stepped outside on the porch, and caught myself listening for the roar of Ole Red's tires coming down the road to get me. But there was nothing. I would leave *alone*. And upon arriving at the Ponderosa's gate, I would walk *alone*. I felt such a deep loneliness but I also felt purpose, determination, and resolve growing within me.

My aim was to get my head together, pray for you, and exit the Ponderosa a different man, a stronger man...a man ready to do whatever it took to help you as much as you have helped me, especially these last few years. I was determined that when I was done, nothing would be about **me** anymore. It would be only about helping **you** recover. I was committed deeply to it.

Where should I sit today? Normally, I would ask you. Today, I couldn't. I thought, *'Go where the food is.'* So, I climbed the hill to the two-seater. I ascended, sat down, and immediately saw 1 Corinthians 15:58 which you had welded into the iron bar in front of me... *'Be ye steadfast, immovable, always abounding in the work of the Lord, forasmuch as you know your labor is not in vain in the Lord.'* Perhaps this was the Lord's first means of comforting me. Again, a tree stand was bringing healing to my soul.

I didn't bow. Instead, I lifted my eyes to heaven. Before I was done, I would raise my arms to heaven. I wasn't thinking much about my posture, it was just pain and fervency spilling out. And then, in the midst of my pain and fifteen minutes into the prayer for you, it was as if a message came to me. An owl broke through the dawn's silence - *'woo, woo, woo, woooooo.'* It was that same wild call you would always make at the end of an evening hunt that said, *"I'm done Jeff. I'm on the ground. I'm at the gate. Let's go."* At that moment, I felt like you were with me. Of course, I knew where you really were...which was why I had left home in the first place. Still, at the time, it seemed to say, *'Jeff, I know you are praying for me. Don't stop. Keep sendin' it up bro.'* It was another grace given to me by God. What else could He do to create a morning to clean out my soul?

I finished my prayer, lowered my head to the food plot, and there she was. A doe! She was just emerging from the thicket to the left. A big smile spread across my face. I thought, 'Lord, what more will You do today? How could You love me more? Only You knew exactly what I needed. It wasn't merely the whitetail I needed to see;

today the whitetail connected me soul to soul with my brother.'
Eddie, God didn't grace me with one deer. He granted me nine;
three of which waddled along because they had babies soon to be
born. I had never seen a pregnant one in the wild because I'm never
there out of season. I had them all around me for more than an hour!
I had to sneak down to escape without busting them. But before I
did, I got the whole show from a doe: stomping, head-bobbing, and
snorting. This was rare. That hill hardly ever sees that much
activity. It was medicine, I tell you! Medicine! I walked out of the
woods that day all cleaned out and was ready to enter into
'Recovery' with you."

I took a picture of those deer with me when I went to see
Eddie in NICU later that day. He was emotional when we arrived.
When I told him about the morning and showed him the picture, he
said with a drawl, *"I wish I had been with youuuuu. Ohhhh, I wish I
had been with youuuuu."* Me too, my friend, me too. My parting
words to him were, *"God is not yet through with you."*

AFTER EFFECTS

We are still waiting to see all the effects of Eddie's stroke
and the degree to which God will bring him back. It is a developing
story, day by day. Let me share a few words to describe some of the
spiritual "after affects."

- *Humility.* A good while before Eddie's stroke I had written a
  line or two for this book that said, *"Each of us still has good
  vigor as Eddie comes to retirement. God willing, we will
  now spend even more time stalking "Sid" (Eddie's name for
  the monster buck)."* Well, at least I said, "God willing."

"Come now, you who say,
'Today or tomorrow we will go into such and such city,
spend a year there, buy and sell and make a profit';
Whereas you do not know what will happen tomorrow.
For what is your life? It is even as a vapor
that appears for a little time and then vanishes away.
Instead you ought to say, 'If the Lord wills,
we shall live and do this or that.' "
James 4:13-17

- *Wait Training*. Eddie has always been a lively, loud and comical person. When he worked full-time, his coworkers always knew when he had entered the canteen at break. He's a mood setter. He lifts spirits. He loves to sing silly songs and create names for people and places. While he was thankful for those trying to help him, he hated the rehab hospital. It was too confining, and he missed home. He called the place, "*Heartbreak Hotel,*" and when he finally was released to go home, he sent me a text that read, *"Elvis has left the building."* While there, Eddie made Isaiah 40:31 his banner.

  But those who wait on the LORD shall renew their strength;
  they shall mount up with wings like eagles,
  they shall run and not be weary,
  they shall walk and not faint."

- *Appreciation.* Since his stroke Eddie's love button stays pressed. He is telling everyone what they mean to him. He couldn't say enough words of love and appreciation for his wonderful wife and children. He's been quick to tell friends he loves them. And he even asked a visitor to forgive him for something he had said to him years ago. When you have tapped on death's door, forgiveness is everything! If there is anything you need to say to someone today, say it. *"Set your house in order"* (2 Kings 20:1). You may one day wish you had.

- *Teaching.* Eddie has always cared for the souls of people but more so now. He looks for a way to talk about spiritual things with every person. He wants people to think about heaven, hell, the brevity of life, and God's plan of salvation. He wants everyone to hear, believe the gospel, repent of their sins, confess their faith in Christ as the Son of God, be baptized for the remission of sins, and remain faithful to the Lord until death (Acts 18:8). He knows what matters.

- *Anticipation.* In typical Eddie fashion he has his own unique expressions. He will call me and say, *"I see a cloud. It's a little one, but it will hold you and me bro."* On another day

he says, *"I see a BIG cloud. It will hold a whole lot of us."*
Here's a man looking into the heavens every day, antic-
ipating meeting Jesus and going home. I personally believe
this stroke was another phase in his life to keep him "packing
lightly," getting him ready for heaven. He sent me a message
recently that simply said, "Sometimes God has to knock you
flat on your back before you are looking up to Him."

"Then we who are alive and remain,
shall be caught up together with them in the clouds
to meet the Lord in the air.
And thus shall we always be with the Lord."
(1 Thessalonians 4:17)

- ***Peace.*** Of course Eddie struggles with what has happened.
  Acceptance is difficult. Nights are hard for stroke victims.
  In a low moment (or should I say high moment) he has even
  said, *"I wish He would come get me now. I want to go see
  Mama."* Eddie's mother was a godly woman who never
  spared any words on helping him stay with the straight and
  narrow (Matthew 7:13-14). He has a picture of her that he
  keeps behind the visor of his Jeep.

  Eddie has peace in God. Recently I took him to the property
  where life changed for him. I guess you might call it
  "returning to the scene of the accident." He said he wanted
  to make peace with the place. I left him beside a fence post
  where he prayed and came to terms with his fall. When I
  later asked him about it, he said...

  "Sometimes we collect bad memories that plague us.
  I had a bad memory of getting hurt on a particular
  day in May. I did something I shouldn't have done.
  I knew better. I knew it was dangerous.
  I climbed up on a high, moss-covered rock
  and paid the price for it.
  Today, I had to picture what happened,
  pray, and ask God to help my memory change
  to a better memory. I thought about Jesus
  in the garden of Gethsemane.

I guess I was asking God in a much smaller way to 'let this cup pass from me.' I gave my rock to the Rock."

- ***Vision and Purpose.*** At the present, Eddie's greatest side effects are his vision, judgment, and distraction. His having a stroke in the right hemisphere of his brain has left him totally dark on his left side. Stand beside him on the left, and he will never see you. However, he is 20/20 with both eyes straight ahead. His greatest concern is whether he will ever drive again. There's a chance with time. He wants it so badly. I understand. But for now, the keys are not in his possession. Love sometimes does hard things.

It occurred to me recently that his physical eyesight is a type of where he is spiritually right now. **He's not focused to the left or to the right, but he's 20/20 straight ahead.** Isn't that what God wants for us spiritually? Don't go to the left. Don't go to the right. Stay focused straight ahead (Proverbs 4:25-27; Deuteronomy 5:32-33).

All things work together for good to those who love God (Romans 8:28). Even bad things work for good. God has brought much of the old Eddie back. He may decide to leave a new Eddie, an Eddie that's somewhat different. I am thankful he's alive. I am thankful he still knows me. I am thankful he remembers all we have done together. I am thankful we still talk every day. I am thankful we may be able to sit together and hunt this winter. And I am thankful that more than ever he is still keeping me focused on things above.

I'm persuaded Eddie will use all he has left to glorify God. He will be used up in His service. He will not be rested up when Jesus comes. He wants to be tired. And Jesus will give Him rest (Hebrews 4:9; Revelation 14:13). May we all do the same. Eddie, thanks for walking with me even though part of the trail has been harder than I wanted it to be. I love you, bro!

I walked a mile with Pleasure.
She chatted all the way.
But left me none the wiser,
For all she had to say.

I walked a mile with Sorrow.
And ne'er a word said she;
But, oh! The things I learned from her,
When Sorrow walked with me.

–Robert Browning Hamilton

THE ARROW STRIKES Do I have a close friend to whom I need to express my appreciation? Do I understand the bond that can build between hunting buddies? Have I learned and benefitted more from the pleasurable times in my life or the sorrowful moments? Do I believe that all things work together for good in a Christian's journey? How have I grown from the bad moments in my life?

WINTER

In the world: It's late December, and Jack Frost is nipping at our noses. Brrrr. We might even get some snow! The neighborhood is quiet as we all head inside to hibernate around a fireplace, enjoying the coziness of home and family. The smell of soups and chili waft in the air. The holiday season is upon us, and the spirit of giving is in the air. There are parties with friends and sweets and treats. We await our hometown Christmas parade, hot chocolate, and pretty lights. Torn wrapping paper, great big smiles, and childhood laughter will soon fill our houses and our memories. Lord willing, fireworks will soon usher in a new year, new resolutions, and a new beginning. And before the season is over...champions will be crowned in High School Basketball, March Madness, the Super Bowl, and NBA playoffs. And don't forget Valentine's Day!

In the woods: Deer are feeling the hard effects of winter in their world, yet God has blessed them with a special winter coat. Hollow tube-like hairs are filled with warm air from inside their body. Love has been in the air, but the rut has taken its toll. No hibernation for these guys! The bucks have lost a lot of weight from the chase. They are hungry and need food badly to restore their energy. Food plots are now the greatest hope for seeing the big one! Sadly, the biggest one sometimes dies post-rut. It is possible for the dynamic chemical changes in his body plus the demands of the rut to overload and poison his system...shutting him down. Even great warriors must eventually return to the dust, while leaving a great genetic legacy to follow them. Those that survive are scarred a bit and will drop the symbol of their strength soon— their headgear. But as surely as a rack hits the ground, there's hope for renewal, a fresh start, and a new beginning.

In the Word: It's the winter of *your* life as a Christian, and it's often hard. It is the difficult days when you say, "I have no pleasure in them" (Ecclesiastes 12:1). No wonder Paul, in prison, told Timothy, "Do your utmost to come before winter; "bring the cloak" and "the books, especially the parchments" (2 Timothy 4:13,21). Even if we can't be where we want to be (such as in the woods), we are always at home in the Word.

The body may ache and look forward to renewal, but the inner man is stronger than ever (2 Corinthians 4:16). A few Bible verses can't be remembered, but the Lord is not forgotten. You rejoice that your once scarlet sins are still white as snow (Isaiah 1:18). The desire to be with Him is ever more intense as you long for the culmination of this love story. You groan for heaven (Romans 8:22-23). The way there involves death but to you it is a simple passageway, a letting go of the "surly bonds of earth to touch the face of God"— an astronaut phrase made popular by Ronald Reagan after the Space Shuttle Challenger disaster. As a dove from prison bars has flown, you will fly away to a home where joy shall never end. Victory (1 Corinthians 15:54)!

The hunt has been long, the pursuit joyful, and the reward is exhilarating. Chapter One of the Great Story will soon begin. As stated by C.S. Lewis in the Chronicles of Narnia, it is the story *"which no one on earth has read, which goes on forever and in which every chapter is better than the one before."* The One we have hunted has been found at last, and we see Him as He is (1 John 3:1). And there are no more goodbyes. Free at last, and it feels so good.

> *"I have fought the good fight,*
> *I have finished the race,*
> *I have kept the faith.*
> *Finally, there is laid up for me*
> *the crown of righteousness,*
> *which the Lord, the righteous Judge,*
> *will give to me on that Day,*
> *and not to me only*
> *but also to all who*
> *have loved His appearing."*
> 2 Timothy 4:7-8

What is That?

Here's something most all deer hunters know. The monster buck goes nocturnal when he knows hunting season has begun. For that reason, a lot of hunters get really worked up on those early morning hunts. They are hoping "big boy" will linger a little too long, and they can intercept him heading back to his hideout at daybreak.

Most every hunter has had the experience of seeing something that looks like a deer before there is ample light. It can really get you excited! I have gotten pumped up at such silhouettes in the shadowy gray light. Don't ever shoot until you are sure!

These blobs can sometimes look just like a whitetail and even appear to be moving. As more light envelopes the scene, you decide, *"No, that's just a small bush."* With even more illumination you can even tell exactly what kind of bush it is. At last you can even see the fine texture of the leaves. Things get clearer and clearer as more and more light shines.

NOT JUST BLOBS

This is exactly the way the Bible brings Jesus to us. Jesus does not appear all at once on earth's stage. The Old Testament first gives us shadowy images of Him. Simply put, the Old Testament prophets foretold His coming. His birth, His death, His resurrection—it's all back there to see if you will look closely and pay close attention. For now, just tuck it away in your mind that the foretelling of Jesus' coming is called *"the prophetic word."* Got it?

It is only the dawning of the New Testament and the day of Jesus' arrival that helps us to see very clearly the meaning of all those passages in the Old Testament. A light comes on for us. We get it. The prophecies about Him make perfect sense now. I believe this is what Peter meant when he wrote his second epistle. He had *read* the prophecies about Jesus, but then He actually *saw* Him when He came to earth. And to top that, Peter even saw a burst of Jesus' glory when His appearance brilliantly changed on the Mount of Transfiguration (Matthew 17:1-8; 2 Peter 1:16-18). Think about all I have said and look closely.

> *"So we have the **prophetic word made more sure**,*
> *to which **you do well to pay attention***
> *as to **a lamp shining in a dark place**,*
> *until the **day dawns and the morning star***
> ***arises in your hearts."***
> 2 Peter 1:19

Let's use a simple illustration. Suppose I told you I was coming to hunt with you the last week of November. If God lets the world stand, the date is sure. It's sure because I told you I was coming, you know me to be reliable, and it's on the calendar. You see it in prospect. But then the day arrives. I come. It was already sure. Now, it's *made more sure!*

And that's the way it is with Jesus. The prophets said He was coming. It was sure. But it was made *more sure* when He actually came. All those Old Testament Bible verses are now very clear. Light is shining on them. And our hearts leap with excitement as we say, "I see it."

FIRST FAITH, THEN SIGHT

Now, listen closely and get this important point. **God wants you to first see Jesus *by faith*, and then He will allow you to see Him *by sight*.** I don't know all the reasons He does it that way; I just know He wants us to see Him on the pages of scripture first. And Jesus was very disappointed when His disciples, who had their scriptures, were so slow to believe that He had risen from the dead. The prophets had said it. He had even said it. The resurrection was sure. It was soon to be more sure. They should have been ready for it.

After His resurrection, He appeared to a couple of sad travelers on the road to Emmaus (Luke 24:13-35). As they saw it, all their hopes were destroyed at the cross. Jesus was dead, or so they thought. But what's interesting is that **God restrained their physical sight**. They didn't know Him. I believe that is because God wanted them to believe the scriptures about Him first. **First, faith. Then sight.** God most often works that way. Are you following me? So what did Jesus do with these dejected, unbelieving travelers? Well, let's see.

"Then He said to them, 'O foolish ones, and
slow of heart to believe in all that the prophets have spoken!
Ought not the Christ to have suffered these things
and to enter into His glory?'
And beginning at Moses and all the Prophets,
He expounded to them in all the Scriptures
the things concerning Himself."
Luke 24:25-27

Wow! Would I have loved to have heard that sermon. Basically Jesus went back to the beginning of the Bible and worked His way through it quoting passages to them and in essence saying, *"Do you see this passage back here? That's Me. And here's another and another and another."*

And what did it do for them when by faith they could see Jesus in their Old Testament scriptures? I've got chill bumps again! Let's listen in on what they said about it.

"And they said to one another,
'Did not our heart burn within us
while He talked with us on the road,
and ***while He opened the Scriptures*** *to us?'"*
Luke 24:32

Their hearts burned! The scriptures did that to them And it was only after they had seen Him by faith that they saw Him by sight. Once they believed, God gave them more. *"Then their eyes were opened and they knew Him..."* (Luke 24:31).

My heart is burning too right now! That's what the Bible does to you when you get into it. And again, the only people who get to *see Jesus by sight* for all eternity are those who are first willing to really study and *see Him by faith*. If we will not believe the scriptures, it is doubtful anything else will do the job. We need to get serious about the scriptures. God is. This is a major point made in the story of the Rich Man and Lazarus.

> *"Then he said, 'I beg you therefore, father,*
> *that you would send him to my father's house,*
> *for I have five brothers, that he may testify to them,*
> *lest they also come to this place of torment.'*
> *Abraham said to him, 'They have Moses*
> *and the prophets; let them hear them.'*
> *And he said, 'No, father Abraham;*
> *but if one goes to them from the dead, they will repent.'*
> *But he said to him, **'If they do not hear Moses and the prophets,***
> ***neither will they be persuaded though one rise from the dead.'"***
> Luke 16:27-31

WILL WE STUDY HARDER?

So, what will we do? Will we take the time to see the Bible is God's word and it is true? Will we see Jesus on the pages of scripture and believe? That's what another traveler did in Acts, chapter 8. He was reading from Isaiah 53:7-8. He knew he was seeing *something,* but he wasn't real sure what it was. It was sort of *"bushy"* to him. He kept looking closely, and then Philip came and *"shed some light on the subject."* He was reading about a lamb being slaughtered. He asked the preacher if the prophet was speaking of himself or some other man. Good. He's asking questions.

This man is looking closely, trying to figure it out. I guess it was much like a deer hunter's shadowy blob before daybreak. Philip looked at the passage with him and *"preached Jesus to him"* (verse 35). The traveler *saw Him by faith that day* and was baptized into Him. On the eternal day, He will *get to see Him by sight*.

IF ONLY GOD WOULD...

Sometimes skeptics say, *"If your God really exists, why doesn't He just open up the heavens and show Himself?"*

Well, first of all that's a death wish because if God did that, we would die. That's what God Himself has said (Exodus 33:18-23). I imagine I may have you wanting to read that. I hope so. I take it that these earthly bodies cannot endure the magnificent glory of God. Only indestructible, eternal bodies can bask in it forever.

Secondly, God is serious about His word. He wants us to read it and trust Him. If we will first see Jesus on those pages, then we can see Him by sight. What a day, glorious day, that will be. The Bible says, *"And now abide faith, hope, love, these three; but the greatest of these is love"* (1 Corinthians 13:13).

Why is love the greatest? Perhaps it is because love is always the same even in eternity. But one day *faith* will become *sight*. And in eternity, we *no longer live in hope. Our dream of being with Him has at last come true* (Romans 8:24-25).

So, walk by faith, not by sight (2 Corinthians 5:7). Besides, it's the unseen things that are eternal. Everything else will be gone one day. The day is coming when every eye will see Him (Revelation 1:7). But only those who have believed in Him and obeyed His gospel will see Him forever. It would be the height of foolishness to give up Jesus because we have never seen Him. Faith goes where the eyes cannot see. That's the point of the entire book of Hebrews. People of faith keep pursuing unseen things (Hebrews 11). It's these people he actually praises.

> *"...Blessed are those who have not seen*
> *and yet have believed."*
> John 20:29

> *"...whom having not seen you love.*
> *Though now you do not see Him,*
> *yet believing, you rejoice with*
> *joy inexpressible and full of glory,*
> *receiving the end of your faith—*
> *the salvation of your souls."*
> 1 Peter 1:8-9

So, keep seeing Him on the pages of scriptures. It's a good kind of heartburn! And get ready to see Him by sight. I can hardly wait.

And I'm really wondering. Has the day dawned for you? Can you
see?

THE ARROW STRIKES Have I ever had an experience where I thought
I saw a deer, but then light helped me see exactly what it was? Do I
believe the testimony of the prophets and the eyewitnesses about
Jesus? Do I need more to believe? Should I expect more to be given
me by God? Does it thrill me to know that my faith will one day be
sight?

The Night Before

From my childhood, I remember some nights I just couldn't sleep. They were nights before something really big was happening the next day.

There was the night before my family would go to Six Flags over Georgia. What a place for a kid! Then there was the night before my birthday, the night before Christmas presents, and the night before the big ballgame. My mind just wouldn't turn off, thinking of what tomorrow might bring!

Well, I'm still a kid in so many ways. You've probably heard that the only difference between men and little boys are the size of their toys. My toy guns, holsters, and broomstick horses have been replaced with a 30-06 rifle, a truck, and a four-wheel drive 4-wheeler. And I still have "nights before."

I can hardly sleep when there is a hunting trip planned to new territory with the guys the next day. Excitement abounds as I think about the comradery, the great food, and the hopes of at least seeing a great buck.

When I shot my first trophy buck, he ran deep into his hideaway. I gave him considerable time, but by then it had become dark. I was afraid to track him for fear I might bump him deeper and deeper into a thick wilderness and never find him. I was also afraid to back out and look for him the next morning. Coyotes might find him first and ruin my chances of putting him on the wall. I also knew I wouldn't sleep a wink! I knew that in my mind I would track him all night long! Nothing makes your pillow harder than dreaming about a big buck. "Nights before" are just that way. Great characters in the Bible had them, and so will you.

"ABRAHAM, ABRAHAM"

When you read Genesis 22, you won't find it shocking that God called out Abraham's name since God once spoke to men in that way. But the next words are enough to stop a man's heart. Abraham answers, "Here I am." And the Lord says,

> *"Take now your son,*
> *your only son Isaac, whom you love,*
> *and go to the land of Moriah,*
> *and offer him there as a burnt offering*
> *on one of the mountains of which I shall tell you."*
> Genesis 22:2

That little white space in your Bible between verses 2 and 3 is the night before. The space may be short, but I doubt the night was. Verse 3 says, ***"So, Abraham rose early in the morning."*** I wonder if he slept. I know I couldn't have. My terrified thoughts would have bounced around my brain's inner walls like a racquetball. I probably would have been thinking, "This can't be. It makes no sense. You promised me this child! You promised a great nation! And You promised me the child would somehow bless all nations. WHY, oh why Lord?"

The Bible records nothing about his night before offering Isaac. It does say that somewhere along the way he was *"accounting that God was able to raise him up, even from the dead"* (Hebrews 11:19). That's giant-size faith but does it make it any easier? What if there is terror in the eyes of Isaac? And won't the knife still hurt? Will not his heart be stabbed as well?

Nevertheless, early the next morning he arose and went. On the way up a young son's voice speaks up and says, *"My Father!...Look, the fire and the wood, but where is the lamb for the burnt offering?"* Oh, break my heart! What those words must have done to Abraham's heart! I love his answer. *"My son, God will provide for Himself the lamb for the burnt offering."* And He did. God stopped Abraham just before the knife came down. Then God showed him a ram caught in a thicket by its horns. But I also believe this is a type, a shadow that matches what God would later do—offer His only Son as a sacrifice for our sins. Indeed, God will provide!

"THAT NIGHT PETER WAS SLEEPING"

Roll the tape forward now to the New Testament. Peter is in prison for preaching the word. In his recent memory is the death of James, his friend and comrade in the gospel. Herod ordered him killed with the sword and evidently had the same plans for Peter. And Peter does what?

> *"And then Herod was about to bring him out,*
> ***that night Peter was sleeping,***
> *bound between two soldiers,*
> *and the guards before the door*
> *were keeping the prison."*
> Acts 12:6

How did he manage to sleep, the night before? May I suggest he knew Who was in control of this storm. Also, he had been with Jesus and had seen Jesus sleep during a storm (Mark 4:35-41). He is not little in faith on this night. He knows that if he lives, his life will be spent serving *the Lord*. If he dies, he has eternity with *the Lord*. It's a "win-win" situation. Either way he has the Lord, so why not sleep? The apostles always knew to trust in God (Philippians 1:20-25).

What happened? Without disturbing the soldiers, an angel came the night before, woke Peter up, loosed his chains, and led him past two guard posts. Even the iron gate that led to the city opened up on its own. He was free! God is good! What a night!

"HIS SWEAT BECAME LIKE GREAT DROPS OF BLOOD"

Then there's the night before Jesus dies. He is so unlike me. I do not know when my last night will be. I don't know when it is the day before...but Jesus did. So He took with Him Peter, James and John, His inner circle of disciples, to one of His favorite places to be alone with God. He went to the Garden of Gethsemane.

As He enters, His burden is of unimaginable proportions. He says to them, *"My soul is exceedingly sorrowful even to death. Stay here and watch with Me"* (Matthew 26:38). Three times He will ask the Father, *"If it is possible, let this cup pass from Me"* (Matthew 26:39). The cup refers to the cross and all the horrible things associated with it. Scourging, a crown of thorns, nails, blood, and spit are all in the cup. Must He drink it? Yes. The Father did not remove the cup. These events show that it is **not possible** for us to be saved without the cross of our Lord! He would drink that cup so you and I might never thirst. Hell is a thirsty place (Luke 16:24). Heaven isn't (Revelation 7:16-17).

Jesus didn't sleep the night before. His three so-called night watchmen did. And we all know how a sleepless night affects the next day. Nevertheless, He prayed fervently. Luke records, *"His sweat became like great drops of blood falling to the ground."* He submitted to the Father's will and drank it...all of it...down to its bitter dregs.

Thank God, Jesus endured through it all! He prepared for His Friday and suffered it all. But He knew Sunday was coming. God would raise Him from the dead and reward Him with joys immeasurable in heaven. He lived with a vision to see beyond death. Heaven was waiting for His arrival, and He knew it (Hebrews 12:2; John 17:5).

WHAT ABOUT YOUR "NIGHT BEFORE"?

It's coming. It may be the night before Jesus comes. It may be the night before you pass from this world. Either way, there will be a night before. Was it last night? Could it be tonight?

Some time ago I read a Facebook post from some parents who lost their child in an automobile accident. Their words resonated with me. *"Last night when we went to bed, you were here. But when we woke up, you were gone."* She left the house the night before and tragically died in a car accident.

Let me ask you a few soul-searching questions. What if you knew you only had one more day to live? Would you do anything differently? Would you make some specific phone calls? Would you write a letter? Would you say anything special to those you love most? Would you forgive someone? Would you become a Christian if you are not one? Would you get your house in order?

Most likely you will not even be thinking about it, the night before. But God will. Some of my thoughts for this piece were prompted by a fellow hunter who wrote in his book, "God knows the death date for every person on earth both Christians and non-Christians alike. He knows *your* death date. He'll be thinking about it, your last night on earth. He'll know if you're walking in a relationship with Him or not, and He'll be aware that the next day holds something either incredible for you as you make the transition from earth to heaven, or that the day is literally going to be hell for you" (Jimmy Sites, *Into The High Country*, pg. 53).

Since there will be a night before, shouldn't you commit your life to God by obeying the gospel (Acts 2:36-41; 2 Thessalonians 1:8)? Shouldn't you live each moment as though it were your last? Shouldn't you stay alert, be ready, and look forward? I pray you will.

Twas the night before Jesus came and all through the house
Not a creature was praying, not one in the house.
Their Bibles were lain on the shelf without care
In hopes that Jesus would not come there.

The children were dressing to crawl into bed,
Not once ever kneeling or bowing a head.
And Mom in her rocker with baby on her lap
Was watching the Late Show while I took a nap.

When out of the sky there arose such a clatter,
I sprang to my feet to see what was the matter.
Away to the window I flew like a flash
Tore open the shutters and threw up the sash!

When what to my wondering eyes should appear
But angels proclaiming that Jesus was here.
With a light like the sun sending forth a bright ray
I knew in a moment this must be THE DAY!

The light of His face made me cover my head.
It was Jesus returning just like He said.
And though I possessed worldly wisdom and wealth,
I cried when I saw Him in spite of myself.

In the Book of Life which He held in his hand,
Was written the name of every saved man.
He spoke not a word as He searched for my name;
When He said, "It's not here," my head hung in shame.

The people whose names had been written with love,
He gathered to take to His Father above.
With those who were ready He rose without a sound
While all the rest of us were left standing around.

I fell to my knees, but it was too late;
I had waited too long and thus sealed my fate.
I stood and I cried as they rose out of sight;
Oh, if only I had been ready tonight.

In the words of this poem the meaning is clear;
The coming of Jesus is drawing near.
There's only one life and when comes the last call,
We'll find that the Bible was true after all!

(Unknown Author)

THE ARROW STRIKES Have I ever had a "night before" experience as a deer hunter? Have there been other exciting, maybe even anxious and fearful "nights before" in my life? Have I thought much about the ultimate "night before" that is coming for me? Could it be tonight? Is such pondering good for me? If so, how?

Read the Instructions

Perhaps you have seen the tree stand commercial on TV where a man is sitting in a tree stand...in his living room! Pretty good decorum, I think. The closing words are *"When hunters are not hunting, they are thinking about hunting."* That's so true. I know it's true of me.

In the off-season, I like to invest some of my time into the industry and give something back to hunting, since it has given so much to me. I teach Hunter Safety courses for the Alabama Department of Wildlife and Freshwater Fisheries. Recently, I took a special class to be certified as a Tree Stand Safety Instructor. I have special interest in that part of safety since more people are hurt by tree stand accidents than are ever hurt by the guns. In fact, when my son and I are going hunting, I often will ask, "What is the most important thing today?" He will answer, "Be safe." That's right. A hunting trip is no fun when someone doesn't make it home. Pencils have erasers to correct mistakes, but some mistakes in the woods can't be erased. Remember that. I had to pass a test to become certified. One of the questions was as follows: *"What is the most important thing a person can do to avoid a tree stand accident or fatality?"* My wife says, "Don't climb up there." I have to admit that sounds pretty safe. But that wasn't one of the choices. Think a moment about how you would answer.

Did you say, "Wear a safety harness"? Great answer. It's the answer I gave. But it's not the answer my instructor was looking for. The answer is "Read The Manufacturer's Instructions." I will not try to use "shock and awe" stories to make my point, but trust me, there are some sad stories to tell of tree stand fatalities. Death could have been prevented by the hunter's reading of the instructions which came with the tree stand. Those instructions make wearing a safety harness a must. Something as simple as a bolt left off or in the wrong place can spell disaster. Another error might be not attaching a five-foot rope from the top to the bottom of your climbing stand. Or you make the fatal mistake of not checking a stand that has been attached to a tree too long. The strap can rot or get chewed apart by a squirrel. You simply must read the instructions and follow them...ALWAYS! The consequences of not reading them may be disastrous.

A while back, in a place I had gone to preach, I met a brother in Christ who was in a back brace. He had broken his back falling out of a lock-on stand. He had not harnessed himself and was giving the stand one final strength check when something gave way, and it threw him to the ground. A year or so later when I saw him, he was all healed up, thanks to the Lord. I asked him, "Do you still hunt from tree stands?" He said, "No! The Lord said, **'Lo**, I am with you always.' So, I go **low**! I'm hunting from the ground."

If reading the instructions is important with our physical lives, it is even more crucial with our spiritual lives. It touches eternity. It doesn't take long in reading your Bible to see that we cannot play loose with or dismiss God's instruction manual. We have to read it and do precisely what it says, or it can be costly. God cares about the details. He designs patterns and demands those patterns be followed carefully (2 Timothy 1:13). When building the tabernacle, Moses was told, *"See to it that you make it according to the pattern which was shown you on the mountain"* (Exodus 25:40). And Moses had it done—*"as the Lord commanded, just so..."* (Exodus 39:43).

DON'T GET ZAPPED!!

One instance in the Bible that catches my attention is when King David wanted to move a special, holy piece of furniture called the "ark of the covenant" to Jerusalem. The ark was normally kept in the Most Holy Place in the tabernacle. More than any other furnishing at the tabernacle, this ark and its resting place were seen as the dwelling place of God (2 Kings 19:14-19). What a tremendously important item it was! God had given detailed instructions for moving this ark. He said it was to be carried with poles which passed through rings on its side. The ark itself was never to be touched.

When King David moved the ark to Jerusalem, it was conveniently and easily carried on an oxcart (Uh oh. Not a good idea). As they moved it, the oxen pulling the ark stumbled and Uzzah reached out to steady the ark, and when He did, God struck him and he died (1 Chronicles 13:10-11). The whole thing compares to a house being wired improperly. It's just a matter of time before somebody gets zapped!

At first, David was angry at God, but when he looked at things more closely, he realized it was not God who was in the wrong. He never is! David later said this tragic death occurred because *"we did not consult Him about the proper order"* (1 Chronicles 15:13). More simply put, David didn't read the instructions.

Even while writing this piece, I have learned of two accidents in my area. One involved a man injured in a tree stand accident. The other was more tragic. A young teenager was killed by another teen while preparing to go hunting. The first could have been avoided by reading the instructions and the second could have been avoided by obeying the first of the Firearm Ten Commandments – "Always keep the muzzle pointed in a safe direction."

Often in scripture, God will give His instructions and then say, *"You shall not turn to the right hand or to the left"* (Deuteronomy 5:32-33). Safety is in what **God has spoken**. Sometimes people say, "Well, God did not say you couldn't..." He doesn't have to. When God says what He wants, that's it. Left or right of that is wrong, sinful and costly! Don't create God in your own image. Let Him tell you how He thinks and operates.

Somewhere in the past, I read of a man who was flying his plane in the afternoon. He stayed up a little too long, and there were no lights on the small landing strip. He passed once and could barely see the runaway. So, he circled again. Another loop around, and it was even darker. He could not land, so he just kept circling. A nearby farmer, hearing the plane, realized there was a problem. He got in his truck, went down to the runway, and drove his truck back and forth on the straight runway with his lights beaming bright. In this way he was saying, "Land here. Land here. Not left. Not right. Land here." What a welcomed sight to the pilot! At last, the farmer parked at the beginning of the runway with his lights shining down the small strip. The pilot maneuvered into position and came down just over the top of the truck and safely on to the strip. That's what we must do as we fly through life. Stay on the strait and narrow.

God's word has the power to save us and give us such a bountiful life, but we must read the instruction manual and never change its words, explain it away, or do it our own way. Read the instructions. Do what they say. Do them exactly as they say. It's that simple and it's that important.

THE ARROW STRIKES Have I ever almost made a costly mistake because I did not read the instructions? Have I thought of God's word as a pattern that must be carefully followed? Am I striving to carefully follow His word? Have I ever thought, "Well, God didn't say I couldn't"? Must I always consult His word before I act?

Dig a Little Deeper

     I was so excited when I saw steady movement on the Tennessee hill in front of me. I knew it was a deer so I got ready. My trigger finger started twitching and was ready to fire. My smoke pole was about to get some action. But when the four-point buck cleared its cover, I realized it was a "no shoot" situation. My trigger finger was on fire, so I blew it out, put it back in my pocket, and reached for my video camera. I like shootin' even if it's just with a camera. What soon unfolded was the best video I have ever shot in the woods.

     This buck was on a mission. The wind was in my face so he came right to the fence in front of me. He stopped and sniffed the barbed wire. I got ready to watch him take to the sky and leap over. But he didn't. He crawled *under* the fence! It was amazing to watch. He did it with such ease, and he never checked up! I thought for a moment, "This deer is going to climb up the tree and sit in my lap!" He came within ten yards, and then looped around in front of me at a salt lick. He was so deliberate. I knew he had been here many times before.

     Rain and dew had dissolved the salt into the ground. This nice four-point started digging into the ground with his hooves. The good, healthy, and helpful stuff he wanted was underneath—buried beneath dirt. He worked real hard at it. His desire for it was obvious. I enjoyed watching him put some muscle into it.

SOME MORE WHITETAIL WONDER

As I sat there admiring his work ethic and handsomeness, he gave me another treat. After a moment or two he lifted his head and became alarmed. I saw concern in his eyes. Next, I detected a change in his breathing. I could see his chest moving in and out. He lifted his hoof, prepared to stomp, but then eased it back to the ground.

Then I saw something I had never seen before. The white on the underside of his tail began to expand. His tail was bristling like a frightened cat. It got bigger and bigger and bigger. I always thought the wind made their tails flare out like that when they bolt away. Not so. I could tell he was about to "flag." He lifted his tail, and there was a burst of white! It's a deer's way of warning other deer there is danger. They have senses that are trained to know when there's trouble in the woods. What in the world was going on? What had him so worked up? And then I saw it. Mr. Wile E. Coyote emerged from the thicket in front of him! He kept his eyes fixed on it, until it moved on. Then and only then did he drop his flag. We can learn a lot from a whitetail.

GO BENEATH THE DIRT

Digging deeper is needed to be truth seekers in our confusing religious world. Being unwilling to dig deep can cause us to miss the truth and only get dirt.

In Jesus' day, there were lots of people who never accepted Jesus' claims because they were shallow in their thinking. They would not dig deep, and it led to false conclusions. Their shallow thinking was as follows:

- Jesus is from Galilee. The scriptures say the Messiah would come from **Bethlehem** (John 7:41-42; Micah 5:2). See...He can't be the Christ!

  All they had to do was dig a little deeper. It would have been so easy to do. Just ask Him, "Where are you from?" It is true He grew up in Galilee, but He was born in Bethlehem. They just wouldn't dig.

- He's not from God. He doesn't keep the Sabbath. He encourages others to break the Sabbath (Matthew 12:1-14; John 5:1-16; John 9:16).

  Jesus never broke the Sabbath. He only broke their man-made laws about the Sabbath. A little deeper thinking would have made all the difference.

- He died on the cross. He can't be the Christ. The law says the Christ will live forever (John 12:34).

  Jesus does live forever. He rose from the dead on the first day of the week, and the evidence for it is abundant. But they would not dig any deeper. See the problem?

IT STILL HAPPENS: UNWILLING TO DIG

Unwillingness to dig deep was not just a problem when Jesus was on earth. It's still a problem in our very confusing religious world.

We need to know that the devil loves to try to hide truth beneath a lot of dirt, beneath false teaching. He knows the truth is in the Bible, he just wants to keep you from going there and digging. Did you know the Bible says that many false teachers are in the world (1 John 4:1)? Even Jesus told us that. Listen to what He says.

> "Beware of false prophets,
> who come to you in sheep's clothing,
> but inwardly they are ravenous wolves."
> Matthew 7:15

The buck I watched digging that day had been taught from "fawnhood" to be cautious of coyotes. Would the deer have been safer if the coyote had resembled a sheep? No, it would have only made him more dangerous. A coyote is underneath the wool! Right?

It's a scary thing to realize that the devil has preachers – men who can dress up in coat-and-tie camouflage and teach you something that's just not true (2 Corinthians 11:13-15). Some do it deliberately while others do it sincerely and unintentionally. But either way, if it's not the truth, it's a lie, and the one smiling all the while is the devil – the father of lies (John 8:44). Of course, I also could teach you something not true. That's why I always encourage my listeners to *"Follow along in your Bible and if you see anything I'm teaching that is not right, you will be my friend to tell me."* I take preaching the truth very seriously (James 3:1; Proverbs 18:21). Life and death are in preaching.

So, how do you protect yourself from getting only dirt? How do you make sure that what you believe is the truth? If we are as smart as a whitetail, we will dig to get down to the good stuff, and we will throw up a flag every time we hear or see something that doesn't seem right.

Don't just go to church and listen to the preacher and accept everything you hear. Don't just swallow everything on the TV or internet. Search for yourself. Prove that what is being said is so. *"Test all things; hold fast to what is good"* (1 Thessalonians 5:21). This is why Jesus taught in parables. He knew that some who didn't really care to learn the meaning would just walk away. Truth seekers would stay and dig (Mark 4:11-12,33-34).

One of my favorite verses to show the kind of students we need to be is in the book of Acts. It shows how some people really studied to find out if what they had been taught was true. It's what you and I need to do too.

"These were more fair-minded than those in Thessalonica, in that they received the word of God with all readiness, and **searched the scriptures daily to find out whether these things were so.**"
Acts 17:11

Truth can easily get buried beneath a pile of surface things that sound good and true. It can be easy to accept them without digging deeper. And the devil also knows that if you say something long enough people will believe it. One of my favorite quotes from an unknown author is ***"It is easier to believe a lie one has heard a thousand times than to believe a fact one has never heard before."*** Another favorite is *"People will occasionally stumble over the truth, but most of the time they will pick themselves up and carry on."* Will you and I be willing to dig past all of our preconceived ideas, false beliefs, and comfortable traditions? Will we take everything we believe and prove it from the scriptures? Will we put the microscope of God's word to it? When we come across a plain Bible passage showing truth, will we accept it?

There are so many things out there that sound very good, and we have heard them for a very long time, but are they true? For example, have you heard any of these one-liners?

"What you believe doesn't matter, because we are all going to the same place. We're just on different roads." Is that true? Do all roads lead to heaven? What if we dug down to John 14:6? What if we were to dig at Matthew 7:13-14?

"To be saved you need to pray this prayer: The Sinner's Prayer." What if we dug in the Bible and discovered that the "Sinner's Prayer" is not in the Bible and no one who asked "What must I do to be saved?" was ever told to pray it. What if *"calling on the name of the Lord"* is really talking about something else (Acts 22:16; Acts 2:21,37-40)?

"One church is as good as another." Oh? Could there possibly be one as good as the one you read about in the Bible, the one we can scratch down to and read of in Matthew 16:18, and the one He bought with His blood and adds us to when we are saved (Acts 2:47)? If one local church teaches the truth, and another one is teaching error, is one as good as the other? Compare two of them Jesus talked about in the book of Revelation. Was Pergamos (Revelation 2:12-17) as good as Smyrna (Revelation 2:8-11)?

"Jesus is the vine and all the denominations are the branches." What if we actually went to John 15, got our hooves into it, and discovered that the branches are individual people, not denominations? "If any *man* does not abide in me..." "If *you* abide in me..." What if we dug and came across 1 Corinthians 4:17 and found that Paul taught the *same thing* in *every church*? What if Paul was to come to our country? Would he preach it one way in one denomination and then another way in another? Would he reject denominationalism all together and simply show people from the New Testament what local churches preached and practiced? Is denominationalism pleasing to God? Maybe we should dig and see.

"People interpret the Bible differently." Actually, we haven't "interpreted" it at all until our understanding matches what the writer intended for us to understand. If John and Jack say two different things about the meaning of a verse, someone hasn't really "interpreted" it. The following are possible: 1) John is right. Jack is wrong. 2) Jack is right. John is wrong. 3) Jack and John may both be wrong. 4) But both Jack and John are not both right at the same time. God wrote a book that can be understood (Ephesians 3:4). To say it can't be understood is to discredit its Author. It is our job to dig and understand.

"Follow your heart. It can't be wrong." Well, read Proverbs 14:12.

Are you seeing what I mean? I need to take all I have been taught, put it on the table next to the Bible, and examine it.

WHY WON'T MORE OF US DIG?

So, if truth is so valuable, why wouldn't I dig? I can think of a few things that commonly get in the way.

It's hard work. The Bible is not hard to understand but work is required. Most deer hunters are willing to get tired sitting for a long time. It's called "doing the time" and "staying power." We are willing to wear out the seat of our pants. Just the other day a deer hunter asked me, "What's the average amount of time you sit in a stand?" I said, "Four hours." He replied, "You are kidding me!"
We need to be just as willing to sit with the Bible open for longer spans of time while we dig. It takes diligence (2 Timothy 2:15; Ecclesiastes 12:12). Why wouldn't we study the Bible like our eternal destiny depended on it? It does, you know. Put some spiritual muscle into it.

I may be afraid of what I might learn. I really do believe that we often don't dig because we don't want to learn. It might require changing what we have always done. So, we just don't dig (John 3:19-21). Surely God will not be upset at us for what we didn't know. Think again (Acts 17:30-31). I don't need to be afraid of truth. "Buy the truth and do not sell it" (Proverbs 23:23).

I may reach some unpopular conclusions. It may be that when I really look close at the Bible's teachings for myself, I may end up in the minority…believing things most people do not.

I may fear the reaction of my friends and family (John 12:42; John 9:22-23). I have a friend who after obeying the gospel was so excited. He was so eager to tell his friends at work about it. He expected them to be so happy for him and the change he was making in his life. They weren't. They dipped his Bible in motor oil.

On the day I watched that buck scooping away dirt, I was struck by the fact that he didn't let anything deter him. A hungry bunch of coyotes nearby might seem like a good reason to quit. But he didn't. He stayed. Once the coyotes moved on, he got right back to digging. A reward was waiting for him.

Let nothing keep you from digging for truth in God's word. A treasure awaits you (Matthew 13:44).

THE ARROW STRIKES Do I hold any beliefs solely because I have heard them a thousand times? Should I dig deeper in God's word to be sure I am on solid ground? Do I desire the praise of men more than the praise of God? Would I be willing to accept truth even if it meant being in the minority? If I am not willing to dig, what might be hindering me: spiritual laziness, traditional thinking, or fear?

Celebrities

If it's about a whitetail, I am passionate about it, all the way up to the celebrities of the hunting world. I love the men and women who make the TV hunting shows because their shows keep me in the woods when I can't be in the woods. They love what I love. They pursue what I pursue. They understand how I tick.

One of the men with a great appeal to southern boys like me is Michael Waddell, from Booger Bottom, Georgia. Michael says his hometown is *"the kind of place where a boy can be a boy and not worry one bit about the fast pace of city life. Man, we need more places like that these days, huh?"* His enthusiasm is contagious.

On his website he says, *"I'm a guitar pickin', blue jeans wearin', backstrap grillin' good ol' boy who was born to hunt. If it gobbles, quacks, bugles or grunts, chances are I've chased it more than a time or two. Droppin' the hammer and closin' the coffin on anything with antlers, feathers or fur just never gets old. I bet you know exactly what I'm talkin' about."* I am watching his schedule. I was thrilled to meet his dad not long ago. I hope to meet him one day.

Also, I recently met Lee and Tiffany Lakosky, one of America's favorite hunting couples. Their on-screen chemistry is tremendous. Lee says he hunts every single day of deer season. Wow! Doing it for a living! Of that privilege, he humbly says, *"I never in a million years thought that we would get the opportunity to do what we do for a living. It truly is a dream come true! There is not a day that goes by that I don't count our blessings"* (Hunting Mature Whitetails The Laskosky Way). It was a thrill to meet these two. They took their time with me and didn't seem to be rushing me away. I hope more women will join Tiffany in hunting.

Then there is the man who has been hiding hunters for years: Bill Jordan the creator of Realtree. That giant company started one day with Bill sitting in his parents' front yard with paper and colored pencils, sketching and coloring the bark of a giant oak tree that grew there. At the time of this writing, he lives somewhere in the woods in Columbus, Georgia, less than an hour from my hometown of Union Springs, Alabama. Do I ever want to meet him!

My list could go on and on, but for sake of time, let me finish with Grant Woods of Growing Deer TV. I watch him weekly on his internet website. He probably has taught me more than anyone. He's a wildlife biologist and a whitetail enthusiast. Literally, he knows a deer inside and out, how that creature ticks, where he wants to live, what he wants to eat, and how to plant food plots and keep them free of weeds. Grant's smart, really smart, but comes across as a good ole down to earth guy.

Now, I know that these people (even the ones who have pictures taken with me) don't know me from "Adam's housecat." They do love their fans and fellow hunters and they can make you feel like you are their best friend. But you are not. I am not. They don't follow my life or my hunting with great interest like I might follow theirs. I'm just another face in the crowd. But still I am having fun watching them and making plans to meet them on life's highway. It's a small world you know. To all of these celebrities, even the ones time and space fail me to mention, I say, *"Thanks for keeping the world of hunting on America's TV screens!"*

Now, let's put all our celebrities in perspective in whatever field they may be - our Hollywood Stars, musicians, athletes, etc. They are people just like us, created by God, and in need of God. I understand that very well. So, for eternal reasons, long ago I made my heroes and friends the faithful men and women of the Bible. Every spiritually-minded hunter I know would encourage us all to do the same.

THE BIBLE HALL OF FAITH

Enter the grand halls of Hebrews 11: the Bible hall of faith. These people are not celebrities. God has none. He only has servants. But that doesn't change the fact that these are the people

God has lifted up to seize my attention. They are people of faith. They are totally good for me spiritually. By following their example, I can one day arrive where they are. What a dream. Nothing, absolutely nothing can match it. And if I fail to meet these people one day—I have missed it all! What they lived for and died for is the purpose of life. It is the whole of man (Ecclesiastes 12:13-14).

They are selected for placement in chapter 11 because they were people who kept serving a God **they could not see**. They kept pressing on when they could not see God's plan with their eyes. *Noah* built an ark having never seen a worldwide flood. *Abraham* traveled thousands of miles, not knowing where he was going, to arrive at a land he had never seen. *Moses* left Egypt and endured all his trials "seeing Him who is invisible" (Hebrews 11:27). Some "no names" suffered terribly and never recanted their faith (11:35-40). It matters not if we don't know who they were. God knows, and that's all that matters. His estimation of their worth is so high He says the world was not worthy of them (Hebrews 11:38).

I too serve a God whom I have not seen. I serve a Lord: Jesus Christ whom having not seen, I love (1 Peter 1:8). I am pressing to my spiritual promised land of heaven which I have not seen. Oh, the evidence abounds for all of these, and by faith I see (Hebrews 11:1; 2 Corinthians 5:7). Folks, we all need to know that the **things we can see are temporary**. They will burn when the earth burns (2 Cor. 4:16-18). If we can see it with our eyes, kiss it goodbye. **It is the unseen that is eternal!** The person who says, *"If I can't see it, touch it, or smell it, I don't believe in it,"* is foolish indeed!

So, these are the people who have become my friends. I feel like I know them because I have spent so much time with them on the pages of scripture. I have contemplated the destruction of a whole world with Noah. I have cried walking with Abraham to offer Isaac. I have felt the frustration of Moses trying to lead a stiff-necked people toward Canaan. See what I mean? These people love the One I love. Their hearts beat with the same passion that courses through my veins. I have a great longing to meet them but an even greater longing to meet the One they gather around. He is the Centerpiece of everything. And when I arrive there, I am home.

These people do take a great interest in me. Hebrews chapter

12 pictures them in the grandstands pulling for me to run well and finish my race.

> *"Therefore we also, since we are surrounded by*
> ***so great a cloud of witnesses**, let us lay aside*
> *every weight, and the sin that so easily ensnares us,*
> *and let us run with patience the race that is set before us,*
> *looking unto Jesus, the author and finisher of our faith,*
> *who for the joy that was set before Him*
> *endured the cross, despising the shame, and has*
> *sat down at the right hand of God."*
> Hebrews 12:1-2

COME ON! RUN!

Not only do these supporters want us to finish, they remove all our excuses for never entering the race or for failing to finish. We may try to say, *"I couldn't see any evidence for God. How can you expect me to believe in an invisible God!"* But we look and see **Moses** in the stands. He saw and followed an invisible God. Even God says the agnostic and the atheist are without excuse (Romans 1:20). We say, *"Sexual temptation was just too strong, I couldn't be faithful."* But then we catch a glimpse of **Joseph** who resisted daily temptation to be sexually impure (Genesis 39). We offer up, *"It was just too hard. I couldn't do it,"* and there is **Abraham**, who in faithful obedience, went to sacrifice his only son. Talk about hard! Or perhaps we bring a broken-hearted, humble spirit and say, *"I've just done too many bad things in my life. God could never forgive me. I can't come to Him."* And we hear **David** in the stands shouting, "Blessed are those whose lawless deeds are forgiven" (Romans 4:7)! He's the very man who in one chapter of his life broke six of the ten commandments, including taking another man's wife and then murdering her husband. Talk about bad! And yet, God forgave him.

See my point? **There's no excuse for not entering and finishing this race.** We have supporters in the stands, some of whom we don't even know! They take away our excuses and say to us, "Yes, you can!" (Heb. 11:36-40). They finished. We can too.

Now look up to the Chief seat in the arena. Who do you see? There's **Jesus**. No one faced a more hostile crowd than Jesus. The opposing team offered Him no help in getting around the track and across the finish line. But regardless, He made the final stride home! With freshly moistened lips and a freed tongue He cried out with a loud voice on the cross, **"It is finished"** (John 19:28-30). We must look to Him and finish! And when we finish, we can run up to our King and receive not a fading crown of laurel but a crown of life (Revelation 2:10). What a joy to hear Him one day say, "Well done!"

Hebrews 11 is not all we have. There are other characters spread throughout the Bible who inspire us. I remember a brother in Christ who asked his suffering sister how he could help her, and she responded, "My brother, tell me about Job. Tell me about Job."

Even Jesus was supplied with such helpers. With the cross looming on the horizon, who appeared to Him? Moses and Elijah. What were they talking about? His approaching death— His exodus from this wilderness to heaven (Luke 9:30-31). I don't know what they said, but I am certain seeing these two finishers encouraged Him!

The bottom line? We have God-given supporters to push us onward...help from heaven! Save me a seat my friends. No, wait a minute. You don't have to. I have a reservation (1 Peter 1:3-4). Jesus is preparing my place (John 14:1-6). But keep cheering for me. The devil will still try to trip me up, and the homestretch can't be too far away.

THE ARROW STRIKES Do I enjoy the celebrities of the hunting world? Which ones have been most helpful to me? Do I love the characters of the Bible? Other than Jesus, who is my favorite and who inspires the most? Do I want to meet the men and women of the Bible one day? Do I imagine they will also want to meet me? Do I expect to meet them one day? Do I need to make any preparations to make meeting them a sure thing?

Deer Season is Almost Over

Well, I am sure by now you can tell just how addicted I am to whitetail adventures. That has surprised some of the friends who grew up with me. Actually it has surprised me too. I never thought I would love it like I do. The first time I went hunting, I was a teenager and I went with a friend. I didn't have adequate clothing or camouflage. I think I wore my "long johns", blue jeans, and a coat; and off I headed to the frozen tundra in my tennis shoes. I saw nothing that day, almost froze to death, and wondered what kind of nut would do this. I had no desire to ever go again. And then, my son was born.

Something kicked in the moment he entered my world. I wanted to raise him to be a man of God and wild at heart, loving creation and the Creator. My friend Eddie later added more fuel to the fire. Growing up, he did lots of hunting with his dad. His father told him, *"Son, if you stay in the woods or by an old fishin' hole, you won't ever get in too much trouble."* It's true. And when it comes to my children, I'd rather hunt *with* them, than hunt *for* them. So, I embarked upon a life of huntin' and fishin' with my kids.

Now someone may wonder why I would be so passionate about writing a book like this, but I have learned that all of life is about God, and He can be seen in everything. Deer hunting for me is about more than the deer. It's what the deer call you into that fascinates me. As you have seen in this book, deer hunting brings to mind so many thoughts from the Bible. The more you know about the Bible, the more you see in the creation that connects to it. References to hunting and the animal world are found all throughout the Bible. Even now, I can hear Isaac telling Esau, *"Now therefore, please take your weapons, your quiver and your bow, and go out to the field and hunt game for me and make me savory food such as I love"* (Genesis 27:4).

Here are a few more reasons why God, deer hunting, and the great outdoors go together so well.

Marvelous lessons are seen about the Creator and Sustainer of it all. We see in nature the greatest evidence of a God who has supreme power and intelligence. Those who can't see it, aren't looking very closely and are without excuse (Romans 1:20). And it's obvious He loves the wild!

Not only did God make the world of the wild, He is the universal shepherd (Job 39:1). To see deer foraging beneath a white oak is to be reminded that God cares for them and feeds them (Luke 12:24; Matthew 6:26). Not only does He feed them, He feeds me (Acts 17:28). I am dependent upon Him! The Bible also teaches that God keeps His creation running. Without Him, it all falls apart (Hebrews 1:3; Colossians 1:17). This is why the woods hold a great attraction for me. As John Eldridge has said in his book, *Wild At Heart*, "Moses didn't meet God at the mall."

Sunrises and sunsets still stir my soul. God takes my breath away with awesome sunrises through a patch of woods. The sun answers to His command (Matthew 5:45; Job 38:12). Did you know it gets colder at sunrise? I don't really know why, but it does for just a little while. I usually grab another layer about then and thank God for giving me clothing. It is also God who brings the sunset and the darkness. It is this darkness that brings out the prowlers (Psalm 104:20). This time of year, a big buck is hard to take. He's smart. He goes nocturnal until hunters leave. It is God who provides darkness for him, keeping everything in balance. God doesn't let predators win every time. When hunting a mature buck, we lose the majority of the time.

Rainy days make for good hunting too. An elder in a church where I once preached was a fisherman. He always said, "Don't ever hold back on going fishin' because it's raining." He's right. Most of the time, it will stop before you leave or not long after you get there. I hunted once in the rain this year. I like it. You can move about without noise because the rain is making plenty. Can't we see God in the rain? He is the Maker of the rain cycle, drawing up the drops of water from the earth and dropping it on man wherever He wills (Job 36:27-28). It is His witness (Acts 14:17). With every drop that drips from the bill of my hat, I thank God.

Even the harvesting of a deer is a solemn moment. I am keenly aware that God is the One who holds the breath of animals in His hand. It may sound "corny" to some, but it is a solemn moment as I stand over the animal God has given to me. They do not die without Him allowing it. In fact, hunters often talk about a "ghost deer," the monster-size one that somehow just keeps alluding them. When I harvest a deer, I know Who gave it. *"What you give them, they gather in; You open Your hand and they are filled with good. You hide Your face and they are troubled. You take away their breath, they die and return to their dust"* (Psalm 104:28-29).

Even birds do not fall without God's knowledge (Matthew 10:29). Not even one is forgotten by God (Luke 12:6). Jesus used these points to teach us that we are more valuable than any of these animals, and if God oversees their lives and cares for them, how much more will He care for us until He is ready to receive us unto Him.

It makes me a more thankful person. God is crushed when He has given us so much to enjoy in the created world and we fail to be thankful (Romans 1:21). Being unthankful is the beginning of a long slippery slope down to the pits of selfish living (Romans 1:20-32). I can't help but bow my head as the sun sets on my last hunt of the year and give thanks. I have also bowed with my hunting partners to do the same. We praise the great Creator and bless Him who *"gives us richly all things to enjoy"* (1 Timothy 6:17).

One season never ends. As much as I enjoy hunting, it is not my greatest love. It must never be. This season is coming to an end as they all do. But the season for teaching God's word will never end until Jesus comes again. While I deer hunt some of the time, I fish all of the time...for men (Luke 5:10).

I do my fishing by teaching the word of God (2 Timothy 4:1-5). I teach men that we ought to thirst for God as the *"deer pants for the water brooks"* (Psalm 42:1). I teach about the Son of God who proved who He was by causing the lame to *leap like a deer* (Isaiah 35:6). I teach husbands to be enraptured with the love of their wives which Solomon compared to a *loving deer and a graceful doe* (Proverbs 5:19). The season of teaching His marvelous word is my favorite season of all.

Maybe you are not a hunter and never intend to be. But do find your quiet places for meditation on God and His word. Maybe it will be a trip to the mountains or a scenic golf course, or a hike on a walking trail. Just be sure to see God and live your life for Him. The sun will set on your life one day, and then only one thing matters. May God be praised in all the world.

THE ARROW STRIKES What thoughts or feelings do I have each year when hunting season is over? Do I take time to thank God for all the joys and memories from the past season? Do I engage in the season that never ends? Have I ever fished for men? If I have fished for men and was successful in making a catch, how did it make me feel? How do I imagine it made the Lord feel? Could anything possibly be more rewarding or important?

Old Fence Post

It was just an old rotting fence post, with tangled barbed wire tenaciously clinging to its side. It was ten yards away from my stand and covered with fresh green moss on its north side. Why does moss always grow on that side? The post leaned severely refusing to give up its place in the earth. It was a bit obscured from sight by a spiny hedge row growing around it. I suppose it would normally be overlooked. And surely it would not provoke much thought in a hunter. But today it did.

My mind ran wild with imagination. Who set this fence post? All the evidence seemed to suggest that while the post still stood, the person who drove it into the ground did not. I feel sure he has gone the way of all the earth (1 Kings 2:1-3). How many times has this land changed owners since the post was set? Was it hard for him to come up with the money to buy it? If only a fence post could talk, it could answer all my questions.

As I stared at the post, I could picture a middle-aged man in overalls sweating in the midday heat with his son, and saying, *"Son, this is such a beautiful place. We will all be really happy here. This will be a great place for our cows and horses and I think I'll build the house near that cluster of trees in the middle of the field. Pull that wire tight now son."*

If the man has passed from the earth, has anyone thought about him in a while? It doesn't seem really fair to me that a man can labor so hard and be forgotten pretty quickly. Oh, the farm or the office may run slowly for a while, but eventually the next man fills the gap, and things roll on. If this was all there was to life, it would be sad wouldn't it? That's what the preacher in Ecclesiastes said about "life under the sun." Wise man or fool…both are forgotten, and they leave their labor for another to enjoy just as I do today in this corner spot.

"For there is no more remembrance
of the wise than of the fool forever,
since all that now is
will be forgotten in the days to come.
And how does a wise man die?
As the fool!

Then I hated all my labor in which
I had toiled under the sun ,
because I must leave it to the
man who will come after me."
Ecclesiastes 2:16,18

A few years ago, I was made to realize how right the preacher was. I was preaching in Kentucky and was privileged to spend the week on the farm of a friend. He, like me, is a sentimental guy who really cares about people and his animals too for that matter. For example, he has a grave on his property where he buried a family dog. He had placed an impressive gravestone there, and when he showed it to me, his voice quivered, and his eyes misted as he said, *"We all loved her so much."* Truly, a righteous man regards the life of his animal (Proverbs 12:10).

The next day, as we made our way into town, we approached a cemetery. The graves on the outer boundary were set very close to the road with no fence. You could almost reach out and touch them as you eased around the curve.

As we got closer, my friend said, *"Jeff, I want you to meet Orville."* We stopped on the side of the road, and I could see Orville's tombstone from the car. He lived a very short life—only about twenty years. Eric said, *"Jeff, I don't know his story. I wish I did. I have asked several townspeople about him and I've also done a little investigating at the library. No one knows who he was or what happened to him."* See my point? It doesn't take long for the memory of us to be lost. I bet that thought doesn't exactly make your day. Are you saying, "Thanks a lot man. What a perfect start to my day"?

REMEMBERED & REWARDED BY JESUS

Oh, how thankful I am that my Lord changes this morbid picture. The Bible teaches that God will never forget those who are His. A fence post may lean, but God's memory of us stands firm (2 Timothy 2:19). He even writes our names in the Book of Life (Luke 10:20). Our names are registered in heaven (Hebrews 12:23). This is the only record book that really matters If your name is there, it matters little if the world forgets you.

It doesn't matter if your awards and trophies and mounts become covered with dust, are set away in the attic, or sold in a yard sale. It doesn't matter if they clean out your desk and put another name tag on the door. It doesn't matter if moss covers the rotting post you placed on the ole home place. If God knows us, all is well. That is what matters! Think of the joy of being able to stand on the day of judgment and hear the Lord say, *"Well done, good and faithful servant"* (Matthew 25:21). But if we are not His and have lived unrighteously, the words are hauntingly sober: *"I never knew you"* and *"depart from Me"* (Matthew 7:23; 25:41).

So, to whoever set this post, I want you to know I thought about you today. You are special. I wish I had known you. I really do. You matter because you lived. You matter because you were made in the image of God (Genesis 1:26; James 3:9). The Lord made you in His image with the dream of your living for Him and being with Him forever. Were you a Christian cleansed in the blood of the Lamb (Revelation 1:5; Acts 22:16)? Was your character of the sort that you will be able to abide with God forever? Did you live your life with integrity, never selling it for any price? Were you the kind of man Psalm 15 praises? I feel sure the day you set this fence post you never imagined another middle-aged man, years down the road, would think this deeply about you. On that day you drove wood into the ground; today you and the Lord stapled great truths on my mind and pounded life lessons deep into my heart. Truth has a barb. It cuts deeply sometimes (Acts 2:37). If you are His child, I look forward to joining you around God's throne, with angels innumerable, to praise Him forevermore. In that case, I will see you later. If you are not His child, with great sadness and grief, I say, *"Goodbye."*

THE ARROW STRIKES Have I thought much about how quickly one can be forgotten on earth after he dies? Does such a thought depress me or really motivate me to live for what matters? Who do I most want to remember me? Is my name registered in heaven, in the book of Life?

Turkey Hunting: Life in Reverse
(A Little Bonus For Those Who Love It)

I love turkey hunting. These All-Stars of spring are growing on me really fast. I can relate to "feather fever." Turkeys are incredible works of God. Their greatest asset is their eyes. If a turkey had a deer's nose to go with his eyes, you never would harvest one! While still a growing interest for me, turkey hunting is mostly a way for me to get back in the woods while I wait for the return of deer season. Every hunter is different, but the whitetail does something for me a turkey has yet to do.

*When you turkey hunt, you are trying to **reverse** nature.* This was the first thing I ever learned about hunting turkeys. There are fascinating spiritual insights to be gained by meditating on it. It also proves the premise of *Hoof Prints to His Prints* – there is always a way *to connect the woods to the Word.* God is in all of life if we will just take the time to see Him.

Springtime is the mating season for turkeys. Gobblers (or as Michael Waddell would say – "thunder chickens") start blasting away with the gobbling. And let me tell you this…you have not heard a turkey gobble until you hear him at less than twenty yards and facing you! It will blow you away. You literally feel it reverberate against your chest. He is trying to court the hens into his harem. His thinking is, *"I'm a bad boy and you should come to me. I might not be very handsome but watch this."* And then he puts on a show. He blows himself up, struts around, and fans out his tail feathers. He looks like a 55-gallon drum with a softball on top! Against the sun, the feathers reflect yellow, gold, pink, maroon, green, blue, and perhaps more. I told someone the other day, *"I think God made up for the ugly head with the artistry in the feathers."*

Now, here's where the **reverse action** comes in. The normal pattern is for the hen to come to the gobbler. But in turkey hunting you are attempting to bring the gobbler to you. So, you hunker yourself down, and act like a woman playing hard to get. You make your call, and he thunders out saying, *"Here I am baby! Come to me."* She woos him a little more with some soft purrs. He gobbles again, but still "she" stays put. Finally, when he can stand it no longer, **he reverses nature** and decides to go to her. That's when the deal gets done. BLAST!! Bird down! Turkey, cornbread dressing, and cranberry sauce are on the way.

YOU CAN TRUST GOD IN REVERSE

When it comes to our lives as Christians, the Bible makes one thing very clear. God is always working for good. Everything might not always be good but He is working for good. And the good thing He is always aiming for is to make us like Jesus. Sometimes He uses difficult things to shape us, because sometimes we can be turkeys too!

> *"And we know that*
> **all things work together for good**
> *to **those who love God**,*
> *to those who are called*
> **according to His purpose**.
> *For whom He foreknew,*
> *He also predestined to*
> *be **conformed to the image of His Son**,*
> *that He might be the firstborn*
> *among many brethren."*
> Romans 8:28-29

Someone has compared the process to the making of a chocolate cake. It has some bad-tasting ingredients in it when eaten by themselves. As a kid, I once got a spoonful of cocoa expecting it to be good, but it turned my mouth inside out. I also don't eat flour by itself or raw eggs for that matter. They taste bad. But when you take cocoa, flour, raw eggs, butter, and sugar and mix it all together, **IT WORKS TOGETHER FOR GOOD!** God does the same.

In order to shape us into the likeness of His Son, He may mix in all manner of things over our lifetime. Some of it we hate, but let God work. You will like what you see at the end. It's what we call "providence." Break the word down and you have two things. *Pro* means *"before."* *Video* means *"to see."* It means that God sees beforehand. He sees the *"end from the beginning"* (Isaiah 46:10), and He is always working toward an awesome end for His people.

It can be very hard to see what God is doing as life runs forward, but when you **look back in reverse,** you can see purpose even in the not-so-easy, maybe even horrible moments of your life. It's sort of like a turkey's feather. The feathers may look brown or black, but turned toward the sun they become beautiful with manifold colors. It just takes looking at it from a different angle with God's light shining on it.

The greatest Bible example of this is Joseph. You probably know the story, but if you don't, it would be great for you to sit down and read in one sitting Genesis 37-50. I can hardly read it without getting misty-eyed. Let me give you the condensed version.

A TROUBLED LIFE TURNED MAJESTIC

Joseph was His father's favorite – evidenced by the "coat of many colors" he made only for Joseph. Joseph also had dreams showing his brothers bowing down to him. The coat and the dreams resulted in the brothers hating Joseph with a cruel jealousy.

One day the brothers contemplated killing Joseph but instead threw him in a pit. They then sold him for silver to a caravan of traders going to Egypt. To convince their father that Joseph had been killed, they tore and dipped Joseph's coat in a goat's blood. His father mourned for many days. How cold-hearted and cruel these brothers were!

In Egypt, Joseph was placed on the slave market and sold to Potiphar, a captain of Pharaoh's guard. Joseph prospered because *"God was with him."* But then Potiphar's wife lusted for Joseph and tried to force him to have sexual relations with her. She took hold of him, and he fled out of his coat and out of the house. She was so angry over his refusing to lie with her that she accused Joseph of trying to rape her.

Potiphar had Joseph put in the king's prison where he met a butler and baker who had been arrested by Pharaoh. By God's enabling, Joseph interpreted dreams for them. When the butler was released and restored to Pharaoh, he was supposed to put in a good word for Joseph to Pharaoh but he didn't. Joseph was left forgotten in the prison. In time, Pharaoh had some troubling dreams and needed an interpreter. It was then the butler finally remembered Joseph.

Pharaoh released Joseph from prison, and Joseph told him the meaning of his dreams. Joseph said the dreams meant that Egypt would have seven years of plenty, followed by seven years of famine, and he recommended that Egypt store up food during the seven good years. Pharaoh was so impressed that he made Joseph second-in-command over all Egypt and over the famine project. Joseph's brothers were forced to come down to Egypt for grain, and **guess who they bowed down to, not knowing who it was? You guessed it…Joseph!**

Joseph tested his brothers to know their hearts but at last he couldn't hold his emotions in any longer. The next shocking words were, *"I am Joseph."* He wept and the brothers were dismayed in his presence. Joseph made plans to bring his father and his family to Egypt to provide for them there. They came and Joseph embraced his father once again! There the family grew in great numbers. In time it became a great nation from which Jesus, the Christ, came!

JOSEPH'S INCREDIBLE PERSPECTIVE

Most of us reading the story are reading it expecting Joseph to be very bitter about all that happened to him. But he wasn't. He had plenty of time to **look at it in reverse,** and he could see God's working. He saw it with God's light shining on it. I am touched by his words to his brothers when he made himself known.

"But now, do not be grieved or be angry
with yourselves because you sent me here;
For God sent me before you to preserve life…
So now it was not you who sent me here, but God,
and He has made me a father to Pharaoh,
and lord of all his house, and a ruler

> *throughout all the land of Egypt."*
> (Genesis 45:5, 8).

THE STORY IN REVERSE

Now, look at the story in reverse. I think you will be amazed.

13. We need a Savior to arise from a great nation.
12. That nation has food and grows mightily in the land of Egypt before leaving.
11. Joseph's family comes to Egypt and Joseph provides lavishly for them.
10. Joseph rises to great power.
9. Joseph interprets Pharaoh's dreams.
8. Joseph meets Pharaoh's butler in prison.
7. Potiphar's wife lies about Joseph, and he is thrown into prison.
6. Joseph is sold to Potiphar's house and has all given to him except Potiphar's wife.
5. Joseph is thrown into a pit and sold to a caravan of traders headed to Egypt.
4. Joseph is hated by his brothers.
3. Joseph has dreams showing that his brothers would bow down to him.
2. Joseph is given a coat of many colors by his father.
1. Joseph is born to Rachel, Jacob's beloved wife.

Can you see how each event could not have happened without the previous event? One led to the other, and the end is God-blessed. And it all happened over several years. God is not in a hurry, and He's never wasting His time.

BRING THE LESSON HOME

So, the next time you rub the striker against your slate call, trying to reverse nature, remember that working backwards is a good teacher.

Strive to be patient when you go through hard times. Hang in there when some of those times seem like they will never end or have a breakthrough. God is working. You may not see His purposes, but He has them. He is proving you, preparing you, and training you for things ahead (James 1:12). Joseph saw that. He was *proven* before he was *promoted*.

At the last, when you sit around the throne of Jesus and resemble Him in your character, you will be thankful for the One who was in control all the while. He is good!

THE ARROW STRIKES Have I ever been through a terribly difficult time in my life? Did I have or still have a lot of "why" questions about it? Am I able to look back and see some purpose in it—some good things that came out of it? Do I believe God works in my life today? As I look at my life in reverse, am I able to see how each piece, whether good or bad, was important to the whole? Even if I can't presently see the purpose, am I willing to trust God with my life?

You Never Know How Big a Tree Is...

Sometimes there are things that happen in the woods that can nearly scare you to death. I've never had it to be anything terribly bad but I can be a little like Shaggy or Scooby-Doo. I get "creeped out" pretty easily and can have a wild imagination.

Because of that, a friend of mine in high school used to love to scare me. One night when I spent the night with him, I slept on the couch. Not too long after turning the lights out and lying down, I heard something move, and I thought I could hear someone breathing (I've got chill bumps, even now). I knew it was him. I just knew it. But knowing it was him didn't make any difference. I then felt a human presence near me. Do you know what I mean? Sometimes you can just feel someone's presence – much like when your little children walk up to your bedside during the night and just stand there. I always hated that!

So, I could feel Ray in the room. I even said, "Ray…Ray… go on now…Ray…!" I slowly turned my head on the couch to look, and there he was, a mere two or three INCHES away from my face…with a hideous, scary mask on. I leaped like a cat! Not funny! Well, maybe it is. But anyway, you get the idea of how I am.

When I started college, our hometown funeral director offered to let me have a room at his newly opened funeral home near the college. He said, *"You can stay there free if you will just look after the place for me. But you will have company sometime."* He meant a body would be there with me at times. With a friend like

Ray knowing I was living there, you better believe there was no way I was going to do that!

JEFF MAY MEET JUSTIN BEAVER

Only a couple of things have scared me really bad in the woods. Both of them were times when something LOUD broke the stone, cold silence of the early morning. My most frightening moment happened on our family farm in South Alabama in the swampiest section of the property. I had not been hunting very long and was growing impatient in my search for some major headgear on a buck. I decided I wasn't paying the price enough and I needed to go into the nastiest section of the woods in hopes of getting a shot at a swamp monster!

I borrowed some waders from my brother-in-law, John, and got directions from him on the best place to go. He gave them to me and told me I would have some water to cross. I asked, "How high?" He said, "Probably just knee high." Keep in mind that I was going to do all of this in the dark. It's one thing to walk in the woods in the dark; it's another to cross water in the dark. Nevertheless, "Shaggy May" struck out on his mission. Somehow, along my trek, I missed a turn I was supposed to take. John never intended for me to go where I went.

I came to some dark water and thought, "This is it." But it wasn't. I stepped into the water and it was quickly over my knees. Then the water was up to my waist. I thought, "Jeff May, you are out of your mind." But I inched further in my determination. The water was now inching up over my belly button and headed toward my chest. I was considering backing out. I was already a little scared, when all of sudden...KABOOM!! It sounded like a cannon had exploded just a few feet away from me. It had to have been a beaver slamming his tail on the water. Put the paddles on me. I think I have just had a heart attack! And break out the Scooby Snacks. I think I deserve them.

And then, there was the day I was lost in my thoughts in the stand, and there was a CRASH followed by an extremely loud BOOM. A tree or at least a big part of a tree had fallen somewhere nearby. After settling down, I wondered how big the tree was, and I remembered a one-liner that has always stayed with me. ***"You never know how big a tree is, until it falls."*** You and I can stand on the ground, look up, admire a huge oak, and each render a guess as to how tall it is. But only when it falls can we measure it and really know.

GET OUT THE TAPE MEASURE

There are a few days in our lives when someone mighty big to us falls. It may be a grandparent, a parent, a sibling, a mentor, or a close friend. It seems like when it does you always think so deeply, and at least with me, I always find myself wishing I had done more with them and more for them. In the days that follow, sometimes even months and years, you are able to see how monumental they were. You can measure their full impact upon your life.

I think a good bit about the day I will fall. I always have. I want my life to really count for something. I want to have served my generation (Acts 13:36). I want to have made a difference in the lives of others. That is why I preach. Preaching touches eternity. To be honest, I want to be remembered. To me, one special "mother in the Lord" (Mark 10:29-30) was a lady I always called "Mrs. Laurette." I loved her, and I miss her. As she prepared for her death, she told her daughter, *"Anne, I don't want a lot of crying at my funeral. But I do want a little bit."* Hilarious! It makes my point.

Most of us want to be remembered, at least a little, and continue to contribute somehow to the lives of those we leave behind. As a deer leaves a hoof print on soft soil, I want to leave my print on the hearts of those who come after me, especially my children. I don't really feel vain in that; I just love people, especially my own family so very much. I want them to be able to pull from their memory bank and still be able to build on their memories somehow. Israel was once told to "look to the rock from which you were hewn"—to Abraham and Sarah (Isaiah 51:1-2). I don't know that I have been a rock to my family, but maybe I can at least be a little stepping stone.

IT'S WHY...

I have written letters to my wife and children through the years on fancy parchment paper and the masters are in a fireproof safe. It's why I have tried to be available to my children and spend time with them especially when they were little. It's probably why I am writing this book – to give them something else, something tangible to hold in their hands, a little piece of Daddy. It's why I have mounted a couple of trophies to pass on to my children. It's not that I want them to remember the hunt – I want them to remember me – and more so, the things I have tried to teach from the word of God. Without His word, I have nothing of any value to say. Truth be known, this book is a classic case of plagiarism. I have stolen from Him.

Some children have dads who have left them mostly wounded or scarred in some way. I don't want that. I want my children to have pleasant memories of me. They don't have to write anything special on my tombstone, I just want to be written on their heart. I heard once of a tombstone that had a horrible message on it. Someone said they saw it in *Ripley's Believe It or Not*. It read, *"Here lies a man who did no good. Had he lived longer, he never would. Where he is now or how he fares...nobody knows, nobody cares."* It can happen. King Jehoram died to no one's sorrow. Nobody cried (2 Chronicles 21:20).

I guess my tombstone is the only place my name will ever be in marble. That means nothing to me. I actually wish I could be buried in the woods under a white oak. Maybe a whitetail could munch on acorns just above my plot. I only want my name to be written in the Lamb's Book of Life (Luke 10:20; Revelation 3:5). That book will remain after this one and all the other volumes written solely by men are gone.

We all have passions in life. Deer hunting has been a major one for me. I feel fully alive when I am doing it. It's life at "full draw." But don't ever let your passions get in the way of what really matters. Don't let them choke the Lord out. Don't let them move your family to the back burner. Live always with the end in mind, and make every decision with a view toward it. Steven Covey, the author of *The 7 Habits of Highly Effective People* encourages a person to envision his own funeral. Who will speak? What will they say? The bottom line is—you are writing your own funeral sermon each day you live. You provide the material. This book never really was about deer hunting. Can you see that? Life is about God, period (Colossians 1:16; Romans 11:36)!

IT'S INEVITABLE

If you are not thinking along these lines right now, you probably will one day. I'm not the first avid hunter to see these things. Just this week, I read a great article from a man who at one time aspired to be one of the greatest hunters ever: a record-book man. Listen to him.

> *"It's inevitable that upon my passing I will leave*
> *a bunch of stuffed deer heads, antlers*
> *and hunting mementos. But if that is all – if that*
> *is all my life amounted to – it sure wouldn't*
> *be much. After all, despite those trophies*
> *being meaningful to me as a result*
> *of the memories they engender, I'm realistic*
> *enough to know they will probably be*
> *wrangled over, sold, given away, relegated*
> *to a dusty attic, placed in a yard sale*
> *or destroyed. No, I want my life to count*
> *for more than just dusty old deer heads."*
> (R.G. Bernier, Whitetail News, Vol. 23, No. 1, pg. 22)

When you fall and your life is measured by those who knew you, will it be like a giant oak or a little sapling? I'm not sure how my life will be measured. I know I've never measured up to what God wanted from me. I am ever thankful for His saving grace, and the older I get, the more aware I am of just how much of His grace I'm going to need. It was the oldest ones in John 8:9 who were the first to drop their stones.

But to be honest, I'm glad He is the One I stand before in judgment. I wouldn't trust anyone else. His measurement is always right. Now that's something to sit in a tree stand or lie in a bed at night and think about it, isn't it? Plant yourself in the rich soil of God's word; let Him feed you; and grow, grow, grow (2 Peter 3:18). May God use your life in some way to bless others and glorify His matchless Name.

THE ARROW STRIKES At the end of my life, when I fall, will I be a sapling or a big oak? Do I think about how much influence my life will have on family and friends after I am gone? Is there anything I could or should be doing to leave a good legacy? Do I value the right trophies?

Going Alone

I stood behind an old-fashioned, screen door at the cabin. You know, the kind that bangs against the door facing as it slams shut. I watched him drive the 4-wheeler down the road headed to the bottoms, and I swallowed a lump. He was going alone. Reluctantly, I had finally given my son, Henderson, the green light to hunt without me.

I know he wanted independence. I know he wanted to cross yet another threshold that told him he was bigger—not a little boy anymore. I felt that he was ready. The lump in my throat was because *I* was not ready. I will miss sitting with him, making sure he is warm, and yes, waking the little boy up after he has fallen asleep. Where does the time go? It sure makes you want to stop the clock a little while and soak in the childhood years. Don't blink! Indeed, life goes faster than you think.

I wonder, did he feel ready? Was there any part of him that was reluctant? If there was, he didn't let me see it. Had I done my job? I recalled all the times hunting when I would ask, *"What is the most important thing today"* He would answer, *"Be safe"*. I had kept him safe while he was with me. It was his job now. He's an extremely focused hunter, the son of a preacher, and the son of a hunter safety instructor. He's heard a lot of good things to keep him safe in the woods and the world. I didn't give him any long speeches before he left. I just simply handed him his 7mm-08 and said, "Henderson, you know this is life and death don't you?" He answered, "Yes sir, I know." Enough said.

THE LAST SIT TOGETHER

My last hunt sitting beside him is forever etched in my mind—my last check on his safety habits and skills. I was determined to give no reminders about safety or any tips on hunting. I had to make sure he had it in him and that it had become second nature.

It was an afternoon hunt, and I had about decided nothing was going to happen. My head had dropped in a little disappointment when Henderson broke the silence with a faint whisper, *"Dad, there's a deer."* I eased my head up and whispered, *"Where?"* *"Right there,"* Henderson whispered emphatically! *"Oh, oh, I see him."* He was standing at the edge of the field, just inside the wood line. When he started walking, he never checked up. He was on a mission. I knew if he was to be harvested, he would have to be stopped.

I wanted to coach Hen a little, but I said nothing. The deer was closing the distance fast and headed off the small "honey hole" food plot. I was so proud when Henderson bleated *"Baaahhh,"* and the deer stopped. He shot, and the round hit its mark. Perfect execution! The only downer about it was that it confirmed it was time for me to go. Clearly, he could go alone.

Life had changed so much for me this hunting season. I was no longer sitting with Henderson. But I was sitting with Eddie in the aftermath of his stroke. Less than a week after Hen's first hunt alone, we had another first. Henderson and I walked down the leafy road leading into the Ponderosa. My mind went back to the first words of this book, *"He led me down a leaf-blanketed road that lead away from one world and into another."* But now it was Henderson matching me stride for stride.

Like Eddie and I would always do, we stopped at the second gate, and said, *"Good luck. Be careful."* After the hunt, I stood at the same gate, watching a hill in front of me. It used to be Eddie's light I would look to see bouncing along the terrain. Today, I was looking for my son's light. Life is all about changes. Hunter friends, it will be the same for you.

Perhaps here is a good time for you to ponder what you want to say to your children when they go alone through life without you. When you are done, you can continue and read a few things I want to say to mine.

AN OPEN LETTER TO MY CHILDREN

Dear Bethany and Henderson,

I want to say that if life runs its usual course the day will come when you will have to go on alone. You will go without me. But in another way, you will never really be without me. And for sure, another Father will always be there (2 Timothy 4:16-17).

Basically, I've tried to work myself out of a job. I can only hope I did it well. If I did anything wrong, please know that I was sincere through it all. I want to charge both of you as David did his son, Solomon:

> *"I go the way of all the earth; be strong, therefore,*
> *and prove yourself a man. And keep the*
> *charge of the Lord your God: to walk in*
> *His ways, to keep His statutes, His judgments,*
> *and His testimonies, as it is written in the Law*
> *of Moses, that you may prosper in all that you*
> *do and wherever you turn..."*
> 1 Kings 2:2-3

I want to leave you a few trail markers. Consider them carefully.

The best looking spot is not always the best. In hunting, there's often a desire to sit in the prettiest spot you have. But it may not be the best place to be. The same is true in the world. Be careful where you live. Find a place with a strong, faithful, scripturally-sound church that's a good place to rear my grandkids. Remember that Lot beheld the well-watered plains around Sodom and Gomorrah and thought he just had to live there. It grieved his soul living in such wickedness (2 Peter 2:6-8), and it cost him with his family (Genesis 13 & 19).

Be careful where you sit. Before every hunting season, I work hard to make sure that every place you sit is safe. I don't want you to fall. Likewise, in life, be careful with whom you sit. Remember that Peter denied the Lord when he sat among the wrong people (Luke 22:55). Read Psalm 1 often and remember, *"Blessed is* *the man who walks not in the counsel of the ungodly, nor stands in the path of sinners, nor sits in the seat of the scornful; But his delight is in the law of the Lord, and in his law he meditates day and night."*

Be watchful. Do you remember the gifts we gave you both for your 13th birthday? Remember to watch and guard the things that are valuable. Jesus often said, "Watch" (Matthew 26:41). In the woods we have been very watchful, very aware of things happening around us. We've tried to move about very carefully so that it would not cost us a trophy. But in life, watching matters even more.

Know when and where to take your stand. How many "stands" have we taken into the woods? Lots of them. In like manner, as you live life, know where and when to take a stand. Some things should not be fought over. They don't matter. But then there are some things you absolutely must fight for. The cost is too great not to fight. Choose your battles. Remember that Paul fought for the "truth of the gospel" even when it was his good friend, Peter, going wrong (Galatians 2:11-21).

Aim well. Both of you have been straight shooters in the woods. Do the same in the world. I hope you achieve all your goals and hit every mark you aim for. When you miss, if it's sin, repent and seek the Lord's grace and keep shooting for greater Christlikeness. He will keep working to finish this wonderful thing He started with you (Philippians 1:6).

Don't forget; it's life or death. *"See, I have set before you today life and good, death and evil...therefore choose life, that both you and your descendants may live, that you may love the Lord your God, that you may cling to Him, for He is your life and the length of your days..."* (Deuteronomy 30:15-20). Life has many choices. Eternity just has two.

Meet me across the river. I'll be waiting.

Remember God is with you, even when you are going alone. He will never leave you, nor forsake you.(Hebrews 13:5).

I love you both, and
I am proud of you,

Dad

Children Are Like Kites
By: Erma Bombeck

You spend a lifetime trying to get them off the ground.
You run with them until you're both breathless
. They crash. They hit the rooftop. You patch and
comfort, adjust and teach.
You watch them lifted by the wind and
assure them that someday they'll fly.
Finally they are airborne;
They need more string and you keep letting it out;
But with each twist of the ball of twine,
There is a sadness that goes with joy.
The kite becomes more distant,
and you know it won't be long
before that beautiful creature will
snap the lifeline that binds you together
and will soar, free and alone.
Only then do you know that you did your job."

THE ARROW STRIKES Do I have any special memories of hunting with my children? What is my favorite memory of them, whether in the woods or elsewhere? Have I prepared them to go alone? Do they have a strong sense that God will be with them and never leave them?

Wake Up, Sleeper!!

When a deer hunter goes to bed at night he never knows what the next day holds for him. His next hunt could be a real dud, or it could be a monumental one with the harvest of a buck that will be remembered for a lifetime. One year after "going alone" for the first time, Henderson harvested his first big buck on Thanksgiving morning.

My alarm went off at 4:00 a.m. and I began trying to wake Henderson. He bucked. I tried three times over the next hour to wake him. He wouldn't budge. I finally said, "Are you going or not?" "No," he said. "Are you really going to sleep in?" "Yes sir," he replied.

I was a little disappointed he wasn't going. I've read too many stories about a big deer being harvested on a day when a hunter almost decided to sleep instead of hunting. He might ought to change his mind. But I knew he was tired and needed some rest. In the physical realm, sleeping is a necessary thing and beneficial to good health. But in the spiritual world, one of the most dangerous things we can do is go to sleep.

ON THE DAY YOU LEAST EXPECT IT

I left the cabin without Henderson. I was doing the hard work today—using my climbing stand so I could watch a fire lane in the heart of the woods. About the time I was firmly settled at the top of the tree, my cell phone vibrated. It was Henderson. The sleeper had risen and was letting me know he had gone to an easy, convenient stand near the cabin. We call it "Cedar Tree."

About thirty minutes later, I heard a blast. And then another text message came that said, "I just shot a big buck." It was such a plain and matter-of-fact text for someone who had just gotten his first great buck. But, that's typical Henderson: laid back, calm, and focused. He's always been that way. If my daughter had dropped this big buck she would have sent a text that said, "Just shot a BIG BUCK!! Hashtag Gotcha! Hashtag Bullseye!"

I think I was as happy, or happier, than he was. Daddies love seeing their children take good bucks. It turned out to be an eight point weighing in at a stout 194 pounds. The rack was perfectly symmetrical with some nice, stately brow tines. He was already talking about the spot on his wall where he wanted to place his mounted deer.

Henderson said at sunrise the buck eased into the beautiful, green, honey-hole food plot, and was following a doe. He thought it was a small buck. He asked himself, "Why does it always have to be a little four point?" He prepared to harvest the doe. But then, the buck turned his head. Upon looking closer, Henderson's eyes bugged out when he saw eight points and tall headgear outside the ears. "It's a shooter," he concluded. By this time, the buck was quartering away, but Henderson knew what shot angle he needed to get the job done. He closed the deal. And he surely was happy he had gotten out of bed. Sleep is not always a good thing.

WHEN SLEEP IS DANGEROUS

The Bible shows us some times when it is especially dangerous to sleep spiritually. They are as follows:

When bringing up children. It just so happens that most every couple is rearing children during the busiest time of their lives. Don't get tired and go to sleep at the wheel. You could wake up to a nightmare. Let's stay awake, train our children, and pray to reap the rewards of our labor.

One of the reasons I am so glad that Henderson's first big buck harvest made its way into this book just before publication, is because it gave me a God-given opportunity. He can be reminded of some eternal principles and lessons long after I am gone.

When the predator (the devil) is closing in on you. We may never know when the devil has found just the right circumstances to plan his attack. We must stay awake at all times and watch carefully. This was Peter's mistake prior to denying Jesus three times in the presence of the Lord's enemies.

Jesus had warned Peter and told him to watch but he didn't. In the Garden of Gethsemane, the night before His death, Jesus did the hard work—praying fervently while Peter conveniently chose to sleep.

When Jesus returned to Peter in the garden and found him asleep, He said, *"What, could you not watch and with Me one hour? Watch and pray lest you enter into temptation. The spirit indeed is willing, but the flesh is weak"* (Matthew 26:40-41). So, what did Peter do? He went back to sleep just as soon as Jesus had gone away to continue praying. And you can easily imagine a heavy sigh from Jesus when He returns once more and Rip Van Winkle is still down under.

You know the rest of the story, don't you? Peter did not perform so well under pressure before those who wanted to know if he was ever with Jesus. He cursed and swore he didn't know the Man! So sad. He prepared for the wrong kind of battle. He had been very proficient at cutting a man's ear off when the poor fellow came to arrest Jesus. I'm persuaded Peter was ready for the most fierce of physical battles. Yet, he never anticipated the spiritual battlefield on which Satan would attack him on the most personal level: his relationship with Jesus.

Doesn't it still happen today? We fall in moments of temptation because we previously chose sleeping over watching. Let's learn to do better. Awake, sleeper!

When landmark decisions are made in the land in which we live. We need to be taking every opportunity to share the Bible with others. Keep teaching what the Bible says, even on controversial issues. John the Baptist certainly cared nothing for political correctness, even when speaking to men in high offices (Matthew 14:1-12).

When does the devil work to spread his corrupt seed? While men sleep.

> *"Jesus told them another parable. 'The kingdom of heaven*
> *is like a man who sowed good seed in his field.*
> *But **while everyone was sleeping**, his enemy came*
> *and sowed weeds among the wheat, and went away.' "*
> Matthew 13:24-25

When we know the Lord could come at any time. The Bible says that Jesus will come as a thief in the night. Thieves don't call to let you know when to expect them. Neither will Jesus. We must stay awake.

Remember the story of the foolish virgins who were not prepared when the bridegroom arrived? Why were they not ready? The Bible simply says, *"But while the bridegroom was delayed, they all slumbered and slept"* (Matthew 25:5). It's so sad to hear their pleas when the bridegroom comes: "Lord, Lord, open to us." But, he refuses to open the door (Matthew 25:12-13). They should have stayed awake and watched. So should we (1 Thessalonians 5:1-11).

> *"Therefore **let us not sleep**, as others do,*
> *but let us watch and be sober."*
> 1 Thessalonians 5:6

When the day of our ultimate salvation is nearing. I do not know when Jesus will come again (Matthew 24:42,44). I also don't know if I will be alive when He comes or if I will die before then. I do know that every day when I wake from my physical sleep, I am one day closer to heaven. What should I do since that is the case? Let the Bible answer once again.

> *"And do this, knowing the time,*
> *that **now it is high time to awake out of sleep**;*
> *for now our salvation is nearer*
> *than when we first believed."*
> Romans 13:11

So, the next time you are tempted to sleep in after you had already planned to hunt, remember that you may very well miss something monumental. And especially make sure that you are not found sleeping on the most monumental day of all—the day He arrives to take the prepared to His prepared place.

THE ARROW STRIKES Have I ever slept in on a day I had initially planned to hunt? Did I later wonder if I may have missed out on seeing or harvesting a great buck? Have I ever felt a little regretful when another hunter came back with a trophy, while I slept? Am I currently very watchful in the spiritual realm? Do I plan to be awake spiritually or slumbering when Jesus comes again? If He came right now, would I be prepared to meet Him?

See, Covet, Take, and Hide

If you hunt long enough, sooner or later a moment of great temptation is likely to come. You will be tempted to do what you know you shouldn't do. I call them "just across the fence" situations. Your integrity will be put to the test. Such a temptation came to a hunter I know several years ago. I need to protect the "not so innocent," so let me see...what would be a good name to use? Maybe a common one. I know! I'll just call him Bubba.

Bubba and Rufus (I changed his name too) were returning from a hunt in another state. They were traveling in a station wagon. Suddenly, Rufus shouted out, *"Wow! What a deer! There's a big ole buck standing out there in the field with the cows."* When Bubba saw his rack, his desire went off the charts! He **saw** him, **coveted** him and he moved to **take** him. So, he whipped the car around and told Rufus, *"Can you give me my gun?"*

"You aren't gonna shoot him from the road are you?"
Bubba replied, *"Yeah I am, if I can hit him."*

Bubba got out of the car, lifted his rifle, and fired. The buck ran a short distance, and collapsed in a ditch with a high embankment. Bubba instructed his partner in crime to go up the road a little bit, give him time to get the deer, and then come back and pick him up. That ought to work.

Well, it might have, but Rufus was so worked up on adrenaline, his thinker was malfunctioning. Brilliantly, he went and looped around in someone's driveway. The family had heard the shot and came out on the front porch to see what was going on. Seeing the station wagon, they figured it was the getaway car. They stared long and hard at the tag number. Rufus and Bubba were busted. They had **seen, coveted** and **taken**. All they could do now was **hide**.

Rufus drove back to Bubba who now had his head high and his chest poked out with pride. But his joy turned to panic quickly when Rufus told him, "I turned around in someone's driveway, and they saw the tag number." "You didn't!" Bubba shouted.

Well, the "Apple Dumpling Gang" dragged the deer up the embankment, threw him in the back of the station wagon, and sped away. It was then that Rufus noticed a big problem. The deer started kicking pretty wildly. *"He's kicking Bubba! He ain't dead yet!"*

Bubba said, *"Take my gun, and if he gets up...shoot him."*
"I can't do that; I'll blow the windows out of this thing," cried Rufus!
"I don't care! If he gets up, he's gonna be in the front seat with us!"

Bubba sped through the next town at a swift 75-80 mph. The station wagon's wheels touched the ground about every mile or so! He got home, pulled in his driveway, while Rufus prepared to "get out of Dodge." Not long after, the county sheriff pulled in the driveway. He got out and started asking questions.

"Did y'all do any good hunting today?"
"Yes sir. I got a pretty nice buck."
"Can I take a look at him? And where did you get him?"
"This side of _____, I think." ("I think?"—Now, that's a real smart answer.)
"Did you shoot this deer from the road?"

Well, Bubba's heart was now beating fast enough to go into cardiac arrest. With pangs of conscience, he hesitantly said, *"I can't lie to you. Yes sir. I did."*

The officer said, "The game warden has been in hot pursuit of you. You can do one of two things. You can ride with me, or you can drive your car with that deer to the little grocery store down the road. The game warden will meet us there." Bubba still had interest in not getting separated from his deer, so he opted to drive the station wagon! And he was a little happy to be going to the grocery store because he had buddies there who might try to help him a little.

Shortly after he parked at the store, "Mr. Game Warden" pulled in and turned on his blue lights. He got out and asked, "Are you Bubba?" When Bubba affirmed his name, the game warden said, "You have the right to remain silent. Anything you say..." (you know the rest). He was read his rights.

By this time a big crowd of Bubba supporters had seen the blue light and wanted to see what all the commotion was about. "Bubba, what have you done?" they asked. "I shot this deer from the road," Bubba said somewhat sheepishly. Well, the Bubba supporters started shouting and prodding the game warden to go easy on him.

I guess Bubba must have been encouraged by all his support, and he felt it was a good time to ask the most important question of the day. You are not going to believe this next question.

"Can I have the neck and the head?"
"No, you can't have the neck!" Mr. Game Warden shouted.
"Aw, come on," all the Bubba fans cried. *"Let him have it. All he wants is the neck."*

Mr. Game Warden said, "Alright, Mr. Bubba. I could take your gun and your car and keep you out of this state for years. But I'm not gonna do that. I'm gonna let you have the neck, but I'm gonna give you a ticket." "How much?" Bubba asked. "That'll be between you and the judge."

Bubba said the hardest thing was having to tell his wife. When he told her, her eyes bugged out, and her mouth flew open, and she said, "Bubba, they are gonna throw you in jail!"

Later in the courtroom, Bubba felt really bad about what he had done. He should have. The judge entered, looked at him, and again he was asked if he was Bubba. He said he was. The judge asked, *"You are guilty?"* He confessed, *"I am, sir."* We have to be proud of what Bubba said next.

"Judge sir, I want to apologize for what I did.
I want to apologize to you.
I want to apologize to this court.

And I want to apologize to the State."

The judge replied, *"Mr. Bubba, the court believes you are sincere and accepts your apology today. I'm going to fine you $100.00 today. If I ever catch you doing something illegal like this again, I will throw you in jail, and you will not hunt in this state for up to ten years."* Bubba was grateful and thanked the judge for his mercy.

The strangest twist to this story is that later on Bubba was hunting on some land he had permission to be on, and he saw the very same game warden running traps on the land without permission. As stealthily as a fox, Bubba eased up on him, and then spoke through the silent air, "Hello, Mr. Game Warden. Do you remember me?" He replied, "You look familiar." "Well, I'm Bubba. You arrested me a few years back for shooting a deer from the road. Do you have permission to run traps on this land?" Mr. Game Warden said he did not. He said something like, "Bubba, I forgave you. Will you forgive me?" Bubba wanted to say, "What goes around, comes around," but he remembered how bad he felt when he himself had done wrong. He remembered the measures of mercy he had received. He also remembered his need to be respectful (Romans 13:1-7). So, he resisted the urge to retaliate. He did say, "You ought to go tell this landowner what you have done." "I will," said Mr. Game Warden. I guess temptation sometimes comes even to those who are sworn to uphold the law. The devil leaves no one alone.

Well, you can imagine how much "ragging" Bubba got for awhile from his hunting friends. One day he walked into a restaurant, and someone said, *"We all know how Bubba gets his deer! He shoots them from the road!"*

Bubba had heard it enough. He walked over to the guy, and said, *"Listen to me. I did wrong. I have apologized to the judge, the court, and to the State. Don't ever bring this up to me again. I will live with this for the rest of my life."* The friend never mentioned it again. Sometime later they bumped into one another, and Bubba was asked how things were going. He said, *"I'm back to deer hunting again. And I'm gonna do it right."*

IT'S AN OLD TERRIBLE TENDENCY

It doesn't take long in studying the Bible to get a little insight into what people often try to do with sin. ***They see, covet, take, and then hide.***

Adam and Eve

Consider the first man and woman: Adam and Eve. Satan, the master deceiver moved in on Eve and convinced her that if she would only eat of the tree of the knowledge of good and evil, she would be like God. Genesis 3:6 says, *"So when the woman **saw** that the tree was good for food, that it was pleasant to the eyes, and a tree **desirable** to make one wise, she **took** of its fruit and ate. She also gave to her husband with her and he ate."* Having seen, coveted, and taken, guess what they did next? They **hid themselves from the presence of the Lord God**.

I'm persuaded that God's question, "Where are you?" was not for God's information. He knew where they were. It was for them to ponder (3:9). Where were Adam and Eve? In sin, alienated from God, and hiding...not a good place to be.

Achan

When Israel conquered Jericho, God said that all the spoil was to be devoted to Him. They were not to take anything from the city for themselves. When Israel lost an easy battle at Ai, Joshua became very upset. How could things go so wrong? God made it clear what the problem was. He said, "...they have taken some of the accursed things...and put it among their own stuff" (Joshua 7:11). Who had done this? God knew and He inched ever closer until Achan was pegged with the sin. In one verse, Achan confesses it all.

*"When I **saw** among the spoils a beautiful Babylonian garment, two hundred shekels of silver, a wedge of gold weighing fifty shekels, I **coveted** them and **took** them. And **there they are hidden** in earth in the midst of my tent, with silver under it"* (Joshua 7:21).

King David

Even David, the man after God's own heart, repeats this awful pattern. While Israel was at battle, he stayed home. He writes a chapter into the story of his life he would later wish weren't there. It cost him so very much.

"Then it happened one evening that David arose from his bed and walked on the roof of the king's house. And from the roof he **saw** *a woman bathing, and the woman was very* **beautiful to behold"** (2 Samuel 11:2). He saw, and he coveted his neighbor's wife (cf. Ex. 20:17).

"Then David sent messengers and **took** *her; and she came to him, and he lay with her..."* (11:4).

And you know what happened next. When he later found out she was with child, he tried to **hide** the relationship he had with her and even had her husband killed in battle. When he was done, he had broken six of the ten commandments. And his life was miserable. He had no peace in his heart.

Because God loved him, He sent Nathan, the prophet, to David. Nathan skillfully drew David to convict himself with his own mouth. He used a powerful story about a rich man who took a poor man's only little ewe lamb and slaughtered it to feed his guests. David, having a shepherd's heart, was filled with anger and said, "The man who has done this thing shall surely die, and he shall restore fourfold." David had stuck his head in the noose, and all Nathan had to do was pull. And pull, he did! Nathan pierced David with the words, "Thou art the man!"

The masquerade was over. David must have felt a gush of relief when the words finally came, *"I have sinned against the Lord"* (2 Samuel 12:13).

Practical Lessons For Us

You simply cannot hide from God (Psalm 139:1-12). *"And there is no creature hidden from His sight, but all things are naked and open to the eyes of Him to whom we must give an account"* (Hebrews 4:13). Most things get caught in this life. To be sure, all things are caught at judgment (Luke 12:1-3). Dear reader, is there anything you or I think we have hidden from Him?

We have all seen, coveted, taken, and hidden. Before our very first sin, we had a perfect relationship with God. We then saw something we wanted more than God. And in the sin we stole a perfect relationship from God. Only Jesus could give a perfect relationship back, atone for our sin, and make us right with God (Hebrews 7:26-27; 1 Peter 1:18-19).

God wants to hide your sin. Here's the good news! If you want to hide it, bring it to Him. He will gladly cover it up in the blood of His Son and never bring it up again (Revelation 1:5; Acts 22:16; Hebrews 8:12). What a relief! It's what King David finally did and it took away all the turmoil in his heart (Psalm 32:1-5; Romans 4:6-8). Now, that's the way to hide!

The unrepentant who have seen, coveted, and taken will most likely want to hide when Jesus comes again. It's what convicted men do when the Lord comes in judgment. The Bible says they *"hid themselves in the caves and in the rocks of the mountains and said to the mountains and rocks, 'Fall on us and hide us from the face of Him who sits on the throne and from the wrath of the Lamb' "* (Revelation 6:15-16).

If you realize that you have **seen, coveted, taken,** and are presently **hiding,** why not bring the sin to God and let Him hide it forever? Great relief awaits you.

THE ARROW STRIKES Have I ever done anything while hunting that was wrong? Does violating my integrity in the woods or the world bother me? Have I ever seen, coveted, taken, and hidden? Is there anything in my life I am currently trying to keep hidden? If so, is it stressful trying to hide it? Is it hidden from God? Is there a part of me that is ready for the masquerade to be over? If Jesus came today, what would be my reaction?

The Paw Paw Patch

"Do you think I'll see one?" Her voice had such a tender longing to it. It was a question I never really thought I would hear her ask. My wife was actually planning to hunt, by herself, on an upcoming Thanksgiving stay at the family farm.

She had already decided this was the year she would start deer hunting. When I asked her why, she said, *"If you can't beat 'em, join 'em."* So she decided to join us.

But I sensed this was more. It wasn't all about joining Henderson and me. I'm pretty sure this planned hunt, her first of the year, was about connecting in some way with her daddy. He had passed away and left her about eleven months before. It was time to start dealing with the firsts—the first birthday without him, the first Thanksgiving, and the first Christmas.

Shortly after Paw Paw Henderson passed away, I remembered we had a new hunting spot on the farm that hadn't been named. It's a quiet little cove, nestled in a recession with a beautiful, green food plot. After the funeral, we made our way to the cabin on the farm, and I asked, "How 'bout us naming that spot 'the Paw Paw Patch?'" Everybody loved the idea. So, the Paw Paw Patch had its beginning...a little memorial to the man we all loved and missed. When Thanksgiving plans were being made, Susan said, *"I want to hunt the Paw Paw Patch this Thanksgiving."* She said it as though she had a purpose.

But now, the question was, *"Do you think I'll see one?"* I think the meaningful things of deer hunting observed through me had rubbed off on my wife. Something tells me that if she sees a deer in the Paw Paw Patch that morning it will somehow be soothing to her heart. She will feel a little connection with her daddy.

I can certainly tell you this: He would be so proud of her. He would think his girl hunting was really neat. He would be talking to her on the phone a few days before and would wish her good luck. He would be calling after the hunt asking, "Did you do any good, Baby?" If the deer is not mature, and she passes on it, he would say, "Why didn't you shoot? That would have been some good, tender meat." Most of his generation never practiced any kind of deer management. If it was brown, it went down. It was always food for the table.

I'm purposely not asking her a lot of questions about her intentions for the hunt. I want it to be hers alone. If a deer gently walks into the Paw Paw Patch, I'm pretty sure that she will take him. I wonder if she will name the deer? If I had to guess, I would say she will. And I can imagine its name being full of meaning to her. Can you tell I am into this? I am more interested in her hunt on this day than any other hunt of the year. I am thrilled that she has chosen hunting as a link to her daddy. And I am thankful that he brought up my wife around country things. Paw Paw was no stranger to cleaning and eating things from the wild.

He lives on in my wife. Just the other day she stayed in the kitchen with me as I cut the bone out of eight hindquarters. She wrapped the meat in freezer paper. She said, *"If I wasn't my daddy's child I probably wouldn't be doing this."* I told my hunting buddies about it, and they thought it was cool she was getting that close to the nasty side of deer hunting. Thanks, honey, for letting me turn our kitchen into a butcher shop. Paw Paw would love it.

When I go way down yonder to the Paw Paw Patch, I miss him now. After he died, I hunted on Henderson Farms, and I couldn't help but get misty-eyed. Our patriarch had left it all to us. He didn't keep it. We leave it all when we go, don't we?

I began to understand why it wasn't easy for him to go to the farm. He missed his daddy and mother and other loved ones who had once lived there and worked the land. I understood now. But I'm a little different, at least for now. I am drawn to the farm. I want to use it with my children to build what he built there in my wife. She remembers driving in the hay field with her daddy, feeding cows, picking peas, fishing, and frying the fish with hush puppies and french fries. I want my kids to make their own memories there.

STILL SPEAKING

Perhaps on Thanksgiving morning in the Paw Paw Patch, his voice will be heard. Like the day he first met me and looked at my feet and said, *"Well, you might not ever amount to much, but you are starting out with a good foundation."*

When I graduated from college, we were renting a U-Haul and didn't know whether to get a 24-footer or one two feet longer. He asked me, "How much more is two feet?" Of course, he was talking money. Stupidly, I thought he was talking distance, so I held out my hands to show him the approximate length of two feet. He chuckled and gave me a look I'll never forget, and said, *"Son, you've got your degree; now you need to get your education."* But seriously, he did value education. He told all his children, "I will pay for your education, but *you* have to get it."

I liked him always telling his children, *"If you make your bed hard, you are gonna have to lay in it."* Or *"Some folks just don't believe cow horns will hook."*

He told his son, John, *"You come here with nothing, and you are only given one thing, and that's your name. And when you leave, you leave with nothing. So, you better take care of your name."* That fits perfectly with Ecclesiastes 7:1-4, which not only talks about a good name, but also shows us how we learn better from sorrow than laughter.

> *"A good name is better than precious ointment,*
> *and the day of death than the day of one's birth.*
> *It is better to go to the house of mourning*
> *than to go to the house of feasting,*
> *for that is the end of all men;*
> *and the living will take it to heart.*
> *Sorrow is better than laughter,*
> *for by a sad countenance the*
> *heart is made better.*
> *The heart of the wise is in the*
> *house of mourning,*
> *but the heart of fools is in the*
> *house of mirth."*

Susan has told me often, *"My daddy was always so supportive of me if I was doing right. If I wasn't doing right, he would tell me. But if it was right, he was always behind me."*

LEARNING TO LIVE A SIMPLE LIFE

When I preached his funeral, I used the word SIMPLE to describe him. He always tried to live humbly. Like me, he wasn't perfect. Like me, he had blemishes. But in his words, *"I'm just ole Billy Henderson."* Simple, he was. Six simple, but powerful things were seen in him.

S – Service to others (He could service small motors over the phone!)
I - Integrity (His word was his bond.)
M - Marriage Commitment (Buried one day shy of his 55th wedding anniversary.)
P - People (He was a real people person.)
L - Loved (His physical way of expressing LOVE was to pinch the children's ear lobes.)
E - Enough (His life was never about stuff.)

As I wrote this book, I would occasionally read a piece to some hunting buddies and they would always share their own similar stories right behind mine. So, I know that you are probably thinking of someone very special to you that has left you. I know you have your own special memories. And it may even be that hunting somehow connects you with them to this day. I remember once reading an article from a hunter telling how he dedicated his entire season to his hunting buddy who had died the year before of an apparent heart attack. If hunting connects you to someone special, that thought makes me smile. I feel sure it makes you smile.

The main thing is to take the good things they shared with you that make for good living and never forget them. Live to make them proud.

So, Paw Paw, I want you to know that we miss you, but you live on in our hearts. Your girl will be at the Paw Paw Patch this Thanksgiving. I hope a whitetail will too. But even if one doesn't show up...that's alright. The main thing is that I know *you will be there* in the cherished memories of this wonderful woman you brought up to be my wife.

I think of a few lines from a Paul Overstreet song called, "Mr. Miller." I insert the words "Mr. Billy" where Paul sings "Mr. Miller."

> *You may have done some wrong things.*
> *But you did a lot that's right.*
> *And my favorite thing you ever did,*
> *Is here with me tonight.*

> *So, thank you, Mr. Billy*
> *for loving your wife.*
> *The love you shared with her back then*
> *today has blessed my life.*

> *Your daughter's all I've dreamed of,*
> *and more than I deserve.*
> *Rest easy, Mr. Billy.*
> *I'll always cherish her.*

A WORD FROM SUSAN

I never thought I'd be writing about ME deer hunting. I'm not sure that I can put into words all the reasons or the feelings stirring within me that brought me to this point. Sometimes when you are healing from a loss, the soul reaches out for something, and you are not sure why.

So, I eased out of the cabin on Thanksgiving morning with my flashlight and my gun all decked out with a pink camo strap! The light of day was still hiding underneath a blanket of night as I eased into the Paw Paw Patch.

Jeff was right when he told me that deer hunting will give lots of time to meditate. I am so thankful for all the memories that went through my mind that cold morning. I thought about my daddy and how this family farm had become such a huge part of him and our family. I could feel the love all around me—love that came in the form of sweat, hard work, devotion, and sacrifice. My daddy, his parents, aunts, and uncles had made it possible for me still to have access to such beautiful things. I thank God for them still.

Memories serve as a bridge to our past and a link to our future. And today, it was the same. My daddy was present in my mind, and my son was hunting by himself in another field. I was living today somewhat in the past but also striving to truly feel the present.

I was taking it all in when a noise to my right interrupted my thoughts. Could this be what I was waiting for? Could this really be a deer? As the leaves continued to crunch and twigs snapped, I knew it wouldn't be long until my deer appeared. Finally, I got a glimpse out of the corner of my eye. Uhhh...a cat. A big cat. A huge cat. A bobcat! Now that was not what I was expecting. I still have lots to learn about hunting, but I figured if a bobcat was around, a deer probably was not.

Not long after watching the bobcat quickly run by, I heard a shot that startled me. That sound signaled at least one of us had seen a deer. Then a voice came over the radio calling Jeff. It was our son. He said, "I got one, Daddy!" I was excited for him and was anxious to go see what he had harvested.

My hunt was over, but the time spent in thought and thanksgiving to God was special. Today, it was not really about the deer after all.

Thank You, God, for the memories you are allowing my kids and grandkids to make on this farm and for the farm being a link to the future.

THE ARROW STRIKES Do I understand Susan's feelings about wanting to go to the Paw Paw Patch? Are there people or places very special to me? What did I learn from them that is so valuable today? Do I need to speak or write a word of thanks? If they have passed away, how can I best honor them?

Breathing Heaven's Air

In the writing of these devotionals I have tried to show that God's creation is a wonderful teacher. You don't have to hunt to see it. And God's teachers are not just whitetail deer. There are lessons to learn from all of God's creatures. Job made this very clear when he said...

> *"But now ask the beasts and they will teach you;*
> *And the birds of the air and they will tell you;*
> *Or speak to the earth, and it will teach you;*
> *And the fish of the sea will explain it to you.*
> *Who among these does not know*
> *That the hand of the Lord has done this,*
> *In whose hand is the life of every living thing,*
> *And the breath of all mankind"?*
> Job 12:7-10

Let me ease out of the woods for a moment to the ocean for one of the most interesting stories I've ever read.

In October of 1988, the world watched as three gray whales, icebound off Point Barrow, Alaska, gasped for breath at a hole in the ice. The whales, which had been discovered by a native hunter, had injured themselves by ramming their heads into the ice in order to breathe and keep the small opening from freezing over. Their only hope for survival was that somehow they might be transported five miles past the ice pack to the open sea. Rescuers began cutting a string of breathing holes about twenty yards apart in ice that was at least six inches thick. For eight days they coaxed the whales from one hole to the next, mile after mile. Along the way, one of the three whales vanished and was presumed dead, but finally with the help of Russian icebreaker vessels, the two whales named Putu and Siku swam to freedom.

Much in the same way, this is what time in the woods and hunting the whitetail have been for me: a breathing hole. A lot of us hunters go to the woods when we feel suffocated and trapped by a cold world with its stresses and strains and problems. In those times, I long for heaven. I want it so deeply. I need to be reminded there is something better ahead. I need a breathing hole.

SPIRITUAL BREATHING HOLES

God has cut into the ice of this world and has created some great breathing holes along our journey. Each hole opens to us heaven's air. We are rejuvenated every time we make it to another hole.

Before we look at these breathing holes, I have to stress a major point. These breaks in the ice are no good to us if we do not come to them. Every deer hunter knows that it's not easy to get out of bed on some of those icy mornings. It takes discipline to get up. I call it "exercising mind over mattress." But once we do, we make our way to a quiet little spot nestled in the woods or on the edge of an open field, and a great blessing awaits us. And it's not always a deer.

Successful deer hunting is a process, and the process has no off-season. Christianity is the same way. Strong Christians have no major secret. They are just disciplined to go to their breathing holes. They do it day after day, week after week, month after month, and year after year. Their spiritual progress is evident (1 Timothy 4:15-16). And as they move from one hole to the next, days are passing and their salvation is nearer than when they first believed (Rom. 13:11).

The top three *daily* breathing holes are as follows:

1. **Pray to God every day.** Here is where you sit before the Lord and talk to God freely and openly (2 Samuel 7:18; 1 Samuel 1:15). But remember, it is not prayer that is powerful. God is the source of great power. Prayer taps

into it. It has been compared to an electrical cord. The power is not in the cord. The cord taps into the power when it is plugged in. The same goes with prayer. We just need to plug in more often. We need *closet prayers,* where we spend concentrated time with God (Matthew 6:6). But we also need *arrow prayers,* those quick shots sent to the throne of God throughout the day when we can't go to a room alone (Nehemiah 2:4). In this way, we can stay in constant touch with God (1 Thessalonians 5:17).

2. **Read your Bible every day** (1 Timothy 4:13; 2 Timothy 2:15)**.** Here is where God talks to you. It serves as a spiritual GPS showing you where you are, where you need to go and how to get there. The first question God ever asked in the Bible was asked to Adam after he sinned. The question was, "Where are you?" That question was not for God's benefit. It was for Adam. He surely was not where he had been. Now, he was in sin and needed to return to God. As you read your Bible, the question God will always be asking is, "Where are you?" As you read, He will guide you on toward home where the air is always fresh and clean.

3. **Meditate on who you are and where you are spiritually every day** (1 Timothy 4:15). You bring God's word back up to your mind and chew on it a while, just like a deer chewing the cud.

My favorite daily time to breath in some spiritual air is in the morning. The first action of the day tends to rule the day.(Psalm 5:3) Prayer, Bible reading, and meditation have a way of staying with you, reminding you of who you are, Whom you serve, and where you are headed. I've always loved the words of Ralph Cushman's poem, "I Met God In The Morning."

> *I met God in the morning*
> *when the day was at its best,*
> *And His Presence came like sunrise,*
> *Like a glory in my breast.*

All day long the Presence lingered,
All day long He stayed with me,
And we sailed in perfect calmness
O'er a very troubled sea.

Other ships were blown and battered,
Other ships were sore distressed,
But the winds that seemed to drive them,
Brought to me a peace and rest.

Then I thought of other mornings,
With a keen remorse of mind,
When I too had loosed the moorings,
With the presence left behind.

So, I think I know the secret,
Learned from many a troubled way:
You must seek Him in the morning
If you want Him through the day!

In addition to these daily breathing holes we seek ourselves, we also thank God for brothers and sisters in Christ who bring a hole to us.

While in the confines of imprisonment, Paul was visited by a man called Onesiphorus. Paul says of him, *"God grant mercy to the household of Onesiphorus, for **he often refreshed me**, and was not ashamed of my chain; but when he arrived in Rome, he sought me out very diligently and found me. The Lord grant to him that he may find mercy from the Lord in that Day—and **you know very well how many ways he ministered to me** at Ephesus"* (2 Timothy 1:16-18).

I know of some men who once took a long trip to find a brother whose wife had been in the hospital a very long time. They went searching for him on his birthday. They found his hotel, found his room, and stood before the door with a cake. After lighting the candles, they knocked on the door. When he came to the door and saw them, tears welled up and he let out a great laugh of incredible joy! A breathing hole was brought to him in the midst of some very difficult days.

But there is also a *weekly* breathing hole God has provided. It is the weekly assembly of the church. A sure way to suffocate is not to assemble with other Christians. God tells us not to forsake the assembling of Christians together (Hebrews 10:24-25). It was my preacher-friend, Steve Klein, who first told me about the Alaskan whale rescue and compared it to our God-given places for fresh air. He says of the first day of the week worship service, "In a way, worship is a string of breathing holes the Lord has opened for His people. Battered and bruised in a world frozen over, with no oxygen for the soul, we rise for air together in worship. We breathe, as it were, the air of heaven itself as we adore and glorify our heavenly Father. In this way, our struggling souls survive the journey through this cold world, until that day when the barrier between us and heaven melts away at last, and we inhale deeply and freely, that we may exhale in voices of eternal praise" ((Heaven: O For A Home With God, pg. 62).

Heaven is the place of the purest air. Think about it. There's no tempter, no sin, no pain, no sorrow, and no tears. I read once where someone asked an astronaut what it felt like when he finally broke free from the gravitational pull of the earth. He said, "Ahhhhh." Heaven will be the greatest "Ahhhh" moment. Free at last! I can breathe freely. I'm planning to go there. Will you go with me?

THE ARROW STRIKES Can I see that God provides breathing holes for taking in heaven's air? Am I currently feeling a little suffocated by the world and its stresses and strains? What would be a good breathing hole for me? Do I keep a good line of communication going with God? Do I use quiet moments to chew on His word and my relationship with Him?

Waiting for the Master

It was a cold, winter morning and I was hunting from a stand Eddie and I named "Nosebleed." We named it that because it was so high, up in the "nosebleed section." The Middle Tennessee hill on which it was placed made it appear even higher.

I know that some hunters say, "Treestand hunting is not really hunting. It's just sitting." Well now, that depends on how you look at it.

We had done all our hunting *before* the season: scouting and choosing very deliberately where we would place the stand. Our treestands are strategically placed where they are for a good reason. And so it was with this location. It was in a great spot.

I could hardly wait to get there. Since it was nestled way back in the woods, it required some patience to cover the distance. Another issue was that the ground was filled with leaves. There was no way to walk there quietly.

Those circumstances made my wait even longer on getting there and getting in the stand. I like to do two things when walking in lots of leaves in the morning. I try to make it without the use of a flashlight. Secondly, I try to walk like a deer. I don't want to sound like a human on a mission. I will take a few steps and stop. Take a few more steps and stop. It also cuts down on the sweat. But another side of me wants to hurry things up because I'm so amped up with anticipation.

It was in my favor that I was on farmland that had cows. Occasionally, a few of them will ease into the hardwoods to eat acorns. Did you know that cows love White Oak acorns? That was a surprise to me, but they do. If a deer hears me, maybe he will think I am a cow. In my mind, everything was going as planned. *Today may be the day!*

The morning was beautiful, and I had been sitting for an hour or so when I heard something running down the hill behind me and into the draw where I was. It was a doe. I thought, *"Get ready, Jeff. She's running for a reason."* I figured "big boy" was chasing her and was soon to appear.

I got ready. I took a few deep breaths, held them for a moment and slowly exhaled. I also was tightening and then loosening my muscles to lessen the effects of the adrenaline rush I was already having. I was so excited. I thought, *"This could be it. Is he coming? Is he coming?"*

But in a matter of a few seconds, I went from the height of anticipation to the pit of disappointment. Dogs!!!!! I've added exclamation points to try to express my let down and frustration. Whose dogs are these? They looked ragged and wild to me. But they were running deer and busting my hunt. I wanted to take them out! But I restrained myself.

BEWARE OF DOGS

Don't get me wrong. I love dogs. I have a good one at home. I just didn't like *these* dogs. Because these kinds of dogs mess things up for me.

The apostle Paul had the same problem in spreading the gospel. Dogs were always nipping at his heels. I don't mean the furry kind. I'm talking about his persecutors he called "dogs." *"Beware of dogs,"* Paul says (Philippians 3:2). We teachers usually call them the Judaizing teachers. They were Jewish teachers who tried to stop Paul from preaching the gospel. They despised him because people were leaving Judaism to follow Christ. They even tried to kill him at Lystra. The text says, *"...having persuaded the multitudes, they stoned Paul and dragged him out of the city, supposing him to be dead. However, when the disciples gathered around him, he rose up and went into the city. And the next day he departed with Barnabas to Derbe"* (Acts 14:19-20).

You have to love this man Paul. He takes a lickin' and keeps on tickin'. Why would he endure so much at the hands of "dogs"? The bottom line: He wanted to save them and all who would listen.

He knew Jesus was alive and was the Savior of the world. He wanted people to obey the gospel and enjoy the same spiritual feast he was enjoying in Christ. He called all the stuff he had left behind in Judaism—"dung." At least that's the way the King James Version reads. I know what dung is. I stepped on a cow patty on the way to the deer stand. It's cover scent.

Listen to Paul's words. *"But what things were gain to me, these I have counted loss for Christ. But indeed I also count all things loss for the excellence of the knowledge of Christ Jesus my Lord, for whom I have suffered the loss of all things, and count them as rubbish* (KJV—dung), *that I may gain Christ"* (Philippians 3:8). He knew that Christ could do for him what the law of Moses could not (Acts 13:38-29).

My studies have indicated that this word translated "dung" or "rubbish" can also carry the idea of "table scraps." We save those at my house to give to the dogs on our family farm. So basically Paul is saying that if the dogs want the scraps, they can have them! He was eating the good stuff. He was eating of Christ. Whether you translate it dung, rubbish, or table scraps, *it's all stuff to do away with* in order to have Christ. You and I may have some dung, rubbish, or scraps we need to throw way. Do you? Do I?

IS HE COMING? IS HE COMING?

Some dogs are incredible. My favorite is one that lived in Tokyo from 1923 to 1935. Let me tell you the true story. There's even been a movie made about it, simply called *Hachi*. If you'd like, check out a few clips on the internet and feel with me.

Hachiko was a golden brown Akita,
owned by a professor at the University of Tokyo.

But Hachi was more than just the professor's dog...
he was his friend.

Hachi was very smart. So, every day,
when Professor Ueno came home from work,
he greeted him at the train station.
But sadly, one day the professor died at work
because of a stroke.

Hachi was given away but he always
escaped to the station...
the train station where he had
always waited...

Hachi waited...
and waited...
and waited.
He waited for 9 years
until he himself
died too.

I don't know how many others did what I did when they first saw the movie, but I was deeply moved with emotion. My heart longed with Hachi for the return of his master. And my thoughts turned easily to thinking about the return of *my* Master.

When He left, He promised me that He was coming again. He said, *"I will come again and receive you to Myself that where I am there you may be also"* (John 14:3). I have come to love Him so much. He is my Friend. With the eye of faith I have walked with Him on the dusty roads of Galilee. I have been gripped by His lessons, awestruck by His miracles, and touched by His love. I watched Him leave that last day. I gazed with the disciples into the heavens until He disappeared (Acts 1:9-11). And I've been looking every day for Him to come back and get me.

So, you see, I "totally get it" with this dog. I feel what Hachi feels as he goes to the train station every day, waits for the doors to open, and looks for a familiar face to step off the train. And when he doesn't step off, loyalty remains and watching continues even though he is told, "You don't have to wait anymore. He's not coming back." Unbelievers may pity me and want to say, **"Poor guy. He's just like that dog. Waiting for something that's not gonna happen."**

That's where they are wrong. Hachi's master didn't return. Mine will. Even though the train station doors open every day, and He's not there, the day will come when He will appear. He promised it. No amount of time changes the faithfulness of His promise and His inevitable return (2 Peter 3:1-13). So, I wait.

THE DAY OF THE LORD WILL COME

There will be no mistaking it when it happens. A trumpet blast will reverberate across the sky; heads will jerk upward; and there He will be! Jesus. Heaven's doors will open, and there He is in the clouds arrayed in all His splendor. Previously, we could not have withstood the brilliant glory. But on this day, we can. As soon as the trumpet blasts, everyone's bodies will change to eternal bodies.

> *"...in a moment,*
> *in the twinkling of an eye,*
> *at the last trumpet.*
> *For the trumpet will sound and*
> *the dead will be raised incorruptible,*
> *and we shall be changed."*
> 1 Corinthians 15:52

Perhaps roots pop in nearby cemeteries, vaults open, and casket lids lift up. The dead, all of the dead, are rising. It may be that those who are saved and have been waiting are so overcome with the joy of His return they hardly notice that others are crying and some are looking for places to hide. It's not a great day for everyone (2 Thessalonians 1:7-10; Revelation 6:14-17).

Those saved by Him begin to rise off the earth. They realize this giant ball has served its purpose, and it too rejoices as the sons and daughters of God meet their Lord in the air to be with Him forevermore (Romans 8:19). This really is the "nosebleed section," the highest stand of all. The last rung has been reached, and they step onto the platform of eternal happiness. All fear is gone as they adore the Master.

> *"For the Lord Himself will descend from heaven*
> *with a shout, with the voice of an archangel,*
> *and with the trumpet of God.*
> *And the dead in Christ will rise first.*
> *Then we who are alive and remain*
> *shall be caught up together with them*
> *in the clouds to meet the Lord in the air.*
> *And thus shall we always be with the Lord."*
> 1 Thessalonians 4:17

Judgment is next, but for the saved it is an awards ceremony. He has brought His reward with Him (Revelation 22:12). The grandest words they have ever heard are said. *"Well done, good and faithful servant; you were faithful over a few things, I will make you ruler over many things. Enter into the joy of your lord"* (Matthew 25:21).

Once inside the eternal city, they see God. Let those last three words sink in. **They see God.** What will we do when we see the Father? I can only imagine. The singing has begun. We hear the song and strive to join. And joy beyond anything we ever dreamed possible is felt as we arrive there with our Master. The most beautiful places we ever saw on earth pale in comparison to the beauty of this place. No wonder it's called *Heaven*! It's opening day in heaven and it's eternal. "We've no less days to sing God's praise than when we first begun."

There are innumerable angels. And there are Abraham and Sarah, Joseph, Peter, Paul, Tabitha, Lydia...all the people we came to love on the pages of scripture. And there are people all around that we knew while we were on earth, people who encouraged us onward and upward. Some of these people we only knew for a short while, but now we never have to say goodbye! What a reunion!

They crafted a bronze statue in honor of Hachi. It still sits outside the train station, as immovable as Hachi ever was. The locals often plan to meet each other there, saying, *"I will meet you at Hachiko."* Like Hachi, I don't desire a statue. All I have ever wanted is the Master. I have simply wanted God, the God who even took a bad day in the whitetail woods with some pesky dogs and led me to think about Him. He has done that with every hunt I have been on. Will you meet me at the station? Today just might be the day!

THE ARROW STRIKES Do I feel for Hachi as he waits and waits for a master that is never going to return? Is it possible for me to love a Lord I have never seen? If so, how can I grow to love Him more each day? Is it possible for me to develop the same longing for Jesus in my life? Can any amount of scoffing from others make me ashamed as I wait for His return? What makes Jesus' promised return a certainty? Where do I expect my eternal home to be when He comes again?

Afterword

There's a bit of sadness as Eddie and I watch our bows being lowered to the ground. But the view from above has been life-changing. Things are better seen when we ascend on high. We see life from the viewpoint of the majestic Lord who made us with great intent and purpose. Our heads are clear, our understanding is keen and our minds are focused. The hunt is over for these two friends but a nice harvest lies on the horizon in front of us—the greatest trophy ever imagined.

Thank you for walking with us through these pages. It's been a great hunt: my most enjoyable ever. I haven't wanted it to end. I hope that you have found Him and that you will place your feet squarely in His footprints. If so, I'll meet you in the air and then at the gate...heaven's beautiful gate. I see a cloud!

Six months after his massive stroke, on
Opening Day of Tennessee Muzzleloader Season,
Eddie placed a perfect shot on a six-point buck
overcoming peripheral darkness on his left side.

He executed flawlessly, like an old veteran hunter on autopilot.
His bodyguard (guess who?) was strapped to the tree with him.
After hearing the crash of the downed buck in the nearby ravine,
he exhaled deeply and simply said, "I needed that."

After locating this whitetail, he stood beside it,

lifted his arms, looked upward, and said, "Thank you, my Heavenly Father."

He named the buck, "Recovery II."

Would you like to read more
"Hoof Prints to HIS Prints"?

Visit our website:
www.woods2word.com

- Short devotionals
- Biblical information on drawing closer to God in your private devotions
- Helpful hints for hunters
- Pictures
- Videos
- Links to some favorite deer hunting sites
- And more

Made in the USA
Charleston, SC
08 June 2015